OXFORD WORLD'S CLASSICS

PERSIAN LETTERS

MONTESQUIEU was born Charles-Louis de Secondat in 1689 at the château of La Brède, south of Bordeaux. He was educated by the Oratoriens at the Collège de Juilly in Meaux and completed a law degree at the University of Bordeaux in 1708. After a few years in Paris he returned to Bordeaux in order to manage the family estates following the death of his father. He married Jeanne Lartigue, a practising Calvinist, with whom he had three children. In 1716 he joined the Academy of Bordeaux and was its director for the year in 1718. On the death of his uncle he inherited the title of baron de Montesquieu and the post of *président à mortier* at the Parlement of Bordeaux where he had begun his career in law. From an early age he manifested a ceaseless intellectual curiosity and devotion to extensive scholarship. He pursued through systematic investigation the numerous factors that shape societies and an understanding of them. In 1721 he published the *Persian Letters* (*Lettres persanes*) anonymously in Holland; his authorship, which became an open secret, gained him entry to the literary salons of Paris, where he lived from 1721 to 1725. Elected to the Académie Française in 1728, he sold his judicial office and travelled around Europe for three years. On his return he continued his scholarly research. His work on the ancient Romans addressed fundamental issues in the philosophy of history and prompted thinking about forms of government that would inform his later work. In 1748 his major work, *The Spirit of the Laws* (*De l'esprit des lois*), was published in Geneva. Despite progressive eye-trouble, he published a *Defence of the Spirit of the Laws* in which he repudiated the allegation that he was a deist, and began work on 'An Essay on Taste' for Diderot's *Encyclopedia*. In 1754 he published an extensively revised version of the *Persian Letters*, acknowledging authorship for the first time. He died in Paris in 1755.

MARGARET MAULDON has worked as a translator since 1987. For Oxford World's Classics she has translated Zola's *L'Assommoir*, Stendhal's *The Charterhouse of Parma*, Maupassant's *Bel-Ami*, Constant's *Adolphe*, Huysmans's *Against Nature* (winner of the Scott Moncrieff prize for translation, 1999), Flaubert's *Madame Bovary*, and Diderot's *Rameau's Nephew and First Satire*.

ANDREW KAHN is Fellow ⌐ ⌐ ⌐ ⌐ ⌐ ⌐ ⌐ Hall, Oxford, and University Lec⌐ ⌐ ⌐ ⌐ rd. He works on the literatur⌐ ⌐ ⌐ ⌐ and Russian Enlightenments. F⌐ ⌐ ⌐ ⌐ on to *Pushkin* (2007), and of Pu⌐ ⌐ ⌐ tories for Oxford World's Classics. His ⌐ ⌐ ⌐ *Lyric Intelligence* (2008).

OXFORD WORLD'S CLASSICS

*For over 100 years Oxford World's Classics have brought
readers closer to the world's great literature. Now with over 700
titles—from the 4,000-year-old myths of Mesopotamia to the
twentieth century's greatest novels—the series makes available
lesser-known as well as celebrated writing.*

*The pocket-sized hardbacks of the early years contained
introductions by Virginia Woolf, T. S. Eliot, Graham Greene,
and other literary figures which enriched the experience of reading.
Today the series is recognized for its fine scholarship and
reliability in texts that span world literature, drama and poetry,
religion, philosophy and politics. Each edition includes perceptive
commentary and essential background information to meet the
changing needs of readers.*

OXFORD WORLD'S CLASSICS

MONTESQUIEU

Persian Letters

Translated by
MARGARET MAULDON

With an Introduction and Notes by
ANDREW KAHN

OXFORD
UNIVERSITY PRESS

OXFORD

UNIVERSITY PRESS

Great Clarendon Street, Oxford OX2 6DP

Oxford University Press is a department of the University of Oxford.
It furthers the University's objective of excellence in research, scholarship,
and education by publishing worldwide in

Oxford New York

Auckland Cape Town Dar es Salaam Hong Kong Karachi
Kuala Lumpur Madrid Melbourne Mexico City Nairobi
New Delhi Shanghai Taipei Toronto

With offices in

Argentina Austria Brazil Chile Czech Republic France Greece
Guatemala Hungary Italy Japan Poland Portugal Singapore
South Korea Switzerland Thailand Turkey Ukraine Vietnam

Oxford is a registered trade mark of Oxford University Press
in the UK and in certain other countries

Published in the United States
by Oxford University Press Inc., New York

Translation © Margaret Mauldon 2008
Editorial material and Appendix © Andrew Kahn 2008

British Library Cataloguing in Publication Data

Data available

Library of Congress Cataloging-in-Publication Data

Montesquieu, Charles de Secondat, baron de, 1689–1755.
[Lettres persanes. English]
Persian letters / Montesquieu; translated by Margaret Mauldon; with an
introduction and notes by Andrew Kahn.
p. cm. — (Oxford world's classics)
Includes bibliographical references.
ISBN 978-0-19-280635-2
I. Mauldon, Margaret. II. Kahn, Andrew. III. Title.
PQ2011.L5E57 2008
843'.5—dc22

2007039894

Typeset by Cepha Imaging Pvt Ltd, Bangalore, India
Printed in Great Britain by
Clays Ltd, St. Ives plc.

ISBN 978-0-19-280635-2

2

CONTENTS

PERSIAN LETTERS

INTRODUCTION

THE *Persian Letters* (*Lettres persanes*) is perhaps the first great popular work of the European Enlightenment. Conceived around 1717, it was published anonymously in 1721 and enjoyed immediate notoriety. The playwright Marivaux was critical of its 'false brilliance' about serious subjects, while the historian and journalist Denis-François Camusat applauded its brilliance but called the contents 'dangerous'. A cleric, stung by its critical attitude to religion, told Montesquieu that his book 'would sell like hot cakes'. The prediction was correct, and Montesquieu later noted that booksellers, eager to cash in, implored members of the public to 'write them some *Persian Letters*'. The original two slim volumes clearly caught the mood of the moment.

Montesquieu now stands as one of the great political thinkers of the modern world. His views on the nature of states and their constitutions had a tangible impact on the world around him. In Russia, Catherine the Great drew on his writing in her legislative reforms of the 1760s, and in America the Founding Fathers looked to his great *Spirit of the Laws* (*De l'esprit des lois*, 1748) in framing their constitution for the new republic. When in the early twenty-first century pundits everywhere worry about the compatibility of Islam and the West, we see Montesquieu's name invoked in discussions about the banning of the headscarf in France, in editorials about the war in Iraq, and in polemics about the separation of powers in the United States.[1]

Yet when encountered first in the 1720s, Montesquieu does not look like an obvious figure to anticipate the tireless scepticism of future *philosophes*. For one thing, they were from less privileged backgrounds, Voltaire the son of a bourgeois lawyer, Diderot the son of a provincial cutler. As an aristocratic landowner and magistrate, Montesquieu might rather have been expected to follow received wisdom about church and state, god and man. He began, however,

---

[1] See e.g. Michael Johnson, 'Revisiting the French Guru of American Democracy', *International Herald Tribune*, 10 Mar. 2007.

by making waves, creating in the *Persian Letters* a style of philosophical fiction in which to pose a wide range of questions about human feeling, institutions, and societies. With typical understatement and irony, Montesquieu retrospectively commented that the *Persian Letters* 'were pleasant and gay and were found pleasing for that reason'.[2] In fact, everything about this book is designed to surprise and even confound, and it made monarchy and religion the subject of rational enquiry rather than the objects of unquestioning acceptance. Of course, Montesquieu was hardly unique in questioning the precepts and role of Christianity in his time. But, for example, in having his Persian correspondents call the pope 'a great magician', he treated the state religion and sacraments with a new spirit of corrosive irony. Even the form is not what we expect. Novelistic without being a novel, the *Persian Letters* combines different modes and creates a new type of writing, which makes ideas come to life as part of the lived fabric of a fictional world. By comparing East and West, his oriental travellers reflect critical curiosity about human behaviour and social structures, turning a mirror both onto the world they left behind in the East and the world they newly encounter in Paris of the 1720s.

The World of the Regency

Montesquieu was born into the gloomy France of Louis XIV's later years. At Versailles, the culture of the court had earlier flourished on a grand scale under the Sun King, but now Louis XIV's devoutness cast a long shadow. Throughout the seventeenth century France had been constantly unsettled by international disputes and a punitive tax burden required to sustain the King's European wars. Poor harvests in the 1690s and a devastating famine of 1707 fomented unrest among the peasantry. By the turn of the century a sense of stultification beset France at a moment when England, in the aftermath of the Glorious Revolution, enjoyed a burst of intellectual energy.

[2] Montesquieu, *Œuvres complètes* (Paris: Bibliothèque de la Pléiade, 1956), 122 (*Mes Pensées* no. 886 [1533]). *Mes Pensées* is the title given to the three large compositional notebook in which Montesquieu (or his secretary) recorded ideas, aphorisms, thoughts on his reading, sometimes extensive drafts of his creative work. Montesquieu said that these were undeveloped thoughts on which he would meditate at a suitable occasion.

Toleration of the Protestant faith had been made the policy of the Catholic state as enshrined in the Edict of Nantes (1585), which ended the catastrophic Wars of Religion that convulsed France in the sixteenth century. Under pressure from the church and Jesuit thinkers, and bent on concentrating more and more power in his own hands, Louis revoked the edict in 1685. The immediate result was the flight of 200,000 Huguenots from France to the more tolerant England and the United Provinces. When Pope Clement XI, following the King's wishes, issued a Bull *Unigenitus* condemning Jansenism in 1714 this was regarded as a further disgraceful example of Christian intolerance.[3] Other policies of a centralizing absolutism had provoked the dissatisfaction of aristocrats and the Parlements, the sovereign courts in Paris and the provinces, manned by the loftiest and wealthiest of the 'Robe' nobility (*noblesse de robe*). In 1673 the King withdrew the right of the Parlements to delay royal edicts, and further consolidated his power by appointing provincial *intendants* directly answerable to the King.

When Louis finally died in 1715 hopes were high for national revival. The King's nephew Philip of Orléans was installed as Regent during the minority of Louis XV. A flamboyant figure, the Regent was famous for a strong hedonistic streak and interest in the arts. His foreign policy was Anglophile, a sea-change that enhanced cultural contacts and affinities between the two nations. Montesquieu, for one, had a keen interest in the advances being made in English science and philosophy. Montesquieu's readership, which included nobles and magistrates, Jansenists and freethinkers, embraced the promise of renewal offered by the Regency.[4] Even if the nobles made only modest headway in restraining the Regent's own absolutist tendency, later writers waxed nostalgic about a period they saw as distinguished by a new sense of freedom. Satirists mocked the Regent's love of luxury, but his patronage of the arts and his love of pleasure banished the prudishness of the previous reign. Although Voltaire

---

[3] See John McManners, 'Jansenism and Politics in the Eighteenth Century', in Derek Baker (ed.), *Church, Society and Politics: Studies in French History* (Oxford: Blackwell, 1975), esp. 253–67.

[4] See Colin Jones, *The Great Nation: France from Louis XV to Napoleon* (London: Penguin Books, 2002), ch. 2.

landed in the Bastille in 1718, and Montesquieu was obliged to avoid
the censure of the church by publishing the *Persian Letters* anonymously in Holland, the Regency gained a reputation for a new spirit
of intellectual liberty. By accepting the dedication of an edition of
Pierre Bayle's *Critical Dictionary* (*Dictionnaire critique*, 1709), the
Regent communicated a new openness to a great Protestant thinker
who was dedicated to religious toleration and the application of
reason to theological enquiry.[5]

As a nobleman and *parlementaire*, Montesquieu was inclined by
background to look warily on centralization by the King, and to value
independence. In 1716 he began service as a magistrate in the
Parlement of Bordeaux. He came of age in a world where scientific
achievements and speculative philosophy, energized by the legacy of
Descartes, were posing profound challenges to theology; and when
the uncertainty created about the workings of the universe, its age,
and size caused numerous thinkers to ponder the origins and practice
of individual societies (allegorized in the celebrated fable of the
Troglodytes in Letters 11 to 14).[6] In 1694, shortly after Montesquieu's
birth, the Académie Française published its dictionary in which the
term *philosophe* is defined as 'a man who by liberty of spirit [*esprit*],
stands above the normal duties and obligations of civic and Christian
life. This is a man who refuses nothing, who is constrained by nothing, and who leads the life of the Philosopher.' By 1721 the 'New
Philosophy', together with the rise of science—not least in the
provincial academies such as Bordeaux, where Montesquieu was an
active member—encouraged a belief among the relatively small educated public that the application of reason would lead to a better
understanding of the natural world and society. Looking beyond
their local domain, scientists and interested amateurs, who shared
intellectual affinities, created an international network often referred
to as the Republic of Letters. By the time he reached the age of 30,
Montesquieu was one of this new generation of men immersed in
the scientific spirit of the age. His membership of the Academy of

    [5] On Bayle and western tolerance towards Islam, see Jonathan I. Israel, *Enlightenment
Contested* (Oxford: Oxford University Press, 2006), 615–20.
    [6] Alberto Postigliola, 'Montesquieu entre Descartes et Newton', in C. Volpilhac-
Auger (ed.), *Montesquieu: les années de formation (1689–1720)*, *Cahiers Montesquieu*, 5
(1999), 91–108.

Bordeaux and adherence to the larger Republic of Letters make him a *philosophe*, and therefore a member of the group of men and women whose activities as writers, intellectuals, and propagandists contributed to the establishment of the Enlightenment as a movement committed to seeking the truth and to bettering life on earth. As a magistrate in the Parlement of Bordeaux, Montesquieu opposed clerical interference in politics (and traces of this hostility to Jesuit activism have been detected in the *Persian Letters*), and his interest in the links between religion, politics, and history—a curiosity that shapes the observations of his Persians—bore fruit in his early *Dissertation on the Politics of the Romans with respect to Religion*. Voltaire, in his story *Zadig* (1747), pithily captured the mentality of the age by saying of his hero that he was 'happy because he possessed the style of reason'—a style which Montesquieu and the more enlightened figures of the *Persian Letters*, both western and Orientals, also possess.

The Regency lasted from September 1715 to February 1723. The narrative of the *Persian Letters* falls within those years, cast as a period of extremes in national spirits and fortunes. The fictional calendar of the text ends in 1720, only a year before the date of publication. The real world can occasionally be glimpsed in the letters when events like the death of Louis XIV (Letter 89) are noted. It has been remarked that Montesquieu had an advantage in creating foreign narrators, because their Parisian chronicle required a minimum of verisimilitude by comparison with the extensive description expected in travel accounts. Yet Lady Mary Wortley Montagu, a famed observer of the East, observed that 'Montesquieu, in his *Persian Letters*, has described the manners and customs of the Turkish ladies as well as if he had been bred up among them'. And if the lightness of touch means that the topography of East and West is spare, Montesquieu's initial readers delighted in seeing parts of Paris—the rue Vivienne and the rue Quincampoix, the Palais-Royal, and the Café de la Régence (immortalized in Diderot's dialogue *Rameau's Nephew*)—strongly associated with the Regency. The effect is to stress the luxury and opulence of Paris as the new focus of attention after the decline of Versailles as the royal seat; and to draw attention to cultural and intellectual spheres, where the arts of conversation and refinement are on display. The austerity of the old regime had given way under Philippe to a delight in sexual pleasure and depicting the erotic. The Persians arrive in Paris just as the elite become enticed by a culture of seduction in which sophisticated role-playing and subtle rules of social comportment shape behaviour. Topical comments about passion and jealousy (Letter 26), the nature of beauty (Letter 32), courtesans (Letters 26 and 55), adultery and divorce (Letters 53 and 113) capture an ethos of libertinism and gallantry explored in the fictions of the younger Crébillon in the 1730s and staged in the plays of Marivaux, and soon to be graphically depicted by Watteau, Fragonard, and Boucher. Such letters are set in striking juxtaposition with the travellers' own sexual politics in their letters about virginity (Letter 56), the comportment of widows (Letter 120), the capacity of eunuchs to experience sexual jealousy (Letter 51), and, most remarkably, the tale of the incestuous love of the siblings Apheridon and Astarte (Letter 65) that anticipates Diderot's *Supplement to the Voyage of Bougainville* (1771), the greatest Enlightenment text on this taboo. Serious-minded as they are, Usbek and Rica move from questions of individual sexual behaviour to questions of national interest and a broader web of connections linking local values and global trends. By speculating (Letters 110 to 120) on the impact of monogamy and polygamy on population growth in Muslim and Catholic countries, they arrive at a critique of colonialism, which in their view undermines the growth of conqueror and conquered. The workings of colonialism and money were a practical as well as theoretical matter in the Regency. For colonialism fuelled the speculative bubble engineered by the Scotsman John Law, the controller-general of the Bank of France, who sold shares backed by putative future profits from France's holdings in Louisiana. Irrational exuberance gripped speculators, and the collapse of his 'System' wiped out individual fortunes and virtually emptied the state's coffers.

The travellers' interrogation of social custom, politics, religious practice, and ecclesiastical authority bespeaks a positive belief in the power of critical examination to better their world. In the nine years during which the two principal travellers, Usbek and Rica, live in Paris, they experience two governments and three currency revaluations, events which sharpen their sense of uncertainty. In the 1750s, when Montesquieu published a new and substantially revised edition of the *Persian Letters* (see the Note on the Text), he had mixed feelings about the Regency, calling its failed projects, its attempts at systems, a 'formless blend of weakness and authority' that was nothing more than a 'beautiful spectacle'. The device of balancing fictional foreground and historical backdrop enabled Montesquieu to reach beyond satire of the immediate context. The sense of historical change just outside the fictional frame adds to the impression that individual fates are inseparable from the national and institutional histories and their instabilities. The delayed news of Roxane's tragedy and the collapse of his eastern world reaches Usbek at precisely the moment when the French state is rocked by financial collapse. If their experiences reflect an element of gloom on Montesquieu's part about France's immediate political prospects, the travellers' energy and openness in recording their experiences still record a positive attitude to the progress Montesquieu sees as possible in an age committed to rational values.

A Novel Form

The *Persian Letters* are often called a novel, but the label is not necessarily an apt one. What would Montesquieu have understood by the term 'novel'? Eighteenth-century neoclassicism favoured the epic poem and the theatre, while the novel remained a less well-defined genre practised outside the control of the academic sphere and its expectations. In the multi-volume romance favoured by aristocratic women writers of the second half of the seventeenth century, it was love and sensibility that made the world go round. The chivalric values of the aristocracy imbued the seventeenth-century adventure novel, which was made up of semi-mythical heroic encounters, escapist plots, and exotic settings. But our modern view of the novel emerges not from these earlier traditions, but rather from some major eighteenth-century works marked by an increase in psychological plausibility and sense of social realism, features that made Prévost's *Manon Lescaut* (1730) an important step in this direction.[7]

---

[7] See Franco Moretti (ed.), *The Novel* (Princeton: Princeton University Press, 2006), vol.1: *History, Geography and Culture*; and Jenny Mander (ed.), *Remapping the Rise of the Novel* (Oxford: Voltaire Foundation, 2007). On the development of the English novel and its great variety, see Patricia Meyer Spacks, *Novel Beginnings* (New Haven: Yale University Press, 2006).

In 1717 Montesquieu's approach to the genre is in the nature of an experiment—indeed, some would argue that Montesquieu was not originally intending to write a novel at all. His book takes the form of a correspondence centred around two Persian noblemen, Usbek and Rica, who are travelling through France. The attraction of an epistolary form lay in its flexibility and openness of plot, structural variety, and capacity for multiple discourses. Although epistolary fictions did exist, and often their subject-matter was exotic, such masterpieces of the genre as Richardson's *Pamela* (1740-1) and *Clarissa Harlowe* (1747-8), Rousseau's *La Nouvelle Héloise* (1761), and Laclos's *Dangerous Liaisons* (1782) had yet to be written. Montesquieu would later claim that he was the first to teach 'how to write a novel in letters', but he did not invent the epistolary correspondence as a literary form. Gabriel Guilleragues's *Portuguese Letters* (1685) first established the letter-form as a type of narrative fiction. Among Montesquieu's models the most interesting is *Letters Written by a Turkish Spy* (1684). Attributed to Giovanni Paolo Marana, the novel's dedication presents it as a genuine translation from the Arabic of a work written in 1683 by one Mahmoud, an agent of the Porte stationed in Paris for forty-five years. The letters present a one-dimensional narrator, as rigid in his loyalty to his faith and masters as Usbek and Rica are by comparison flexible and questioning. And while Montesquieu shares more common ground with Marana than has been acknowledged—in particular, the latter's interest in the scientific and philosophical questions of the Enlightenment have been underestimated—the narrative focuses mainly on diplomatic and military issues.

At the same time Montesquieu was also drawn to the new form of the periodical, that was having a sensational success as best represented by Addison's *The Spectator* (and imitated in France by Marivaux). The emergence of periodicals in England implied a new readership and sphere of debate. While the public sphere was emerging more slowly in Paris, there was such a readership, as Rica observes in Letter 124 (and see Appendix, p. 235). The periodical made it possible to discuss serious things in what Dr Johnson called the 'middle style', that is, in a conversational tone of voice. To this style, Montesquieu joined the exotic visitor and the intellectual preoccupations of Bayle, while also looking back to the seventeenth-century moralist tradition and the study of types that he learned from La Bruyère's satirical portraits in his *Characters* (1688).

While Montesquieu follows Marana's example of the foreign observer embedded in a new culture, Usbek and Rica owe their tone of humour and sophistication to the model set by Joseph Addison's Mr Spectator. The Addisonian speaker instructs by entertaining, provoking, charming, and puzzling. Like the articles in *The Spectator*, the chapters of the *Persian Letters* often begin as vignettes before advancing to a more general, abstract level of discourse, and they fold journalistic observation of current events into an essayistic style written in the neutral middle register. Their diction is the educated speech of polite society. Coupled with the multiple perspectives in which the epistolary novel excelled, the elegance of Montesquieu's fleetly punctuated and conversational style represents an innovation. Some twenty different voices can be heard in the *Letters*, including the travellers, friends, Muslim clergy, and eunuchs. The use of the letter-form means that the writer is freed from the essayist's obligation to engage in thorough argumentation and exposition of a topic, and can therefore sound more chatty. When Montesquieu wishes to increase the degree of amusement and satire, he stages scenes as in a comedy. And when he wishes to underscore emotional drama, he shows equal facility in using a tragic register.

The type of organic growth that we expect from fictional characters is not a fundamental part of Montesquieu's understanding of how the novel works. Nonetheless, the letters are often psychologically revealing, showing shifting attitudes juxtaposed with inflexibility on certain points. This openness to experience seems to reflect Montesquieu's interest in John Locke's empiricism.[8] Nothing in the *Persian Letters* suggests that he wishes us to believe that ideas are innate to the human soul. If anything, the experience of the travellers, whose spirit of discovery causes them to question the religious and domestic practices of their native Persia, suggests that part of their mission is to approach the world in the spirit of a Lockean epistemology, where sensation is seen as the basis of all ideas. Formed by other cultures and experiences, Usbek and Rica are hardly blank slates; yet they possess the sensibility to experience the new and the

---

[8] Edwin Curley, 'From Locke's Letter to Montesquieu's *Lettres*', *Midwest Studies in Philosophy*, 26: 1 (2002), 280–306.

rational means to assess how it challenges the values they hold. With the exception of faith, what they know depends on their experience of the outside world and does not come from within. At the same time, the presence of two main letter-writers constantly varies the perspective, and events prompt both to considerations that lay bare their individual psychologies in their reaction to a new environment. The usual critical tendency to see Rica as superficial and Usbek as morose and profound is too simple. They both exhibit qualities of intelligence, but their modes of observation are different. Rica's characteristic approach is to channel his bemusement and surprise through anecdote, often deflecting conclusions through wit. Without pointing the moral of his stories, he leaves it to the addressee of his letters and the reader to ask the necessary questions. While there are a number of letters where Usbek works inductively from his empirical observations to more abstract questions, it is more often the case that he begins with a general proposition and organizes his narrative to corroborate his view. Usbek's identity develops through a double procedure. We understand him through letters that treat his relationship to the institutions of his home culture; through letters that capture his naive and then increasingly sophisticated perspective on French manners, customs, and institutions; and through the letters to the seraglio which capture an emotional self over which he has seemingly little control.

Questions about the sources of individual identity, whether approached in essentialist terms or in terms of cultural determination, are raised over and over again. The *Persian Letters* does not offer a conclusive verdict, because its aim is to pose the question. A Persian can play at being both a Frenchman—and, surprisingly, a Persian. In Letter 28 Rica recounts how his Persian dress made him an object of fascination in Paris, to the point that:

old men, young men, women, children, they all wanted to see me; if I went out, everyone crowded at the windows; if I went walking in the Tuileries, I would instantly find a circle forming round me; even the ladies encircled me with a rainbow of a thousand delicate shades; if I went to a theatre I would immediately be conscious of a hundred lorgnettes focused on my face; in a word, no man has ever been seen as much as me. It sometimes made me smile, to hear people who had scarcely ever ventured from their chambers saying to one another: 'One must admit he looks very Persian!'

Such celebrity inspires an experiment. Shedding his Persian costume, he dresses as a Parisian and now fails to persuade anyone who will listen that he is the same fascinating foreigner. Rica also finds himself in a position to see the question of identity through the eyes of a Frenchman. Letter 52 is one of the most theatrical in the entire work. Rica sets the scene in the first paragraph, as he describes a conversation overheard from the neighbouring room. The story concerns a man who has fallen on hard times and can no longer cut the figure of an *honnête homme* or gentleman in society. He catalogues the defining qualities of the Parisian 'bel esprit':

'I must say, the reputation of being a wit is very difficult to maintain; I don't know how you have managed it.' 'I've had an idea,' said the other man, 'let's work together on being witty; we'll team up to do it; every day we'll agree what we're going to talk about, and we'll be such a help to one another that if someone comes and interrupts us in the middle of our thoughts we'll get him to join us, and if he won't come willingly we'll make him; we'll agree on where to show approval, and where to smile; on other places where we should really laugh, laugh heartily; you'll see, we'll set the tone for all the conversations, and we'll be admired for our razor-sharp wit and the felicity of our repartee; we'll protect one another with prearranged signals; today you'll shine, tomorrow you'll support me; I'll arrive at a house with you, and exclaim, gesturing towards you: "I must tell you a very funny reply that M. just made to a man we met in the street," and I'll turn to you: "He wasn't expecting it, it certainly took him aback." . . . So, my friend, that's how to go about it; you do what I tell you, and I promise you a seat in the Academy before six months are out; in other words, you won't have to work for long, because you can then abandon your study of the art; you'll be a wit no matter what you do.'

The performance displays conviction in the notion that only appearance is authenticity. This Parisian is no more a native of his world than Rica, unless he can satisfy social expectations of his identity. At the end of the letter Rica observes that, in France, 'as soon as a man joins an association, he immediately acquires what is termed *esprit de corps*'. If clothing and manners make the external man, will the inner man change to follow suit? This remains an open question, left for the characters and reader alike to ponder.

Irony affords a sense of distance from the France under observation, while a feeling of erotic anxiety makes Persia feel near. During the nine years that Usbek spends in France the largest number of letters that he receives are from the harem: there are eleven from his wives, five from the chief eunuch, and six from others in the seraglio. He is portrayed in these letters as being unable to transfer his new-found views on the question of women's emancipation to the situation of his own wives, who even in the absence of their lord and master remain abject slaves of their eunuch guardians, deprived of rights and in a state of virtual incarceration (on which see the Appendix, pp. 240–3). In counterpoint to the conversational tone that Usbek and Rica maintain, the language of the correspondence between Usbek and residents of the seraglio is highly dramatic. In letters to the chief eunuch and his subordinate, Usbek becomes another person: he commands and brusquely threatens all his wives, apart from Roxane.

By the time Montesquieu produced a revised edition in 1754, with eleven new letters, the novel as a genre was well established. In this context the original Regency work looked old-fashioned alongside fictions where plot drove the narrative. Keen to gain a second success on these new terms and to deflect criticism, yet at pains to minimize the obviousness of any changes, Montesquieu offered a new interpretative key in 'Some Reflections on the *Persian Letters*'. He claimed that 'Nothing has given readers of the *Persian Letters* greater pleasure than finding, without expecting to, a kind of novel in it . . . These passages are invariably associated with a feeling of surprise and amazement, and never with any idea of scrutiny, even less with that of criticism.' In adjusting the order of the letters and supplementing it with new letters that reinforced the plot-line, Montesquieu aimed to realign his fiction with new conventions and to underscore the drama of the seraglio, Usbek's loss of control and blindness about the degree of rebellion and disenchantment. He called this the 'secret chain' that linked the disparate letter-writers of his work, and their diverse subjects.

Although the *Persian Letters* has traditionally been read in French (and in English translation) in this later version, encrusted with the older writer's changes, the present translation, for the first time in English, gives the initial version as it was first read in the 1720s. In both texts the major plot-line of the book is built on the episodic exchanges of these letters about the seraglio. But in the original text they are interspersed within the travel narrative at such irregular intervals that the building suspense might go unnoticed were it not for the arrival of urgent news almost at the end of the book, where we are reminded that even in his absence Usbek remains an actor on a different stage. In the original edition Usbek's final letter to his wives, enjoining them to show obedience, is sent on 4 October 1719. Written with anxious urgency, Usbek's appeal goes unanswered until Roxane writes on 2 March 1720 to describe the chaos of the rebellion. Letters 143 and 149, reporting on the complete breakdown of order in the seraglio, come twenty months after Usbek wrote Letter 63 ordering that measures be taken to end the chaos. Roxane's final letter, in which she exposes her own role in the revolt and declares her intention to commit suicide, is written on 8 May 1720, and will reach Usbek long after she has killed herself. While the 1754 text adds letters in order to bolster the seraglio intrigue, arguably the effect of the revolt is more dramatic in the earlier version because it is more sudden and violent. Turning-points, while prepared for, can only be spotted with hindsight. Montesquieu uses the time-lag between Usbek's sending and receiving letters to create a sense of helplessness: the characters' emotions escalate, but their reactions cannot be synchronized, and their passions dictate their fates.

In this respect Montesquieu learned much from neoclassical stage technique, and especially from the timing and reversals that create tension in Racine's tragedy *Bajazet* (1672). Set in the East, the play concerns an adulterous hero and heroine (the latter shares her name with Usbek's wife Roxane) whose fate depend entirely on the absent emperor Bajazet: if he perishes in battle they are safe, if he returns victorious then false friend and unfaithful wife will pay with their lives. An unreliable rumour from the battlefield arrives, keeping the protagonists on edge (and spectators in suspense) until Bajazet's unexpected and late return seals their doom. Montesquieu's final letters stand in stark contrast with the urbane tone maintained for most of the work, and with the deceptive earlier reports that allayed Usbek's fears of Roxane's restiveness. The unexpectedness of the revelations, together with their bluntness, create a stunning *coup de théâtre* at the end. If the travellers in their letters attempt to penetrate the appearance of French polite society, Usbek's letters to the seraglio perpetuate the performance that he must maintain according to the sexual politics of the harem. In the final letters, where a genuine voice of unvarnished emotion speaks, all pretence of deference and subservience vanish. Where so many of the earlier letters concerned the institutions of a newly explored civilization, these later ones convey the breakdown of the order Usbek took for granted. When Usbek defends suicide in Letter 74 as a legitimate choice—a position that was regarded as heretical by the church and therefore as a provocation on Montesquieu's part—it is without any foresight into the outcome of his own affairs. At the end Usbek scales the heights of reproach and anger as he fathoms the extent of the unrest in the harem. In Letter 148 Roxane writes that 'Horror, darkness, and terror hold sway in the seraglio'; she, too, speaks as a character from a tragedy. Only the reader is in a position to appreciate the dramatic irony created by the juxtaposition of the suicide and Usbek's earlier views.

Montesquieu and Orientalism

'Orientalism' has been a productive, if contentious, critical term since the appearance in 1978 of Edward Said's influential analysis. In his view, Orientalism is an imperial discourse devised by colonial powers, which extended their hegemony by casting the Orient as a world of inimical and alien values that needed to be civilized and tamed. Debate over Said's argument has generated important criticism and corrections to a picture that, while stimulating and conscience-raising, was distorted by tendentiousness.[9] Although his account begins with the seventeenth century, the real starting-point of his views on the literary and historiographical treatment of the East and its peoples is the later history of nineteenth-century European empires. Reactions to Said's description continue to produce a more balanced picture of a long tradition of serious study of the Orient by explorers, ethnographers, philologists, and anthropologists who anticipated and then sometimes accompanied colonial expansion without necessarily being supporters of an imperialist ideology. From the seventeenth century, the expansion of trade with the East paved the way for travel writers who provided highly detailed accounts of oriental civilization, most specifically its Turkish and Persian variants. Barthelemy d'Herbelot's enormous *Bibliothèque*

---

[9] See Robert Irwin, *For Lust of Knowing: The Orientalists and their Enemies* (London: Penguin Books, 2006), esp. ch. 9; and Maya Jasanoff, 'Before and After Said', *London Review of Books*, 8 June 2006, pp. 14–15.

orientale (1697) provided a cultural handbook to the East culled from a wide range of sources. Despite Said's polemical exaggerations, not all Orientalists or Orientalisms were implicitly racist or tainted by the hegemonic culture's sense of superiority. Montesquieu himself does not fit easily into Said's paradigm. While he does play to popular perceptions of a brutal and uncultivated Orient, it is only to bring out the parallels more forcefully. An enlightened sensitivity to the distinctive shape and histories of other cultures informed his *Spirit of the Laws*, a seminal comparative study of systems of government and perhaps the most influential work of political and social theory to come out of the Enlightenment. Without being normative or prescriptive, Montesquieu famously argued that nations, governments, and peoples were the product of their environment.

Yet, whether or not we subscribe to the view that a colonialist ideology pervades all representations of this other, Eastern world, Said nonetheless provided a valuable service in focusing attention on the inescapable fact that a particular image of the East crystallized in the minds of writers and readers of Montesquieu's lifetime. No matter how scientific the observations of travel writing could be, from the early eighteenth century the Orient appears as a place of fabulous luxury and sensuous delight in fiction, painting, and the decorative arts. Antoine Galland's sensational and highly popular French version of *The Thousand and One Nights* (1704–17) cast a spell. The compendious anthology of Scheherazade's tales fixed standard features of this orientalist mirage, from the image of grand vizirs to the odalisques of Ingres in the nineteenth century. Harems, eunuchs, secret apartments, and seductive visions were only extreme manifestations of the Regency's delight in pleasure. Hot on Galland's coat-tails, Louis XIV's expert on the East, Pétis de la Croix, published two further original collections that were sold as translations, *The History of the Sultan of Persia and his Vizirs* (1707) and *A Thousand and One Days, Persian Tales* (1710–12).

The discovery of the East created an intellectual need to re-evaluate the West. Travel—or at least the virtual travel of fiction—was not in one direction. Real-life visits by foreign travellers also had a powerful mystique. While a Turkish ambassador's appearance at the court embassy to Louis XIV proved to be a diplomatic fiasco, the occasion mesmerized writers and painters with an eye for the exotic. Several contemporary authors anticipated Montesquieu in making their Orientals go west. Charles Dufresnay's *Serious and Comic Pleasures of a Siamese in Paris* (1707) was light on philosophy but generous in Watteauesque tableaux of pleasures. But other works, such as J. F. Bernard's *Moral, Comic and Satirical Reflections on the Manners of our own Century* (1711) and J. Bonnet's *Letter Written to Musala Concerning the Manners and Religion of the French* (1716), turn to the foreign traveller as a satirical commentator on local society. In the main, these writers played up the more sensational stereotypes of the East as the antithesis of western values. Their fictional Orient is a world where corruption and absolutism reign, where women, relegated to the seraglio, are oppressed, where luxury on an unprecedented scale saps moral strength. Such decadent visions undoubtedly encouraged among moralists of the eighteenth century and the Victorian period the disapproval Said associated with western discourse on the Asiatic. But for Montesquieu's readership, the escapism of the Orient appealed as part of the pleasure of literature.

We can only guess at the precise impulse that led Montesquieu to conceive his oriental fiction. Montaigne's reputation had lapsed during the height of French classicism, and he ceased to be reprinted for about fifty years from the 1670s; but, as we know from his notebooks, Montesquieu read and esteemed him and would certainly have known Montaigne's great essay *On Cannibals* of 1580. There he created a naive perspective from which to illuminate 'the opinions and customs of the country we live in', showing the 'savage' to be civilized and throwing the very meaning of 'civilized' into question. This was a clear influence. But Montesquieu's imagination may have been more immediately stimulated by a footnote in the *Critical Dictionary* in which Bayle wondered what the effect would be if a work written by a westerner attempted to convey the views of a Japanese or Chinese traveller who had lived in the great cities of Europe. It is equally possible that the figure of the philosophical traveller originates with an event recorded in the pages of Joseph Addison's *Spectator*. In April 1710 four Iroquois chiefs visited London on a mission for aid in their struggle against the French in Canada. Their appearance aroused public curiosity and also captivated the imagination of Addison, who in *The Spectator* provided a description of the sights of London and the mores of the English as seen through their foreign gaze. In *The Spectator* (No. 50, April 1711) Addison produced a cultural commentator and satirist of western institutions in the fictional figure of Sa Ga Yean Qua Rash Tow, the visiting emperor of the Iroquois Indians and author of a satirical letter that was translated into French in 1714.[10] Through their naive perspective, where facts were only half-understood or comically reproduced, the Iroquois offered English readers a different perspective on the political circumstance and cultural landscape of their country. Addison puts the technique of defamiliarization, where what we know is described in simpler terms as something alien, to good use. The Iroquois gather that two 'kinds of Animal', namely, Whig and Tory, are important; they wonder at the size of St Paul's and its religious purpose; and comment on the performance of a preacher or 'Man in Black who was mounted above the rest, and seemed to utter something with a great deal of Vehemence' (Jonathan Swift, who had hatched his own plan to write a work of *Indian Letters*, regretted sharing the idea with Addison who was quicker into print). Addison's account was a gift to an ironist like Montesquieu, and in the *Persian Letters* he launched the career of a new type of narrator who would be a mainstay of classic Enlightenment fictions like Voltaire's *Philosophical Letters* (1734), Oliver Goldsmith's *Citizen of the World* (1762), and Diderot's *Supplement to the Voyage of Bougainville* (1771).

Montesquieu's Orientalism does not fall precisely into the style of writing about the Orient that was immediately available. The vogue for the Orient was inseparable from its image as a place of marvellous storytelling. By contrast, the *Persian Letters* scarcely indulge this tendency, with few tales spun solely for the sake of entertainment. Montesquieu's scrupulous attention to descriptive detail is not about realism. It attests to the sensitivity of the historian and student of cultures determined to create out of the novel a plausible narrative vehicle for the philosophical questions he wishes his readers to consider. In his descriptions of Islam, the seraglio, and even in the chronology of the Persians' outward journey Montesquieu drew on documentary descriptions. The most important accounts were by the explorers Jean Chardin (*Journeys in Persia*, 1711) and Jean-Baptiste Tavernier (*The Six Journeys of Jean-Baptiste Tavernier . . . in Turkey, in Persia and in the Indies*, 1719). The travellers' itinerary is based on

---

[10] Joseph Addison and Richard Steele, *The Spectator*, ed. Donald F. Bond, 5 vols. (Oxford: Clarendon Press, 1965), i. 211–15 (no. 50).

Tavernier, while the Islamic dating of the letters follows the data provided by Chardin. The reader can glean a picture of the East and its mores, but this is of secondary importance in a work that is primarily about seeing French and European life and institutions from an outside perspective. Although the East acts as a contrast and provides subversive parallels to what is seen in France, it chiefly enables Montesquieu to sharpen his satire. Despite its novelistic sub-plot of the seraglio, the world of the *Persian Letters* does not replicate Galland's entertainments. Montesquieu remained more faithful to the world of the travel accounts than the world of the fictions. Unlike other writers, Montesquieu downplays expectations for wondrous description, avoiding the obvious clichés and manner of oriental fictions. The letters emanating from the seraglio, whether from the chief eunuch or Usbek's wives, focus on the psychological reality of feelings like passion and love that are universal. Unlike Scheherazade, Usbek's wives do not relieve their captivity or win love or even entertain the reader with amazing stories; their storytelling is manipulative rather than exotic. Montesquieu pulls away from the dominant trend of associating the Orient with entertainment by not creating a fabulous Orient: the most extensive interpolated stories, such as those about the Troglodytes and the story of the incestuous brother and sister, are didactic fables dressed up in an appealing mode. By equalizing the tone of western and eastern discourse, and by keeping a bifocal balance between the Parisian and oriental narratives, he is able to suggest both comparison and parity. Men and women from East and West emerge in this work as products of their environment; yet, at a profound level, French or oriental, they are also recognizably similar. For all his concern to satirize a specific moment in French history, and for all his similar concern to give his Persians life as characters, Montesquieu's larger aim is to depict a process of questioning. In the event, the tension between the conclusions of reason and the modes of custom and behaviour may be so deeply ingrained by virtue of birth and culture that they cannot be changed.

A Literary Perspective on Enlightenment

More than Montesquieu's other predecessors, Marana's *Turkish Spy* made it possible for him to combine fiction and cultural commentary. Marana set an important example by including letters on subjects that Montesquieu would later take up, such as the question of progress, the religious repercussions of Copernicus's theory, the status of scientific academies, and Cartesian philosophy (see the Appendix, pp. 232–4). On all these questions, as a true follower of Muhammad and the revelation of the Qur'an, the Turkish spy sets his mind firmly against European values and learning. Marana's work emphasizes the gulf between East and West, whereas Montesquieu's travellers are caught in a double bind owing to their newfound belief in the power of reason. Sceptical about Europe, they are intrigued by and attracted to its modes of thought and its forms of civilization. Sceptical about the Orient, they cannot tear themselves away from beliefs and customs that are no less problematic yet fundamental to their personal lives.

This ambivalent sense of belonging and observing emerges in the explicit cultural comparisons of manners and institutions and, more subtly, through small linguistic details that create an effect of defamiliarization. In Letter 47 the priest who accosts Rica is called a 'dervish'; the description of this figure makes the reader see him through Rica's eyes, and renders him as bizarre to the French reader as he is to Rica. Such questioning brings a refreshing distance. In Letter 34 Usbek gives his account of what seems to him an obscure doctrinal dispute convulsing the 'beaux ésprits' of Paris. In fact, he has stumbled on an important moment in the history of European aesthetics, namely, the second part of the so-called 'Quarrel between the Ancients and the Moderns'. In the 1680s and then again in the 1710s French Academicians debated whether, as the Ancients held, priority should be given to perfecting imitation of classical culture, in the knowledge that it could never be surpassed; or whether, as the Moderns argued, cultures could indeed make progress and advance beyond their predecessors. The first stage of the Quarrel marked a turning-point in French culture, and its repercussions continued to shape attitudes to notions of taste and aesthetics not only in France, but in England as well. The second phase of the Quarrel erupted in 1714 around a famous translation of Homer by Anne Dacier, who believed that fidelity to the literal meaning of the original was the acid test of excellence. Her ideal was contested in another translation by Houdar de La Motte, who, as a Modern, believed it was possible to perfect even the ancients. Usbek's letter on the controversy is a masterly example of the naive viewpoint. Homer, never referred to by name, is called the 'Greek poet'. Stripping away the hallowed name conveys Usbek's stupefaction that such vitriolic discussion relates to an obscure figure from the very distant past, whose country of origin and date of death remain unknown. Unfamiliar with scholarly conventions, he refers to Latin as a 'barbaric language', rather than the language of scholarship in the period, and also misses the point that the Moderns wished to champion the vernacular. By reducing the episode to a common-sense description of its basic elements, the foreign observer as satirist gains a distance that its participants lack.

Elsewhere a clash of perspectives can be implicit, its purpose to underscore the degree to which unvoiced assumptions determine individual conclusions. When Usbek's friend Rhedi writes from Venice (Letter 29), he complains about the lack of running water. In this he resembles many other contemporary and future travel writers, who are chiefly anxious about cholera. Fear of illness in this case is communicated entirely in terms of ritual piety. Rhedi fears that he will be unable to carry out his ritual ablutions as a Muslim, and consequently sees Venice as a 'profane' city. In other respects he casts himself as a model traveller, keen to learn about advances in medicine and physics despite mocking them as 'superstitions'. Even so, the gap between European and oriental perspectives is distilled into the different uses of water.

The theme of religion surfaces in various registers, from apology to pastiche, from theological dissertation to mockery of rituals and anti-ecclesiastical satire. Religion is present as an issue in almost forty letters, vividly reminding us that Montesquieu and his contemporaries were as profoundly troubled by questions about the political role of the church as they were concerned with theological problems. The perspective on religion emanates from Muslims who, even before they arrive in France and attempt to interpret Catholicism, have already started asking questions about their own faith and its practices. Even before he subjects western Christianity to sceptical analysis, Usbek has already developed a comprehensive approach to religion as a phenomenon determined by social structure rather than revealed truth. In Letter 7 he explains the circumstances of his departure from Isphahan, and describes how a feigned interest in 'science' (meaning secular knowledge) turned into real curiosity. In Letter 11 he overtly expresses piety for 'certain truths of which one cannot be persuaded, that have to be felt'. This frame passage is, however, an ironical introduction to the ensuing three letters in which he narrates the story of the Troglodytes, essentially a myth about the way political power makes use of religion to consolidate structures. Letter 12 discusses religious festivals and worship in terms of a universal human need to make sense of the world by positing causality: in the absence of any other explanatory mechanism, people will follow a natural impulse to ascribe their good fortune to the gods. Having set out this theory in letters to a friend, Usbek immediately follows with a profession of faith in Letter 15 to the guardian of a shrine. This is a prelude to a series of questions that he wishes to put to the sage, Mehemet Ali (for a model, see the Appendix, p. 231). A master of rhetoric, Usbek opens with a flattering tribute to the wisdom of the holy man who, in his view, must be a recluse from life because he fears that the brilliance of his wisdom would 'obscure the sun'. He praises his 'science as an abyss more profound than the ocean'. By force of juxtaposition with the letters on the Troglodytes, it is impossible not to read this profession ironically, a tone that Mehemet Ali catches when he castigates Usbek for asking too many questions when he would be better off reading 'the traditions of our Doctors'.

Out of this fundamental premiss—that religious belief is a historical phenomenon conditioned by political and social factors—comes the scrutiny to which Usbek subjects Christian practice. The letters on the Troglodytes constitute a sophisticated use of parable.[11] Other letters make use of literal description to create an effect of defamiliarization, showing practices that would have been entirely commonplace to Montesquieu through the naive gaze of the Persians; this is the case, for instance, in letters that treat seemingly arbitrary dietary practices. By the end of the *Persian Letters* there is a distinct feeling that religion is seen as a man-made system that serves a useful function. When it produces evils like intolerance, dogmatism, religious wars, and even depopulation (because strict rules of celibacy threaten birth-rates), then religion undermines its own purpose.[12] Montesquieu's view is anthropocentric, in seeing

[11] Alessandro Crisafulli, 'Montesquieu's Story of the Troglodytes: Its Background, Meaning and Significance', *PMLA* 54 (1943), 372–92.

[12] David B. Young, 'Libertarian Demography: Montesquieu's Essay on Depopulation in the *Lettres Persanes*', *Journal of the History of Ideas*, 36: 4 (1975), 669–82.

religion as a mechanism for coherence in society rather than a revelation of transcendent truth.

In his first letter Usbek claims that he and Rica travel in 'the arduous quest for wisdom', and that despite their wonderful country of
origin 'they did not believe its boundaries should be the boundaries
of our knowledge'. And yet in Letter 57 Rica, who seems to have
been acculturated effortlessly into his European world, puts his
finger on the paradox of their experience. True to the Lockean tenet
that the world comes to one as experience and must be understood
empirically, the travellers also recognize that they cannot overcome
the perspectives that are part of their own character. As Rica states,
'it seems to me, Usbek, that we never judge anything without secretly
considering it in relation to our own self'. The letters from the
seraglio, while essential to the creation of a novelistic plot-line, form
an important counterpoint to Usbek's narrative of Enlightenment.
For however great his curiosity and seeming open-mindedness about
gender relations in his Parisian experiences, Usbek seems always to
revert to type as a despotic husband and master, tragically incapable
of change. Reason and understanding make it possible to see the
other point of view without necessarily invalidating his own bias.
The 'unenlightened' East, of which the seraglio seems only to be a
microcosm, collapses in chaos and suicide. Meanwhile, the 'enlightened' West, as represented by France, seems equally despotic, has no
moral advantage, and goes bankrupt.

This is a small book about huge questions. Montesquieu's travellers
are curious anthropologists of both the old and the new, and while
they remain attached to the core beliefs in which they were raised—
and may not in fact be able to shed them—they cannot refrain from
interrogating basic assumptions about the whole range of human
enterprise. What is the place of women? Does the value of a woman
reside in her chastity or in her intelligence? What proof of the existence of God is sufficient when there are only myths and stories
to rely on? How many books does one need to know? Do manners
and clothes really 'make the man', or are residents of different
nations different at an essential level? Scepticism about unproven
assumptions flows out of the pens of the letter-writers. Their observations take the form of a wide variety of modes, frequently entertaining and never narrowly didactic. These narrators reflect Montesquieu's

command of the intellectual tools of the Enlightenment. If their oriental provenance makes it hard for them to be open-minded, they see the bigotry of others and apply reason as experience compels them to compare their European and Persian worlds. Usbek and Rica are still decades from La Mettrie's radical discussion of the nature of human feeling in the 1740s, Jean-Jacques Rousseau's seminal writings on political theory in the 1750s, and the materialist and atheistic reflections of Diderot and d'Holbach in the 1770s. But the Persians are Montesquieu's spokesmen for a new attitude, critical of an old order and hopeful, if uncertain, about the new, an achievement acknowledged by the editors of the *Encylopédie* in the tribute published in the fifth volume after his death. Montesquieu does not reflexively dismiss ideas and institutions, but makes them the subject of debate through the method of relative comparison. If he and his contemporaries had yet to use the name of the European Enlightenment, *Aufklärung* or *Siècle des Lumières*, they were already talking its language and manifesting its spirit. For the mentality of that European movement was already in place and being actively promoted by the generations of thinkers from Descartes, Locke, and Newton to Montesquieu, Voltaire, and Benjamin Franklin.

Tribute has often been paid to Montesquieu's prescience in bringing together a range of philosophical, social, and scientific topics that would become mainstays of the intellectual activity later in the eighteenth century. While such a retrospective assessment is of value, another way to appreciate the striking achievement of the *Persian Letters* is to see his work in its historical context, and to suggest that Montesquieu conveyed in his fiction how far advanced the process of Enlightenment already was, and why the Enlightenment was worth capturing in an early stage of ferment and in all its forms of discovery. For students of the Enlightenment as a pan-European movement, the true importance of the *Persian Letters* should lie in how it distils the spirit of a new age, capturing the changing patterns in the history of thinking about philosophy, science, and the institutions of culture and government that took root from the mid-seventeenth century onward. Montesquieu's genius lies in his creation of a philosophical fiction, written with grace, wit, and humour, that conveys the pressure that a new spirit of reason and scepticism brought to bear on some of the political and religious certainties of *ancien régime*

institutions. If the great Enlightenment themes such as moral rela-
tivism, tolerance, compassion, and gender equality captivate the
imagination of Montesquieu's characters, it is because these themes
are already present and active in his world, and are not merely
spectres on the horizon.

NOTE ON THE TEXT

MONTESQUIEU first published the *Lettres persanes* anonymously, in 1721. He apparently took no part in the production of a second edition that appeared in the same year. In 1754 he oversaw a revised edition. In 1758, after Montesquieu's death, a printer produced a fourth version. Surprisingly, it is this posthumous edition of 1758, and neither of the two overseen by Montesquieu in his lifetime, which has become the standard version in French and in translation. The authoritative critical edition of Philip Stewart and Catherine Volpilhac-Auger, published as the first volume of the *Oeuvres complètes de Montesquieu*, now establishes the definitive text once and for all. For their base text the editors of the Voltaire Foundation edition have gone back to the 1721 version. The present translation is based on this edition, and makes available in English the version that first won Montesquieu acclaim, inspired imitations in France and England, and is truest to his thinking at the time.

The editorial apparatus of the Voltaire Foundation edition gives a full account (pp. 15–43) of the differences between the first edition and the major revision of 1754. The main points of the editorial history can be briefly stated. The first edition of 1721, printed in Holland (with a false imprint of the printer Pierre Marteau of Cologne), contained a total of 150 letters. (A second edition appeared in the same year, but it can be disregarded here because Montesquieu had no hand in its production.) After 1748 Montesquieu was embattled because of the controversy surrounding *The Spirit of the Laws*, but demand for his work only increased. The first 1721 edition of the *Persian Letters* had become a rarity by this time, and he was encouraged to produce a new one. In 1754 Montesquieu brought out his own second edition of the *Persian Letters*, making numerous 'micro-textual' changes at the level of punctuation and word-choice to his 1721 original. The overall effect, arguably, was to simplify the style and diminish some of the sparkling irony in favour of more blunt statement. The most significant changes, however, relate to the total number of letters. The volume contained, at the end, a supplement of eleven letters as well as the author's 'Some Reflections on the

Persian Letters'. Montesquieu was keen to give his work a new relevance and to modernize it by giving the seraglio plot greater coherence and continuity. The supplementary letters represented a substantial modification to the content of the work. Especially noteworthy is the third supplementary letter (no. 77). Insofar as it appeared to temper the advocacy of suicide presented in the adjacent letter (no. 75 in the present numbering) it may have been an attempt to mollify the church authorities, who openly accused Montesquieu of impiety. But, for whatever reason, Montesquieu in 1754 did not slot them into the original sequence, and his decision to append them as a separate supplement counteracted the cumulative impression of change.

After his death the publisher Huart brought out, in 1758, the first posthumous edition containing all 161 letters as revised in 1754, and assimilating into a single consecutive sequence the letters that were first published separately in the supplement of 1754. Ever since the eighteenth century it is this posthumous edition that has been regarded as the standard text, and the form familiar both to French readers and in translation.

Despite the weight of tradition, there are two arguments against using the 1758 version. First, it is simply not a version that Montesquieu authorized, whereas the two versions from 1721 and 1754 bear his authority. In choosing between these two, there is a case for saying that the first edition, with its original stylistic choices, should take priority because of its freshness and its historical importance as the text that influenced the Enlightenment. Montesquieu had a fine sense of how innovative the work was in its time, and wrote in his *Pensées*, 'of all the editions of this book, it is only the first that is good and it never belied the courage of the booksellers'. True to that spirit, the Voltaire Foundation critical edition restores the 1721 text as printed. But the eleven supplementary letters that were composed subsequently represent Montesquieu's own revision, and need to be made available to the reader without violating the form of the 1721 original. Following the practice of the Voltaire Foundation edition, the present translation prints the eleven supplementary letters after the original sequence of letters. Much writing about the *Persian Letters* refers to the 1758 edition, which has a different sequence because the supplementary letters have been integrated throughout. In order to make any cross-references to the 1758 edition accessible the Concordance of Letter Numbers gives the equivalent numbering.

ACKNOWLEDGEMENTS

For their learned help I would like to thank Nicholas Cronk, Jonathan Mallinson, Catherine Volpilhac-Auger, and Wes Williams. I would also like to thank Judith Luna for expert advice and encouragement from the start of the project.

Andrew Kahn

SELECT BIBLIOGRAPHY

Critical Editions

Lettres persanes, ed. Jean Starobinski (Paris: Gallimard, 1973).

Lettres persanes, ed. Philip Stewart and Catherine Volpilhac-Auger, in *Oeuvres complètes de Montesquieu* (Oxford: Voltaire Foundation, 2004), vol. 1.

Lettres persanes, ed. Paul Vernière, revised by Catherine Volpilhac-Auger (Paris: Le Livre de Poche, 2005).

Lettres persanes, ed. Alain Sandrier (Paris: Gallimard, 2006).

Critical Studies in English

Ballaster, Ros, *Fabulous Orients: Fictions of the East in England 1662–1785* (Oxford: Oxford University Press, 2005), ch. 2.

Cronk, Nicholas, 'Voltaire, Lucian, and the Philosophical Traveller', in John Renwick (ed.), *L'Invitation au voyage: Studies in Honour of Peter France* (Oxford: Voltaire Foundation, 2000), 76–84.

Frautschi, R.-L., 'The Would-be Invisible Chain in the *Lettres persanes*', *French Review*, 40 (1976), 9–22.

Grenby, M., 'Orientalism and Propaganda: The Oriental Tale and Popular Politics in Late-Eighteenth-Century Britain', *Eighteenth-Century Novel*, 2 (2002), 215–37.

Grosrichard, Alain, *The Sultan's Court: European Fantasies of the East*, trans. Liz Heron (London: Verso, 1998).

Gunny, Ahmad, 'Montesquieu's View of Islam in the *Lettres persanes*', *Studies on Voltaire and the Eighteenth Century (SVEC)*, 174 (1978), 151–66.

Haskins Gonthier, Ursula, 'Montesquieu and England: Enlightened Exchanges in the Public Sphere (1689–1755)', DPhil. thesis, Oxford University (2006).

Kra, Pauline, 'The Invisible Chain of the *Lettres persanes*', *SVEC* 23 (1963), 7–60.

—— 'Religion in Montesquieu's *Lettres persanes*', *SVEC* 72 (1970).

Mallinson, G. J., 'Usbek, Language and Power: Images of Authority in Montesquieu's *Lettres persanes*', *French Forum*, 18 (1993), 23–36.

Mason, Sheila, 'New Perspectives on the *Lettres persanes*: Montesquieu and Lady Mary Wortley Montagu', in Margaret Topping (ed.), *Eastern Voyages, Western Visions: French Writing and Painting of the Orient* (Bern: Peter Lang, 2004), 113–33.

O'Reilly, R. F., 'The Structure and Meaning of the *Lettres persanes*', *SVEC* 67 (1969), 91–131.

Peirce, Leslie P., *The Imperial Harem: Women and Sovereignty in the Ottoman Empire* (New York and Oxford: Oxford University Press, 1993).

Said, Edward, *Orientalism* (London: Routledge & Kegan Paul, 1978).

Shackleton, Robert, *Montesquieu: A Critical Biography* (London: Oxford University Press, 1970).

—— *Essays on Montesquieu and the Enlightenment* (Oxford: Oxford University Press, 1988).

Vartanian, Aram, 'Eroticism and Politics in the *Lettres persanes*', *Romantic Review*, 60 (1969), 22–33.

Yegenoglu, Meyda, *Colonial Fantasies: Towards a Feminist Reading of Orientalism* (Cambridge: Cambridge University Press, 1998).

Yeazell, Ruth Bernard, *Harems of the Mind: Passages of Western Art and Literature* (New Haven and London: Yale University Press, 2000).

Young, David B., 'Libertarian Demography: Montesquieu's Essay on Depopulation in the *Lettres Persanes*', *Journal of the History of Ideas*, 36: 4 (1975), 669–82.

Critical Studies in French

Ehrard, Jean, *L'Invention littéraire au XVIIIᵉ siécle: fictions, idées, société* (Paris: PUF, 1997).

Hoffman, Paul, 'Usbek Métaphysicien: recherches sur les significations de la 69ᵉ "Lettre persane"', *RHLF* 92 (1992), 779–800.

Postigliola, Alberto, 'Montesquieu entre Descartes et Newton', in Catherine Volpilhac-Auger (ed.), *Montesquieu: les années de formation (1689–1720)*, *Cahiers Montesquieu*, 5 (1999), 91–108.

Schneider, Jean-Paul, 'Les Jeux du sens dans les *Lettres persanes*. Temps du roman et temps de l'histoire', *Revue Montesquieu*, 4 (2000), 127–59.

Stewart, Philip, 'Toujours Uzbek', *Eighteenth Century Fiction*, 11 (1998–9), 141–50.

Volpilhac-Auger, Catherine, and Philip Stewart, 'Introduction: Pour une "Histoire véritable" des *Lettres persanes*', in *Oeuvres complètes de Montesquieu*, vol. 1: *Lettres persanes*, ed. Jean Ehrard and Catherine Volpilhac-Auger (Oxford: Voltaire Foundation, 2004), 15–71.

Background Reading

Brockliss, L. W. B., *Calvet's Web: Enlightenment and the Republic of Letters in Eighteenth-Century France* (Oxford: Oxford University Press, 2002).

NOTE ON THE CHRONOLOGY
OF THE *PERSIAN LETTERS*

The definitive discussion of calendar time in the text is Robert Shackleton, 'The Moslem Chronology of the *Lettres persanes*', in his *Essays on Montesquieu and on the Enlightenment* (Oxford: Oxford University Press, 1988), 73–83. Montesquieu appears to be following the lunar months of the Muslim calendar. Shackleton identified a number of features from which he concluded that Montesquieu had lost sight of the fact that lunar months did not have a fixed number of days. He tried, perhaps half-heartedly, to align his itinerary with time-lines given in Chardin and Tavernier, but the result is more an effect of local colour than strict adherence to the Muslim calendar. In effect, Montesquieu gave Muslim names to the months of the solar or Gregorian calendar, as follows. These differ from current Islamic renderings, but because there are various transliteration systems, this translation retains Montesquieu's original French spellings:

January	Zilcadé
February	Zilhagé
March	Maharram
April	Saphar
May	Rebiab 1
June	Rebiab 2
July	Gemmadi 1
August	Gemmadi 2
September	Rhegeb
October	Chahban
November	Rhamazan
December	Chalval

A CHRONOLOGY OF MONTESQUIEU

1674 Birth of Philippe d'Orléans, nephew of Louis XIV, who will become Regent in 1715.

1685 Revocation of the Edict of Nantes; 200,000 Huguenots leave France.

1685 Publication of André Du Ryer's French translation of the Qur'an.

1688 Café Procope opens in Paris. In England, the Glorious Revolution installs William of Orange as king. Catholic priests take refuge in France. Jean de La Bruyère publishes the first edition of his *Les Caractères* (*Characters*).

1689 18 January, birth of Montesquieu, Charles-Louis de Secondat, at the château de La Brède in the Bordeaux province.

1700 Publication of John Locke's *Essay on Human Understanding* in French translation.

1700–5 Education at the Collège de Juilly, which is run by the Oratoriens. He returns to Bordeaux in 1705 and pursues legal studies.

1704 Antoine Galland publishes his translation of the *Thousand and One Nights*. Locke's *Letters on Tolerance* published.

1708 Licensed to practise law at the Parlement of Bordeaux.

1709–13 Resident in Paris; makes the acquaintance of Fontenelle, the permanent secretary of the Academy of Sciences, whom he greatly admires, and Nicolas Fréret, the secretary of the Academy of Inscriptions and Belles-Lettres, whose special interest was China.

1713 Pope Clement XI issues the Bull *Unigenitus* condemning Jansenism.

1714 Elected to the Parlement of Bordeaux. Treaty of Utrecht, ending the War of the Spanish Succession. Embassy of Mehemet Riza Beg, Persian ambassador, to Paris.

1715 Marriage to the wealthy, Protestant, Jeanne de Lartigue; the union reportedly lacks great affection. Publication of J. F. Bernard, *Reflexions morales, comiques et satiriques sur les moeurs de notre siècle* (Cologne, 1715: *Moral, satirical and comic reflections on the manners of our age*), in which a Persian protagonist journeys to Europe. Death of Louis XIV (1 September). Philippe, prince d'Orléans, installed as Regent, restores to the Parisian Parlement its right of 'remonstrance'.

1716   Elected a member of the Academy of Bordeaux, on which occasion he reads his *Dissertation sur la politique des Romains dans la religion* (*Dissertation on the Politics of the Romans with respect to Religion*). Comes into his fortune and the baronetcy, succeeds his uncle as president of the Parlement of Bordeaux. French translation of Addison's *The Spectator*, containing a story of the visit of Iroquois kings to London.

1717   In Paris from January to March, active in the Academy of Bordeaux later in the year. Formation of the Quadruple Alliance (France, England, Holland, Austria) against Spain. Turkish conquest of Belgrade.

1718   Composes scientific works on various subjects like the cause of the echo, the function of the renal glands, as well as works on the mines of Germany and the sobriety of the residents of ancient Rome. Plot against the Regent uncovered; the duc de Maine is arrested. John Law, as finance minister, establishes the Banque générale and the Mississippi Company (which becomes the Compagnies des Indes Orientales et de la Chine), aimed at developing investment in the North American French colony of Louisiana. Voltaire's tragedy *Oedipe* brings his first important triumph.

1720   A crash ends Law's schemes between January and June, bankrupting large numbers. He flees and dies penniless in Venice in 1729.

1721   Anonymous publication, to acclaim, of the *Lettres Persans* (*Persian Letters*) in Amsterdam under imprint of Pierre Marteau, Cologne, a pseudonym for Jacques Desbordes of Amsterdam, one of the most important publishers of the Enlightenment. In his *Essai d'observations sur l'histoire naturelle* (*An Essay on Observations on Natural History*), read to the Academy of Bordeaux on 20 November 1721, Montesquieu reports on botanical and biological experiments; he espouses Cartesian mechanics, although his views continue to evolve. The Russian tsar, Peter the Great, visits Paris.

1721–8   Active at La Brède, where he takes an interest in viticulture; long periods in Paris, where he frequents the fashionable salons, especially that of Madame de Lambert, meeting with the philosopher Fontenelle and cultivating the acquaintance of freethinking libertines, and economists such as the members of the 'Club de l'Entresol'. He continues to produce scientific work as well as writings on moral issues.

1723 Writes the *Letter from Xenocrates to Pheres*, a tribute to the late regent.

1724–5 Publishes the *Temple de Gnide* (*Temple of Gnidus*), a prose poem in seven cantos, which is presented as a 'translation' from the Greek.

1726 Sells the *privilège* of his presidency to raise funds.

1728 Elected to the Académie Française, despite objections of impiety aimed at the unidentified author of the *Persian Letters*

1728–31 Embarks on a Grand Tour, which offers a wealth of opportunity for the comparative study of institutions and cultures. He starts with Vienna and joins Waldegrave, nephew of James Fitzjames, the duke of Berwick and natural son of James II. He visits Genoa and Florence before arriving in Rome in January of 1729, where he remains until July, during which period he also visits Naples. He then visits Innsbruck, Munich, Augsburg, Frankfurt, and Hanover. From October he is in Holland, until returning to England in November. He spends the year of 1730 in London, where he strengthens his contacts with political figures and men of science. Elected to the Royal Society. He becomes a Freemason. Throughout the journey he keeps a record of his itinerary and activities.

1731–41 Return to Bordeaux in May. Scholarly activities include further writings on political theory and geology. In 1733 publishes a second major work, *Considérations sur les causes de la grandeur des Romains et de leur décadence* (*Considerations on the Causes of the Greatness of the Romans and their Decline*). He resumes his Parisian life, but devotes himself 'eight hours daily' to work on a book about laws. From the early 1740s his vision is impaired by a cataract.

1747 Elected to membership of the Berlin Academy of Sciences.

1748 Anonymous publication of *De l'esprit des lois* (*The Spirit of the Laws*) in Geneva. Vigorous attacks on his theories follow, prompting him to reply with his *Défense de l'Esprit des lois* (*A Defence of the Spirit of the Laws*) in 1750.

1750 Jean-Jacques Rousseau's *Discours sur les sciences et les arts* (*Discourse on the Sciences and the Arts*) awarded a prize by the Academy of Dijon.

1751   The Jansenist abbé J.-B. Gaultier attacks the *Persian Letters*, citing the work's un-Christian attitude to suicide and its whiff of materialism. The Vatican places the *Spirit of the Laws* on the Index.

1753   Having declined to write the articles on despotism and democracy, Montesquieu produces the *Essai sur le goût* (*Essay on Taste*) for volume 7 (published in 1757) of the *Encyclopédie*, edited by D'Alembert and Diderot. Addresses a *Mémoire sur la Constitution* (*Memoir on the Constitution*) to the king, in which he defends religious toleration against a background of continued persecution of Jansenists.

1754   Publishes a revised edition of the *Persian Letters*, containing a refutation ('Réflexions') of the abbé Gaultier's criticisms.

1755   Dies in Paris on 10 February. Volume 5 of the *Encyclopédie* contains a 'Eulogy to Montesquieu'.

LIST OF CHARACTERS

Travellers

    Usbek
    Rica

Characters from the seraglio

    wives of Usbek:
        Fatmé
        Roxane
        Zachi
        Zelis
        Zephis
    head black eunuch (also called chief eunuch, head of the black eunuchs)
    Jaron, black eunuch
    head white eunuch
    Pharan, black slave
    Narsit, black slave
    Solim, black slave
    Cosrou, white eunuch
    Nadir, white eunuch
    Zelide, slave to Zephis and Zelis
    Ismael, black eunuch

Letter-writers

    Rustan, friend of Usbek in Isphahan
    Mirza, friend of Usbek in Erzeron
    Mehemet Ali, guardian of sanctuary in Qum
    Ibben, friend of Usbek
    Rhedi, nephew of Ibben
    Haggi Ibbi, author of a single letter (Letter 37) on religion
    Nargum, Persian ambassador in Moscow

PERSIAN LETTERS

PREFACE

THIS is not a dedication, and I seek no patron for this book; if it is good it will be read, and if it is bad, I do not particularly care if it is read.

I have selected these first letters to test the public's taste; I have kept, among my papers, a great many more, which I can make available at a later date.

But that is conditional upon my remaining anonymous,* for if my name becomes known, from that instant I shall keep silent. I know a woman who walks quite well, but limps as soon as people watch her. The faults of the work are sufficient, without my offering the critics the faults of my person as well. If people knew my identity, they would say: 'His book is not consistent with his character; he ought to spend his time on something better; this is not worthy of a serious man.' The critics never fail to make comments of this kind, because they can be produced without great mental effort.

The Persians who wrote these letters lodged with me; we spent our lives together. As they thought of me as a man from another world, they concealed nothing from me. Indeed, men transplanted from such a distance could no longer have any secrets; they showed me most of their letters, which I copied; I even happened upon some that they would have been most reluctant to let me see, so mortifying were they for Persian vanity and jealousy.

My role, therefore, is simply that of translator; all my effort has been directed at accommodating the work to our customs and tastes; I have relieved the reader of as much of the Asian style* as I could, and have saved him from a vast number of high-flown expressions, which would have bored him to tears.

But that is not all I have done for him. I have abridged the long compliments with which Orientals are no less generous than we ourselves are; and I have skipped over a great many trifling details which withstand the glare of public scrutiny so poorly, and should always disappear after two friends have shared them.

If most of those who have given us collections of letters had followed my example, they would have seen their work vanish to nothing.

One thing has often amazed me: to find that these Persians are sometimes as knowledgeable as I myself am about the customs and manners of this nation, so much so as to be familiar with the finest points; and that they notice things which, I am certain, have escaped many Germans who have travelled in France. I attribute this to the long period of time they have remained here, quite apart from the fact that it is easier for an Asian to learn about French ways in the space of one year, than it is for a Frenchman to learn about Asian ways in the space of four; the reason being that the former are as frank as the latter are reserved.

Custom authorizes every translator, and even the most uncouth commentator, to embellish the head of his version, or commentary, with a panegyric of the original, and to point out its usefulness, merit, and excellence. I have not done this; to guess my reasons will be easy: one of the best is that such remarks would be very boring, appearing in a place which on its own is very boring anyway, namely, a preface.

LETTER 1

Usbek to his friend Rustan, in Ispahan

We spent only one day at Qum:* when we had finished our prayers at the tomb of the Virgin who gave birth to twelve prophets,* we resumed our travels; and yesterday, the twenty-fifth since leaving Ispahan, we reached Tabriz.

Rica and I are perhaps the first Persians whom the appetite for learning has prompted to leave the land of their birth, and forsake the charms of a peaceful life in favour of the arduous quest for wisdom.

We were born in a prosperous realm, but did not believe its boundaries should be the boundaries of our knowledge, and that the light of the Orient need be the only light to illuminate our path.

Tell me what people are saying about our journey; do not flatter me; I do not expect many supporters. Address your letter to Erzeron,* where I'll be staying for some time.

Goodbye, my dear Rustan, never doubt that wherever I may be in the world, you have in me a faithful friend.

Tabriz,* the 15th of the Moon of Saphar* 1711

LETTER 2

Usbek, to the chief black eunuch of his seraglio* in Ispahan

You are the faithful custodian of the most beautiful women in Persia; to you have I entrusted the worldly possessions I hold most dear; you guard the keys to those fateful doors which open solely for me. While you watch over this precious treasure of my heart, my heart is at ease, wholly free from apprehension. You keep watch equally in the silence of the night as in the bustle of the day; your tireless attentions support virtue when it wavers. If the women you guard wished to deviate from their duty, you would make them lose all hope of doing so; you are the scourge of vice, the pillar of fidelity.

You both command and obey them; you carry out their orders unquestioningly, and you see that they obey the laws of the seraglio in like manner; you take pride in performing the meanest tasks for them; you comply respectfully and fearfully with their legitimate demands: you serve them as if you were slave to their slaves, but by a reversion of power, you exercise complete command in my name when you fear some infringement of the laws of chaste and seemly behaviour.*

Always remember the abyss* from which I raised you, when you were the least of my slaves, by placing you in this post and entrusting you with the delights of my heart; always bear yourself with the deepest humility in the presence of those that share my love, but at the same time make them aware of their total dependence; see that they enjoy every innocent pleasure, distract them if they seem worried, amuse them with music, dancing, delicious drinks; encourage them to meet together often. If they desire to go into the country, you may take them there; but show no mercy to any man who dares appear in their sight; exhort them to cleanliness, which reflects the purity of the soul; speak to them sometimes of me: I long to see them again in that lovely place which they make yet more beautiful. Farewell.

Tabriz, the 18th of the Moon of Saphar 1711

LETTER 3
Zachi to Usbek, in Tabriz

We ordered the chief eunuch to take us to the country; he will tell
you our journey passed without incident. When we reached the river
and had to abandon our litters in order to cross it, we climbed into
boxes* as is our custom; two slaves carried us on their shoulders and
we were safe from all eyes.

How could I have gone on living, dear Usbek, in your seraglio in
Ispahan, in those apartments which, reminding me constantly of past
pleasures, made my desire burn with a fiercer flame each day?
I would wander from room to room, always seeking you and never
finding you, but finding everywhere some cruel reminder of my past
felicity; picturing myself now in that room where for the first time in
my life I took you in my arms; now in that other room, where you
decided the famous quarrel among your women. Each claimed to be
the most beautiful of us all; after adorning ourselves with every garment and ornament that the imagination could devise, we paraded
before you; you delighted in the miracles of our art; you were amazed
at what our passion to please had inspired us to achieve, but soon you
wanted those borrowed charms replaced by a more natural grace, and
you undid all that we had done; we had to set aside those ornaments
which now you found inconvenient, and appear before your gaze in
the simple garb of nature. To modesty I gave no heed, my only
thought was for my own honour and glory. Happy, happy Usbek,
what delights were displayed before your eyes! For a long time we
watched you wander from enchantment to enchantment; for a long
time your wavering heart remained irresolute; each new delight
exacted a tribute from you; soon we were all covered with your
kisses; your questing eyes explored the most secret places; you kept
asking us to assume a thousand different poses; always there were
fresh demands, and always fresh obedience. I confess to you, Usbek,
that a passion more powerful than ambition made me long to please
you. I saw myself gradually become mistress of your heart; you chose
me; you left me; you returned to me, and this time I kept you;
victory was for me alone, and despair the lot of my rivals; you and I

felt as if we were alone in the world, as if now nothing else was worthy of our attention. Would to heaven that my rivals had had the courage to remain to see all the tokens of love I received from you; if they had witnessed my raptures they would have understood the difference between my love and theirs; they would have seen that although they might be able to compete with me in physical beauty, they could not compete with me in sensibility... But where am I? Where are these futile words leading me? It is a misfortune to be not loved; but it's an insult to be no longer loved. You have left us, Usbek, to journey through savage lands. How can you hold as worthless the blessing of being loved? Alas, you do not even know what you are losing! I sigh, but you do not hear my sighs; my tears flow, but you feel no delight in my tears; the seraglio is filled with the breath of love, yet your indifference takes you ever farther from it: ah, my dear Usbek, if only you knew how to be happy!

Fatmé's seraglio, the 21st of the Moon of Maharram 1711

LETTER 4

Zephis to Usbek, in Erzeron

That black fiend has finally decided to drive me to despair: he'll use any means whatever to deprive me of my slave Zelide, Zelide who serves me with such devotion, and whose skilful hands bejewel and embellish my entire body; he's not satisfied that this separation should be painful: he claims also that the grounds for it are discreditable. The perfidious creature asserts that my reasons for trusting Zelide are criminal, and because he gets bored waiting outside the door, where I always send him, he dares suppose that he has heard, or seen, things that I cannot even imagine. I am terribly unhappy; neither my seclusion nor my virtue can protect me from his wild suspicions: a base slave has attacked me in your very heart, Usbek, and I must defend myself there. But no, I have too much self-respect to stoop to justifications; I want no other guarantee of my conduct than you yourself, your love and mine, and—I must tell you this, dearest Usbek—and my tears.

Fatmé's seraglio, the 29th of the Moon of Maharram 1711

LETTER 5

Rustan to Usbek, at Erzeron

You are the subject of every conversation in Ispahan; people talk of nothing but your departure: there are those who attribute it to frivolity, others to some sorrow; only your friends defend you but no one believes them; no one can understand how you could leave your wives, your parents, your friends, your homeland, to travel into lands unknown to Persians. Rica's mother is inconsolable; she begs you to return to her her son whom you have, she says, carried off. For my part, dear Usbek, I am by nature inclined to commend everything you do; but I cannot forgive you for this absence, and whatever reasons for it you may give me,* my heart will never approve them. Farewell, love me always.

Ispahan, the 28th of the Moon of Rebiab 1 1711

LETTER 6

Usbek to his friend Nessir, in Ispahan

At a day's journey beyond Erivan* we crossed out of Persia, and entered lands which owe obedience to the Turks; twelve days after that we reached Erzeron, where we plan to remain for three or four months. I must confess to you, Nessir, that I felt a secret pang on taking a last look at Persia, and finding myself surrounded by perfidious Ottomans.* The further I penetrated into the land of those infidels, the more I felt an infidel myself. My homeland, my family, and my friends filled my thoughts; my affections reawakened; a nagging anxiety added to my unease, and made me realize that I had embarked on an enterprise too great for my own peace of mind.

But above all, my heart is troubled about my wives: I cannot think of them without being overcome with distress.

It's not that I love them, Nessir: in that respect I am so lacking in feeling that all desires have abandoned me. In the large seraglio where I have lived, I've forestalled love, and let it destroy itself: but out of my very indifference has come a deep-seated jealousy, which devours me; I see a band of women left almost to themselves: I own only base souls to watch over them, and I would scarcely feel secure were my slaves faithful to me. What will happen if they are not? What painful news may not reach me in the distant lands I plan to travel? This is an evil for which my friends can offer no remedy: its setting a place of whose sad secrets they must remain in ignorance: and indeed what remedy could they provide? Would I not a thousand times prefer having crimes silently left unpunished, to having them noisily and publicly corrected? I am confiding all my troubles to your loving ears, Nessir; it's my sole remaining comfort, in my present state.

Erzeron, the 10th of the Moon of Rebiab 2 1711

LETTER 7
Fatmé to Usbek, in Erzeron

Two months have passed since you left, dear Usbek, and I, in my dejection, still cannot quite believe it. I hurry through the seraglio as if you were still here; even then I cannot accept the truth; what is to become of a woman who loves you, who was used to holding you in her arms, whose sole occupation was to discover ways to prove her love? A free woman by her high birth, but a slave to the violence of her passion.

When I married you, my eyes had not yet seen the face of a man; you are still the only one whose features I have been permitted to look upon, for I don't regard as men those hideous eunuchs, whose least significant defect is that they are not men. When I compare the beauty of your face with the ugliness of theirs, I cannot but think myself happy; my imagination is unable to conceive anything more beautiful than the alluring charms of your person. I swear to you, Usbek, that were I permitted to leave this place where I am kept imprisoned by the laws of my condition; were I able to escape the guards surrounding me and choose freely among the men living in this capital of nations—Usbek, I swear to you that I would choose no one but you; there can be no one but you in this world who deserves to be loved.

Do not imagine that your absence has made me careless of a beauty you treasure; although I can be seen by no one, and the ornaments with which I adorn myself can give you no pleasure, I still try to maintain the habit of pleasing: I never go to my bed without first perfuming myself with the most delicious essences: my memory dwells on those happy times when you would come to my arms; a delightful, seductive dream shows me the dear object of my love; my imagination, lost in its desires, is lulled by hope: sometimes I think that, wearied by the vexations of travel, you will return to us; the night passes in dreams I dream between waking and sleeping; I seek you at my side, but you seem to be eluding me; soon my overpowering desire itself dispels these enchanting fancies and brings me to my senses: I find then that I am so aroused... You may not believe me, Usbek, but it is not possible to live like this; fire runs in my veins; why can I not describe to you what I feel so vividly! And how can I feel so vividly what I cannot describe to you! In those moments, Usbek, I would relinquish power over the entire world, in exchange for one of your kisses. How wretched is a woman, to feel such violent desires when she is denied the very person who alone can satisfy them; when, left alone with herself, without any distraction, she is forced to pass her life between continual sighs and the violence of awakened passion, and, far from being happy herself, she is not even granted the blessing of promoting the happiness of another; a useless ornament of a seraglio, guarded for the sake of honour, and not for the happiness of her husband.

You men are so cruel! You are delighted for us to feel desires we cannot satisfy: you treat us as if we were insensible, yet you would be very angry were that actually the case; you believe that our long-suppressed desires will be aroused on seeing you; it's a difficult task to win someone's love, it's quicker to rely on our amorous susceptibility to obtain what you dare not hope to win by personal merit.

Goodbye, my dear Usbek, goodbye; you may be sure that I live only to adore you; my heart is full of you, and your absence, far from making me forget you, would inflame my passion, were it possible for it to become more violent.

The seraglio in Ispahan, the 12th of the Moon of Rebiab 1 1711

LETTER 8

Usbek to his friend Rustan, in Ispahan

I received your letter in Erzeron, where I now am. I had assumed that my departure would cause quite a stir, and this does not disturb me, for ought I to heed my enemies' prudent counsels, or my own?

I was extremely young when I first appeared at court, and I can say that my heart remained uncorrupted there; I even formed a great design, for I dared to be virtuous. As soon as I became aware of vice, I distanced myself from it, approaching it later only in order to expose it. I brought truth to the very foot of the throne, where I spoke a language unknown until that time; I confounded the flatterers and simultaneously astonished both the worshippers and the idol.

But when I saw that my sincerity had made me enemies, that I had provoked the jealousy of ministers without gaining the favour of the prince, and that all that protected me in a corrupt court was my impotent virtue, I determined to leave. I affected a deep devotion to the sciences and, by dint of affecting it, in fact grew to feel this devotion. I no longer played any part in affairs at court, and retired to a house in the country. But even this course of action had its drawbacks: I was still vulnerable to the malice of my enemies, and I had deprived myself almost entirely of any means to protect myself. Some confidential warnings made me think seriously about my own safety, and I resolved to exile myself from my native land; the very fact of my retirement from court provided me with a plausible pretext. I went to the king; I told him of my desire to instruct myself in the sciences of the West; I insinuated that my travels could be advantageous to him; my request found favour in his eyes; I departed, and deprived my enemies of a victim.

There, Rustan, you have the true reason for my travels; let Ispahan talk, do not defend me except to those who love me; let my enemies repeat their spiteful interpretations. I am only too glad that that is the sole way they can harm me.

At present people are talking about me; perhaps I shall be forgotten only too completely, and my friends… But no, Rustan, I will not give way to these sad thoughts; I shall always remain dear to them, and I believe in their loyalty, as I do in yours.

Erzeron, the 20th of the Moon of Gemmadi 2 1711

LETTER 9

The chief eunuch to Ibbi, in Erzeron

You attend your former master on his travels, journeying through provinces and kingdoms; grief and cares cannot affect you, for every moment brings something new; everything you see diverts you, and makes the time fly past unnoticed.

It is not so for me, confined as I am in a dreadful prison, surrounded always by the same objects and tormented by the same cares; I groan beneath the burden of the tasks and the anxieties that have been mine for fifty years; I cannot say that in the course of a long life I have known one day of serenity, or one moment of peace.

When my first master conceived the cruel plan of entrusting his wives to me, and forced me, with flattering attentions that veiled a thousand threats, to part for ever with my very self, I was weary of the harsh tasks that were my daily lot, and believed I was sacrificing my passions to my repose and to my fortune. Unhappy man! My distracted mind showed me the compensation, and not the loss: I expected to be freed of the pangs of love by the inability to satisfy them. Alas! The effect of passion was extinguished without extinguishing the emotion that sparked it, and far from being free of passion, I found myself surrounded by objects that constantly excited it. I entered the seraglio, where everything inspired in me regret for what I had lost; I felt perpetually aroused; it was as if a thousand natural beauties revealed themselves to my eyes simply in order to oppress me and—worst of miseries—I always saw before me a fortunate man. During those years of torment never did I conduct a woman to my master's bed, never did I undress her, without returning home with my heart full of rage and my soul full of terrible despair.

That is how I passed my miserable youth: I had no one to confide in but myself. Oppressed by troubles and afflictions, I was forced to stifle and deny them, and on those same women upon whom I felt tempted to gaze so tenderly, I invariably turned a severe eye; had they guessed my feelings I would have been lost, for to what purposes might they not have used their advantage?

I remember that one day, when assisting a woman into the bath, I felt so overcome that I completely lost my head, and dared lay my hand in a fearsome place. My first thought was that that day was my last upon this earth; I was lucky enough to escape dying a thousand deaths, but the beauty to whom I had revealed my weakness exacted a high price for her silence; I completely lost my authority over her, and since that time she has repeatedly forced me to do her favours which have endangered my life.

At last the fires of youth have died down, I am old, and in that regard I now know peace; I look upon women with indifference; I return with interest their scorn and every torment they made me endure; I remember always that I was born to command, and I feel I am again a man on those occasions when I still command them. I have hated them ever since I looked at them with dispassionate eyes and my reason showed me all their frailties; although I guard them for another, the pleasure of making them obey me fills me with a secret joy; when I deprive them of everything, I feel I do it for myself, and it always gives me indirect satisfaction; the seraglio is like a little empire of my own, and my ambition, the sole passion remaining to me, knows a measure of gratification. It gives me pleasure to see how everything depends on me, and that I am always indispensable; I welcome the hatred of all those women, for it strengthens my position here; nor do they find me unappreciative, for I am always one step ahead of them in even their most innocent pleasures; I invariably present myself as an unmovable obstacle; they make a plan, and I suddenly put a stop to it; refusals are my weapons, scruples my barbs; the only words upon my lips are duty, virtue, shame, and modesty; I drive them to despair with my perpetual harangues on the weakness of their sex and the authority of their master; then I deplore having to treat them so severely, seeming to imply that my sole motivation is their own interest, and my deep devotion to them.

Never imagine that I in my turn do not experience an infinite number of vexations, or that those vindictive women do not constantly try to pay me back in like coinage; they devise terrible revenges; between us there exists a kind of flux and reflux of power and submission. They always ensure that I be given the most humiliating tasks; they feign the most extreme contempt; and without any consideration for my years, they make me rise ten times during the night, for the least little trifle; I am continually overwhelmed with orders, commands, tasks, and whims; it is as if they take turns in keeping me overworked and concocting capricious demands; frequently they find great pleasure in making me do my work twice over; they arrange for me to be given secret confidential information which is in fact untrue; perhaps it might be that a young man was glimpsed near these apartments, or again that noises were heard, or a letter changed hands; all this worries me, and they laugh at my anxiety, delighted to watch me make myself uneasy. Another time they might tie me up behind a door and keep me chained there day and night; they are skilled at feigning sickness, fainting, and frights; they can always find ways of manipulating my reactions to fit their purpose; at such times I must show blind obedience and absolute compliance; a refusal on the lips of a man like me would be unthinkable, and were I to hesitate in obeying their command, they would have the right to punish me; I would sooner lose my life, my dear Ibbi, than suffer such a humiliation.

That is not all: I can never be confident, for one instant, of my master's favour; I have many enemies who are close to him, whose single thought is to bring about my downfall; they have their moments in the sun, when my voice goes unheard, when nothing is refused them, when I am always in the wrong; the women I lead to my master's bed are angry; do you suppose that they argue there on my behalf, or that my interests ever prevail? I have every reason to fear their tears, their sighs, their embraces, and even their pleasures; they are at the site of their triumph; their charms fill me with dread; in that moment their services blot out all my past service; and nothing can assure me of the trust of a master who is no longer in control of himself.

How many times have I gone to my bed in favour, and risen from it in disgrace? That day when I was so shamefully flogged round the seraglio, what had I done? I left a woman in the arms of my master; as soon as her charms had aroused him, her tears began to flow, and she began to complain, cunningly spacing her grievances so that their gravity intensified as his passion increased. What hope was there for me at a time like that? I was lost when I least expected it; I was the victim of an amorous negotiation, of a treaty written in sighs. Such, my dear Ibbi, is the cruel and constant condition of my life.

How fortunate you are! Your responsibilities are limited to the personal care of Usbek; it is easy for you to please him, and to remain in his good graces until the end of your days.

The seraglio in Ispahan, the last day of the Moon of Saphar 1711

LETTER 10

Mirza to his friend Usbek, in Ispahan

You were the only person who could console me for Rica's absence, and there was no one but Rica who could have consoled me for yours.

We miss you, Usbek, you were the soul of our circle: what violence is needed to break the bonds that the heart and mind have forged!

We debate here constantly; usually our debates are about philosophical and ethical issues. Yesterday we discussed whether man's happiness depends on pleasure and the satisfaction of the senses, or on the practice of virtue. I have often heard you say that man was born to be virtuous, and that justice is a quality as natural to him as existence itself. Explain, I beg you, what you mean.

I have consulted mullahs* who drive me to despair with their citations from the Qur'an, for I do not address them as a true believer, but as a man, as a citizen, and as the father of a family. Farewell.

Ispahan, the last day of the Moon of Saphar 1711

LETTER 11

Usbek to Mirza, in Ispahan

You set aside your own intellect in favour of mine; you condescend to consult me; you believe that I am capable of instructing you. My dear Mirza, what flatters me even more than your good opinion of me is your friendship, from which it springs.

To fulfil your request, I think it best not to employ purely abstract reasoning: sometimes simply to persuade people of a truth is not sufficient, one must also make them feel it; moral truths belong in this category, and perhaps this little narrative will impress you more deeply than would a subtle philosophical argument.

There lived in Arabia a people known as the Troglodytes;* few in number, they were the descendants of those ancient Troglodytes who, if we can believe historians, resembled animals rather than men. These men were not so ugly, nor had they fur, like bears; they did not whistle when they spoke, and they had two eyes; but they were so cruel, so savage, that they were wholly devoid of principles of equity or justice.

They had a king, a foreigner, who, hoping to reform their wicked natures, ruled them severely; but they conspired against him, killed him, and wiped out the entire royal family.

This done, they assembled together to choose a government, and after much discussion, they appointed magistrates; but barely had they finished the elections than they found they could not stand these magistrates, so they slaughtered them as well.

Freed of this fresh yoke, the Troglodytes now let themselves be guided solely by their natural savagery; they agreed that they would no longer obey anyone, but that each would consult his own interest without reference to others' needs.

Every man found this unanimous resolution greatly to his liking; they all said: 'Why bother wearing myself out working for other people who are no concern of mine? I'll consider only myself; I'll be happy; why should I care whether others are? I'll get myself everything I need, and as long as I'm alright, all the other Troglodytes can rot in misery for all I care!'

It was the month for sowing the fields with seed; they said: 'I'll only cultivate as much of my land as I require to grow the corn I need for food; a larger area would be no use to me; I'm not going to go to a lot of trouble for nothing.'

The arable terrain of this little kingdom was not all similar in nature: parts were arid, parts mountainous, while other, low-lying areas were watered by numerous streams. That year the drought was extreme, so that the fields on the high ground had no water at all, while those that could be irrigated were very fertile; thus the Troglodytes living in the mountains almost all starved to death, because their neighbours showed them no mercy, and refused to share their crop.

The following year was extremely wet; at higher elevations the fields were extraordinarily fertile, while the lower areas flooded. Once again half the Troglodytes cried 'Famine!' but those wretches found others as hard-hearted as they themselves had been.

One of the principal inhabitants had a very beautiful wife; his neighbour fell in love with her and carried her off; a tremendous quarrel ensued, and after much cursing and many blows they agreed to refer the matter to the decision of a Troglodyte who, during the period of the republic, had gained some respect. They approached him and attempted to tell him their story. 'What do I care whether this woman belongs to you, or to you? I've my field to till; I'm not about to spend my time settling your differences and working for you, while I neglect my own affairs; leave me alone, I beg you, and don't bother me any more with your quarrels'; whereupon he left them, and went off to work on his land. The abductor, the stronger of the two, swore that he'd sooner die than give this woman back: the other, bowed down with thoughts of his neighbour's injustice and the judge's hardness, was walking home in despair when he encountered a beautiful young woman returning from the well; he no longer had a wife; this woman pleased him, and she pleased him all the more when he discovered that her husband was the man he had asked to act as judge, and who had been so unsympathetic to his misfortune; he took her and carried her off to his house.

There was a man who owned quite a fertile field which he cultivated with great care; two of his neighbours banded together, drove him out of his house, and took his field; they joined forces to defend themselves against those who tried to seize it, and in fact did so successfully for several months; but then one of them, tired of sharing what he could have all to himself, killed the other and became sole master of the land. His dominion did not last long; two other Troglodytes came and attacked him, and he was too weak to defend himself against them; he was butchered.

An almost naked Troglodyte, seeing some wool for sale, asked the price; the merchant thought: 'Of course I shouldn't expect to get for my wool more than I need to buy two measures of corn; but I'm going to ask for four times as much, so I can get eight measures.' There was no recourse, the price had to be paid. 'I'm so pleased,' said the merchant, 'now I'll have some corn.' 'What did you say?' continued the stranger. 'You need corn? I've some to sell; it's just that the price may well astound you, because at present corn is terribly dear, famine being so widespread. But give me back my money, and I'll give you a measure of corn; otherwise I won't part with it, even if you were dying of hunger.'

Meanwhile, a cruel disease was ravaging the country; a skilful doctor came from a neighbouring land, and dispensed such appropriate remedies that he cured everyone who consulted him. When the sickness had abated he went to all the patients he had treated and asked for his fee: but he encountered only refusals, and returned home, exhausted by the fatigues of such a long journey; not long afterwards, however, he heard that the same disease had surfaced again, and was afflicting this ungrateful land even more severely; this time they came to him, not waiting for him to come to them: 'Be off with you, you unjust men,' he told them, 'your souls are sick with a poison deadlier than that for which you seek a cure: you are not worthy of occupying a place on this earth, because you are devoid of humanity, and know nothing of the rules of fairness; I believe I would offend the gods, who are punishing you, if I opposed the justice of their anger.'

Erzeron, the 3rd of the Moon of Gemmadi 2 1711

LETTER 12

Usbek to the same, at Ispahan

You have seen, my dear Mirza, how the Troglodytes perished through their own wickedness, and became victims of their own injustice. Out of all those families, there remained only two that escaped the misfortunes of the nation. Two most unusual men lived in that country: they were humane, they understood what justice was, and they loved virtue; bound together as much by the purity of their hearts as by the corruption of their fellow-men, they saw the general desolation and felt only pity; bound even more closely together by this, they worked with equal zeal for the common good, knowing no disagreements other than those arising out of their sweet and tender friendship; and in the remotest part of the country, isolated from compatriots undeserving of their presence, they led a happy, peaceful life, while the earth, worked by those virtuous hands, seemed to produce of its own bounty.

They loved their wives, who cherished them tenderly in return; they devoted their whole attention to raising their children in the path of virtue; they told them repeatedly of the misfortunes of their compatriots, and showed them those piteous examples; above all, they made them feel that the interest of the individual is always identical with the common interest, and that to attempt to separate oneself from it is fatal; that we should not find virtue arduous, or regard it as a painful exercise, and that justice to another is a charity to oneself.

Soon they knew the consolation of virtuous fathers, which is to have children like themselves. The young folk that grew up in their care married happily and multiplied: their numbers increased, but their unity remained the same, and virtue, far from becoming weakened in the multitude, was instead fortified by the greater number of examples.

What pen could depict here the happiness of those Troglodytes? So just a people should surely be cherished by the gods. As soon as the Troglodytes became aware of the gods, they learned to fear them; and the softening influence of religion tempered those customs which still retained a certain harshness from earlier primitive times.

They instituted festivals in honour of the gods: young girls, wearing flowery garlands, and young men celebrated with dances and pastoral music; feasts would follow, where joy and moderation ruled side by side; it was at these gatherings that the voice of innocent nature let itself be heard, where the young men learned to offer and to accept a heart, where the modest virgin would be surprised into a blushing admission, which the fathers' approval would quickly ratify, while the tender-hearted mothers took pleasure in the prospect of a sweet and faithful union.

They went to the temple to beg favours of the gods, not riches or an onerous abundance, for such desires were unworthy of the happy Troglodytes, and it was only on behalf of their compatriots that they asked for these; no, they approached the foot of the altars solely to beg that their fathers enjoy good health, that their brothers marry loving wives, and that their children be loving and obedient; the young girls came to the temple to offer the tender sacrifice of their heart, and asked no other blessing than that they might make a Troglodyte happy.

At sundown, when the flocks came in from the meadows and the tired oxen returned with the plough, they gathered together; and while they ate a frugal meal, they sang of the injustices of the first Troglodytes, and their misfortunes; of virtue born anew in the heart of a new people, and its felicity; then they sang of the greatness of the gods, their everlasting favours to those who prayed to them, and their inevitable anger towards those who feared them not; next they described the delights of country life, and the happiness of an existence always attended by innocence; soon, they would be overcome by sleep, which no anxieties or sorrows ever interrupted.

Nature provided them as readily with what they desired as with what they needed; in that blessed country cupidity was unknown; when they gave one another gifts, it was always the giver who saw himself as the more fortunate. The Troglodytes thought of themselves as a single family; as a rule their flocks were intermingled, and the sole task that they ordinarily avoided was that of dividing them up.

Erzeron, the 6th of the Moon of Gemmadi 2 1711

LETTER 13

Usbek to the same

I cannot speak too highly of the virtue of the Troglodytes. One day a son said: 'Tomorrow my father is going to till his field; I'll get up two hours before him, and when he reaches his field he'll find it all tilled.'

Another Troglodyte thought to himself: 'I believe my sister is very attracted to a young man who is a relative of ours; I must speak to my father and persuade him to arrange this marriage.'

Another was told that thieves had stolen his flock. 'I'm upset,' he said, 'because I had a pure white heifer which I intended to sacrifice to the gods.'

Another was overheard saying: 'I must go to the temple to give thanks to the gods, for my brother, whom my father loves so dearly and I adore, has recovered his health.'

Or again: 'There's a field that abuts my father's land, and the men who work in it are constantly exposed to the fierce rays of the sun; I must plant a couple of trees there, so that those poor folk can sometimes rest in their shade.'

One day, at a gathering of Troglodytes, an old man spoke of a youth whom he suspected of an evil deed, and reproached him with it. 'We do not believe that he committed this crime,' said the young Troglodytes, 'but if he did do so, may he die the last of his name.'

A Troglodyte was told that some strangers had sacked his house, and taken everything. 'If they were not unjust men,' he replied, 'I would hope that the gods might grant them a longer enjoyment of my possessions than they did to me.'

Such great prosperity was not seen without envy; neighbouring peoples assembled together, and under some vain pretext resolved to steal all their flocks. As soon as this news reached the Troglodytes they dispatched ambassadors, who addressed these neighbours in the following manner:

'How have the Troglodytes offended you? Have they carried off your wives, stolen your cattle, pillaged your land? No, we are just men, and we fear the gods. So what do you want of us? Do you want wool to make yourselves garments? Do you want milk for your flocks, or fruit from our trees? Lay down your arms and come amongst us, and we will give you all those things; but we swear by all that is most sacred, that if you enter our land as enemies, we will regard you as an unjust people, and will treat you as we would wild animals.'

These words were dismissed with contempt, and those barbarous people took up their arms and invaded the land of the Troglodytes, whom they believed had only their innocence to defend them.

The Troglodytes, however, were well prepared for their defence, and had placed their women and children in their centre. They were amazed by the injustice of their enemies, not by their numbers; their hearts were filled with fresh ardour: this Troglodyte wished to die for his father, that one for his wife and children, another for his brothers, and yet another for his friends; all wanted to die for the Troglodyte people. Those that died were promptly replaced by others who now, in addition to the common cause, had particular deaths to avenge.

Such was the battle between injustice and virtue; those cowards, who sought only plunder, were not even ashamed to flee; they were defeated by the virtue of the Troglodytes, without being influenced by it.

Erzeron, the 9th of the Moon of Gemmadi 2 1711

LETTER 14

Usbek to the same

As the Troglodytes were every day increasing in number, they decided it would be appropriate to choose a king, and agreed that the crown should be conferred upon the most just among them. They turned unanimously to an elderly man who had earned their deep respect by his long and virtuous life; he had been unwilling to attend their assembly, and had withdrawn to his house with a heavy heart.

When they sent deputies to inform him that they had chosen him as king, he said: 'God forbid that I might so wrong my countrymen, that anyone should suppose that there lives no Troglodyte more virtuous than I; you are bestowing the crown upon me, and if you are absolutely determined to do so I must perforce accept it; but you may be certain that I shall die of misery, having at birth seen the Troglodytes free, and today seeing them subjects.' With these words, he began to weep bitterly, saying: 'Oh cursed day, why have I lived this long?' Then, in stern tones, he exclaimed: 'I can see exactly what is happening, Troglodytes; your virtue is becoming burdensome; in your present situation, without a leader, you have to be virtuous in spite of yourselves, for otherwise you could not survive, you would fall into the misfortunes of your earliest forefathers; but you find this yoke too heavy to bear, you prefer to be subject to a prince and to obey his laws, which would be less strict than your own customs; you know that then you will be able to satisfy your ambition, amass riches, and live a life of ease and self-indulgent pleasure; and that, as long as you avoid serious crime, you will have no need of virtue.' For a moment he fell silent, his tears more copious than ever. 'And what do you require of me? How can I give an order to a Troglodyte? Do you want him to do a virtuous deed, because I command him to do it, he who would do it anyway without my intervention, simply because it is how Nature guides him? Oh Troglodytes, I have reached the end of my days, my blood runs cold in my veins; soon I shall be meeting your sacred forebears; why do you want me to grieve them, by having to tell them that I left you under the rule of something other than virtue?'

Erzeron, the 10th of the Moon of Gemmadi 2 1711

[SUPPLEMENTARY LETTER I]¹

LETTER 15

Usbek to the mullah Mehemet Ali, guardian of the three tombs at Qum

Why do you reside among tombs, divine Mullah? You are most surely better suited to life among the stars: no doubt you hide yourself lest

---

[1] For Supplementary Letters, see pp. 214–27, and the Note on the Text.

you darken the sun; you have no blemishes like that star, but like the sun, you cover yourself with clouds.

Your learning is an abyss deeper than the ocean, your mind is more penetrating than Zufagar,* that sword of Ali's with two points; you know what is happening in the nine choirs of the celestial powers; you read the Qur'an upon the breast of our divine Prophet, and when you find a passage obscure, an angel unfolds swift wings at his command, and descends from the throne to reveal to you its secret meaning.

I could, through your intercession, enjoy close contact with the seraphim; for after all, Oh thirteenth Imam,* are you not the centre at which the sky and the earth converge, and the point of communication between the abyss, and the empyrean?

I am in the midst of an ungodly people; allow me to purify myself with you; permit me to turn my face towards the holy places that you inhabit; single me out from the wrongdoers, just as at dawn you can see clearly the streak of bright light against the blackness; help me with your counsel; watch over my soul; intoxicate it with the spirit of the prophets and nourish it with the science of paradise; and allow me to lay its wounds at your feet. Address your sacred letters to Erzeron, where I shall remain for several months.

Erzeron, the 11th of the Moon of Gemmadi 2 1711

LETTER 16

Usbek to the same

I cannot, Oh divine Mullah, calm my impatience, I cannot await your sublime reply: I have doubts, they must be settled; I feel my reason is going astray; I beg you to lead me back onto the right path; instruct me, Oh source of enlightenment, and with your pen strike down the difficulties I am about to propound to you; make me ashamed of myself, make me blush at the question I am about to ask.

Why is it that our Legislator forbids us the flesh of the pig, and all meats* that he calls unclean? Why is it that he forbids us to touch a corpse, and commands us to wash our body constantly in order to purify our soul? It seems to me that nothing is either pure or impure in and of itself; I cannot imagine any quality inherent in a thing that would render it such. Mud looks dirty to us, because it offends our sight, or another of our senses; but in itself it is no dirtier than are gold and diamonds; the idea that we are defiled by touching a corpse comes from a certain natural repugnance we feel on doing so; if the bodies of those who do not wash offended neither our sense of smell nor our sight, how could anyone have supposed that they were unclean?

Therefore the senses, divine Mullah, must be the sole judges of the purity or impurity of things; but, since objects do not affect all men in the same way—since what gives a pleasant sensation to some, strikes others as disgusting—it follows that the evidence of the senses cannot serve us as the rule; at least, unless it is said that each of us may decide this matter, and distinguish, as far as he personally is concerned, what is pure from what is impure.

But would not that very statement, Oh holy Mullah, overturn the distinctions established by our divine Prophet, and the basic tenets of the law inscribed by the hand of the angels?

Erzeron, the 20th of the Moon of Gemmadi 2 1711

LETTER 17

Mehemet Ali, servant of the prophets, to Usbek, in Erzeron

You persist in asking us questions that have been asked a thousand times of our holy Prophet. Why do you not read the Traditions of the Doctors? Why do you not turn to that pure source of all intelligence? You would find all your doubts resolved.

Unhappy man! Constantly perplexed about things of this world, you have never gazed fixedly upon those of heaven; you revere the status of the mullah, but do not dare embrace or follow it.

Impious men, who never penetrate the secrets of the Eternal; the light of your understanding is like the shadowy darkness of the abyss; the reasoning of your intellect is like the dust your feet raise when the sun is at its highest point in the blazing month of Chahban.

Moreover the zenith of your intellect does not reach the nadir of that of the least of our imams. Your empty philosophy is the lightning that heralds a storm and darkness; you live in the heart of the tempest, and drift at the will of the winds.

It is quite simple to respond to your difficulty; all I need do is tell you what happened one day to our holy Prophet, when, tempted by the Christians and tested by the Jews, he confounded both in equal measure.

The Jew Abdias Iben Salon* asked him why God had forbidden people to eat the flesh of the pig. 'He had good reason to do so,' replied the Prophet, 'as I am about to prove to you.' With his hand he fashioned the figure of a man out of mud, then he flung it to the ground, crying: 'Arise!' Immediately, a man stood up and said: 'I am Japhet, son of Noah.' 'Was your hair this white when you died?' the Prophet asked him. 'No,' he replied, 'but when you woke me up, I believed the Day of Judgement had come, and I was so terrified that my hair suddenly turned white.'

'Now then, tell me', God's envoy said to him, 'the whole story of Noah's Ark.' Japhet obeyed, and described exactly everything that had happened during the first months; then he continued: 'We collected the excrement from all the animals on one side of the Ark, which made it lean over so much that we were all very frightened, especially our wives; never have you seen such weeping and wailing! Our father Noah, having sought counsel from God, was ordered by him to take the elephant and stand him with his head towards the side that was sinking. This huge animal produced such a vast quantity of excrement that a pig was born of it.' Is it hard to believe, Usbek, that ever since that day we have abstained from pork, and considered the pig an unclean animal?

However, since the pig stirred the excrement about every day, such a stench arose in the Ark that the pig itself could not help sneezing, and from its nose emerged a rat. The rat began to gnaw everything that lay around it: Noah found this so unbearable that he thought it appropriate to consult God once again. God commanded him to give the lion a hearty kick upon its forehead; this animal also then sneezed, and produced from its nose a cat. Do you not believe, Usbek, that these animals also are unclean? What is your opinion?

Therefore, when you do not grasp why certain things are unclean, that is because there are many other things that you do not know, and you lack the knowledge of what passed between God, the angels, and men. You are ignorant of the History of Eternity, you have not read the Books that are written in the Heavens; that which has been revealed to you is but a tiny part of the divine library, and those who, like ourselves, approach a little closer while on this earth, still dwell in darkness and shadows. Farewell: may Muhammad dwell in your heart.

Qum, the last day of the Moon of Chahban 1711

LETTER 18

Usbek to his friend Rustan, in Ispahan

We spent only one week at Tokat:* after thirty-five days of travel,*
we have now arrived in Smyrna. Between Tokat and Smyrna we did
not see a single city worth describing. I was astonished at the weakness of the Ottoman Empire: its sick body is sustained not by a gentle
and moderate regime, but by violent remedies which persistently
weaken it, leaving it exhausted.

The pashas, who have to buy their positions, are financially ruined
when they arrive in the provinces, which they then lay waste like
conquered lands. An arrogant militia does exactly as it pleases;
fortifications are demolished, cities deserted, farmland despoiled,
and land cultivation and commerce completely abandoned.

This harsh regime operates with complete impunity; the
Christians, who work the land, and the Jews, who levy the taxes, are
subjected to endless persecution.

There is no security in owning land; consequently, the urge to
make the best use of it is greatly diminished; no legal title or physical
possession can ever prevail against the caprice of those who govern.

Those barbarians have so totally abandoned the arts that they have
even neglected the military art; while the nations of Europe constantly refine their military skills, they remain as ignorant as their
forebears, and never think of adopting the new European inventions
until these have been used against them a thousand times.

They have no experience on the sea, no skill in manoeuvres; it is
said that a handful of Christians materializing out of a rock* make the
Ottomans tremble, and harass their empire.

Incapable of engaging in commerce, they can scarcely tolerate that
Europeans—invariably industrious and enterprising—should do so;
they believe they are granting them a favour by allowing these foreigners to enrich them.

In this whole vast country that I have crossed, I have found
only Smyrna that can be considered a rich and powerful city; it is
Europeans who make it such; had it been left to the Turks, it would
be just like all the others.

Here, Rustan, you have an accurate picture of this empire which, in less than two centuries' time, will provide some conqueror with a theatre for his triumphs.

Smyrna, the 2nd of the Moon of Rahmazan 1711

LETTER 19

Usbek to his wife Zachi, at the seraglio in Ispahan

You have offended me, Zachi, and there are feelings in my heart which should make you fearful, were it not that my absence leaves you time to change your ways, and calm the violent jealousy tormenting me.

I am told that you were found alone with the white eunuch Nadir, who will pay for his faithlessness and perfidy with his head. How could you so far forget yourself as to receive a white eunuch in your room, when you have black eunuchs to serve you? It is pointless to tell me that eunuchs are not men, and that your virtue makes you immune to thoughts which an imperfect resemblance might inspire. That is not enough for you or for me; not for you, because you are doing a thing forbidden by the laws of the seraglio; not for me, because you rob me of my honour, by exposing yourself to the gaze—what am I saying, the gaze—perhaps to the *actions* of a traitor who may have sullied you by his crimes, and still more by his regrets and despair at his own impotence.

Perhaps you will tell me that you have always remained faithful to me. How could you be otherwise? How could you have deceived the vigilance of those black eunuchs who are so astonished by your conduct? How could you have broken down those bolts and those doors that keep you imprisoned? You boast of your virtue, but it is not a virtue freely chosen, and perhaps your impure desires have wiped out, on countless occasions, the value and merit of that fidelity you so proudly vaunt.

Would that you have not done all that I have cause to suspect, that the traitor never touched you with sacrilegious hands, and that you refused to let his eyes feast upon delights that are his master's; would that, covered by your garments, you preserved that feeble barrier between him and you; that he, overcome with holy respect, lowered his eyes; that, his boldness faltering, he trembled at the punishments he was bringing on himself; even were all that true, it is still a fact that by this act you transgressed against your duty: and if you did this gratuitously, without satisfying your dissolute desires, what would you have done in order to satisfy them? What more would you do, were you able to leave this sacred precinct, which you see as a cruel prison, but which is, for your companions, a refuge from the lures of vice; a sacred temple, where your sex can set aside its frailty and becomes invincible, despite all the disadvantages bestowed upon it by nature? What would you do if, left on your own, your only defence was your love for me, whom you have so grievously offended, and your duty, which you have so shamefully betrayed? How holy are the customs of the country where you live, for by them you were rescued from violation by the vilest of slaves! You should be thanking me for the constraints I impose upon you, for it is only because of them that you deserve to live.

You cannot stand the head eunuch, because he keeps a watchful eye on all you do, and gives you wise advice; his ugliness, you say, is so extreme that you cannot look at him without suffering; as if those posts were ever entrusted to the best-looking slaves! The real reason for your distress is that in his place you no longer have the white eunuch, who has dishonoured you.

But how has your head female slave offended you? She told you that the familiarities which you were taking with that young Zelide were improper; that is why you hate her.

I should, Zachi, be a severe judge, but I am only a husband, who wants to find you innocent. The love I feel for Roxane, my new wife, has not lessened the tenderness I feel for you, who are no less beautiful; I share my love between you both, and Roxane enjoys no other advantage than that which virtue can add to beauty.

Smyrna, the 12th of the Moon of Zilcadé 1712

LETTER 20

Usbek to the head white eunuch

You should tremble upon opening this letter, or rather you should have trembled when you permitted Nadir's perfidy to occur; you, who even in your passionless old age cannot without crime let your eyes rest upon the awe-inspiring objects of my love; you, who are forbidden ever to put a sacrilegious foot upon the threshold of that formidable place which hides them from all eyes; you allow those for whose conduct you are accountable to do what you yourself would never dare; and yet you do not see the thunderbolt poised to strike down both them and you?

And what indeed are you, other than base instruments that I can shatter as I please? You exist only in as much as you know how to obey; you are in the world solely to live under my law or to die when I so command; you draw breath only in as much as my happiness, my love, and even my jealousy have need of your baseness; in a word, your only portion is submission, your only soul, my desires, and your only hope, my felicity.

I am aware that some of my wives find it hard to submit to the austere rule of duty, that the constant presence of a black eunuch irks them, and that they are weary of those hideous objects which are there to foment their love for their husband; I am aware of this; but you, who countenance this licentiousness, you deserve a punishment of such severity as to terrify anyone who abuses my trust.

I swear by all the prophets in the sky, and by Ali the greatest of them all, that if you deviate from your duty, I shall consider your life as I do that of an insect I find beneath my feet.

Smyrna, the 12th of the Moon of Zilcadé 1711

[SUPPLEMENTARY LETTER 2]

LETTER 21

Usbek to his friend Ibben, in Smyrna

We have reached Livorno after forty days at sea. Livorno is a new city that bears witness to the genius of the dukes of Tuscany, who transformed a swampy village into the most flourishing city of Italy.

The women here enjoy great freedom; they can look at men through certain lattice-screened windows; they can go out every day accompanied by elderly women;* they wear only one veil;* their brothers-in-law, their uncles, their nephews can see them, and the husband hardly ever objects.

When he first sees it, a Christian city presents a wonderful spectacle to a Muslim. I do not mean things that make an immediate impression on every visitor, such as the difference in the buildings, the dress, and the principal customs: but even in the tiniest details there is something so strange, something I can feel, but cannot put into words.

Tomorrow we leave for Marseilles; we do not mean to stay there long, for Rica's plan, and mine, is to travel on without delay to Paris, which is the seat of government of the empire of Europe. Travellers always seek out the great cities, which provide a kind of homeland common to all foreigners. Farewell, be assured of my faithful love.

Livorno, the 12th of the Moon of Saphar 1712

LETTER 22

Rica to Ibben, in Smyrna

We've been in Paris for a month, and we've been constantly on the go: it's a complicated business to obtain lodgings, and track down the people whose names we'd been given, and provide ourselves with basic necessities, all of which were lacking simultaneously.

Paris is as large as Ispahan;* its houses are so tall that you'd swear they're occupied only by astrologers. As you'll imagine, a city built in the air, where six or seven houses are piled one upon the other, has a huge population, and when all the people come down from their houses the crowding and confusion in the street is amazing.

You'll find this hard to believe, but in the month I've been here I have yet to see anyone walking; there can be no nation in the world that makes their bodies work harder than the French. They run, they fly;* the slow conveyances of Asia, the deliberate, even steps of our camels, would give them a heart attack. For me, who am not used to such speed, and usually walk at a steady pace, I sometimes fret and fume like a Christian; it's not so bad being splashed from head to foot, but I can't forgive the digs and thrusts from elbows that I regularly receive; periodically a man who's overtaking me from behind turns me halfway round, while another, passing me on the opposite side, suddenly returns me to my original position; barely have I gone a hundred paces than I'm more exhausted than if I'd walked ten leagues or so.

Don't expect me to be capable, at present, of giving you a deep understanding of European ways and customs; I myself have only formed a vague notion of them, and I've barely had time to do more than feel astonishment.

The king of France is the most powerful prince in Europe. Unlike his neighbour the king of Spain, he owns no gold-mines, but he possesses greater riches than that king does; he draws these riches from the vanity of his subjects, which is more inexhaustible than mines; he has been able to undertake or support great wars with no other resources than titles and honours to sell, and by a miracle of human vanity, his troops have been paid, his strongholds provisioned, and his fleets equipped.

Furthermore, this king is a great magician:* he exerts his dominion over the very minds of his subjects, for he makes them think whatever he wishes: if he has one million gold pieces in his treasury,* and he needs two, he has only to persuade them that one gold piece is worth two, and they believe him. If he has a war that is difficult to support, and he has no money, he has only to suggest to them that a piece of paper is money, and they are convinced upon the spot; he even goes so far as to make them believe that he can cure them of all kinds of ills simply by touching them, so great is the strength, and the power, that he exerts over their minds.

What I tell you about this king should not astonish you, for there is another magician even greater than he, who exerts no less a mastery over his mind than he himself enjoys over the minds of others. This magician is called the pope; sometimes he makes the king believe that three are only one, that the bread he eats is not bread, or that the wine he drinks is not wine, and countless other things of that nature.

And to keep him constantly on the alert, and not let him lose the habit of believing, from time to time he gives him, as an exercise, certain articles of belief. Two years ago he sent him a very long document that he called a *Constitution;** he wanted to force this king and his subjects, under penalty of harsh reprisals, to believe everything that it contained. He succeeded as regards the king, who quickly submitted, setting an example for his subjects; but some of these rebelled, saying they would not believe any part of this document: it is the women who were the fomenters of this revolt,* which divides the entire court, the entire kingdom, and every family. This *Constitution* forbids women to read a book which all Christians claim was brought down from heaven; it is, in fact, their Qur'an. The women, indignant at this insult to their sex, are raising every possible objection to the *Constitution*; they've won over the men, who in this case don't want to be privileged. One must admit, however, that this mufti presents quite a well-reasoned argument; and by almighty Ali, he must have been instructed in the principles of our holy law; for since women are a creation inferior to ours, and our prophets tell us that they will not enter paradise, why should they read a book whose sole purpose is to teach the way to paradise?

I've heard tales about the king which verge on the miraculous; I doubt not that you will unhesitatingly believe them.

It's said that while he was waging war against his neighbours,* who were all allied against him, he was surrounded in his kingdom by innumerable invisible enemies,* and that for over thirty years he searched for them; but despite the indefatigable exertions of certain dervishes whom he trusts, he has been unable to discover a single one; they live with him, they are at his court, in his capital, among his troops, in his tribunals, and yet it's said that he will know the bitterness of dying without having found them; it's as if they did exist in principle but do so no longer in any particular case: a body with no members. No doubt heaven wishes to punish this king for not being sufficiently merciful towards the enemies he vanquished, since it sends him invisible ones whose genius and destiny are superior to his own.

I shall continue to write to you, and will tell you of things quite alien to the Persian character and nature: we both tread the same earth, but the men of the country where I now am, and those of the country where you are, are very different beings.

Paris, the 4th of the Moon of Rebiab 2 1712

LETTER 23

Usbek to Ibben, in Smyrna

I have received a letter from your nephew Rhedi: he writes that he is leaving Smyrna to travel through Italy, and that the sole purpose of his journey is to educate himself and become worthier of you; I congratulate you upon a nephew who one day will be a consolation in your old age.

Rica sends you a long letter; he tells me that he has described this country to you at length; his lively mind enables him to grasp things in a flash; but I, who think more slowly, am not yet in a position to tell you anything.

Our most heartfelt conversations are about you; we cannot say enough about the warm welcome you gave us in Smyrna, and the services your friendship renders us every day. Generous Ibben, may all your friends be as grateful and loyal as we are!

May I see you again soon, and once more enjoy, with you, those happy hours which pass so sweetly when two friends are together! Farewell.

Paris, the 4th of the Moon of Rebiab 2 1712

LETTER 24

Usbek to Roxane, at the seraglio in Ispahan

How fortunate you are, Roxane, to be in the sweet land of Persia, and not in this poisonous place where modesty and virtue are unknown! How fortunate you are! You live in my seraglio as in the home of innocence, safe from the evil intent of all humans; you take delight in your blessed powerlessness to sin; no man has ever sullied you with his lascivious glances; not even your father-in-law, in the intimacy of our feasts, has ever seen your beautiful mouth; you have never failed to cover it with a sacred veil. Fortunate Roxane! When you have travelled to the country, you have always had eunuchs to precede you and slay any man so reckless as not to flee from your sight; heaven gave you to me to ensure my happiness, yet with what difficulty did I gain possession of the treasure which you defended with such resolution! What disappointment for me, in the first few days of our marriage, not to see you! And what impatience when I did see you! Yet you did not satisfy my impatience; instead, in your frightened modesty, you exacerbated it with your obstinate refusals; you confused me with all other men, from whom you always concealed yourself. Do you remember that day when I lost you among your slaves, who did not betray you, but hid you from my pursuit?

And that other day, when, finding your tears of no effect, you invoked the authority of your mother to check the violence of my passion? And do you remember, when all other resources had failed you, what you found the courage to do? You took a dagger and threatened to sacrifice a husband who loved you, if he persisted in demanding what you valued more highly even than your husband! Two months passed in this duel between love and virtue; you clung too long to your chaste scruples; even after you were vanquished, you did not surrender, but defended to the last your dying virginity: you saw me as an enemy who had violated you and not as a husband who loved you; more than three months passed before you dared look at me without blushing; your air of mortification seemed to reproach me for taking advantage of you; I could not even possess you in tranquillity, for you did your utmost to deny me enjoyment of your charms and graces, so that I found myself intoxicated by the ultimate favours, without having obtained the lesser ones.

If you had been brought up in this country, you would not have been so distressed: women here have lost all sense of decorum; they appear before men with their faces uncovered, as if courting their own defeat; they encourage them with their glances; they see them in the mosques, when they take walks, and in their own homes. The custom of having eunuchs to serve them is unknown here; in place of that noble simplicity and pleasing modesty which reigns among you, a visitor encounters crass effrontery, to which he finds it impossible to accustom himself.

Yes, Roxane, if you were here you would be outraged at the ignoble disgrace into which your sex has fallen; you would flee these abhorrent scenes, you would sigh for that sweet retreat where innocence dwells, where you are sure of yourself, where no danger makes you tremble and where, in a word, you can love me without fear of ever losing that love, which it is your duty to feel for me.

When you enhance the brilliance of your complexion with the most beautiful hues; when you perfume your whole body with the most precious essences; when you put on your prettiest garments and vie with your companions in grace of dance and melodiousness of song; when you compete with them so delightfully as to which is the loveliest, the sweetest, and the liveliest, I cannot imagine you having any object other than to please me; and when I see you blushing modestly, and your eyes seeking mine, and that you insinuate yourself into my heart with pleasing, flattering words, I cannot, Roxane, doubt that you love me.

But what am I to think of the women of Europe? Their artfully painted complexions, the ornaments with which they adorn themselves, the care they lavish on their persons, their incessant pre-occupation with the desire to please, are so many blemishes upon their virtue, and insults to their husband.

It is not, Roxane, that I believe they pursue their efforts as far as such conduct might make one suppose, and that their dissolute ways lead them into the horrifying, terrifying excess of a complete betrayal of conjugal faith; there are very few women so profligate as to carry their crime to that extreme; they all bear in their heart a certain quality of virtue which is imprinted there, bestowed by nature at birth and, though weakened, not destroyed by education; they may well ignore the outward observance of the rules modesty imposes, but when it is a matter of the final step, nature rebels. Therefore, when we keep you so carefully shut away, and have you guarded by so many slaves; when we so severely frustrate your desires if they are excessive: it is not because we fear the ultimate infidelity, but because we know that purity cannot be too great, and the smallest stain can corrupt it.

I pity you, Roxane; your chastity, tested for so long, deserved a husband who would never have left you, and who could himself have quelled those desires which only your virtue is able to subdue.

Paris, the 7th of the Moon of Rhegeb 1712

LETTER 25

Usbek to Nessir, in Ispahan

We are now in Paris, that magnificent rival of the City of the Sun.

On leaving Smyrna, I entrusted my friend Ibben with a casket containing some gifts for you; he will forward this letter by the same route. Although separated from him by a distance of 500 or 600 leagues, I send him my news and receive his as easily as if he were in Ispahan and I in Qum. I send my letters to Marseilles, whence ships constantly set sail for Smyrna; from there he forwards those addressed to Persia by the Armenian caravans, which leave daily for Ispahan.

Rica is blessed with perfect health; his iron constitution, his youth, and his naturally high spirits make him immune to all ills.

For my part, however, I am not well. I feel low both in body and in spirit, and I am prey to thoughts which every day grow gloomier: my health, which is failing, makes me turn to my homeland, and makes this country seem more alien to me.

But I beg you, dear Nessir, to make certain that my wives do not learn of my condition; if they love me, I wish to spare their tears, and it they do not love me, I have no wish to encourage their daring.

If my eunuchs believed my health to be in danger, if they could hope for impunity from a complaisant coward, they would soon cease to be deaf to the beguiling voice of that sex, a voice which can melt rocks, and quicken inanimate objects.

Farewell, Nessir; it gives me pleasure to demonstrate the trust I have in you.

Paris, the 5th of the Moon of Chahban 1712

LETTER 26

Rica to ***

Yesterday I saw something I thought rather singular, although it takes place daily in Paris.

All the people assemble in the late afternoon* to act a kind of scene, which I have heard called a play; the main action is on a platform which is called the theatre;* on either side you can see, in little alcoves called boxes, men and women who together enact scenes without words, very much in the style of those we see in our Persia.

Sometimes we watch a woman crossed in love express her despair; sometimes we see a different woman, whose sparkling, passionate eyes devour her lover, while he returns her gaze with equal ardour; every passion is depicted on those faces and expressed with an eloquence that is all the more intense for being wordless. In the boxes the actors are visible only to the waist, and as a rule their arms are modestly concealed in a muff. Standing on the floor below is a group of men who jeer at those that are above them on the stage; they, in their turn, make fun of those below.

But those who have the hardest job are some young men who are purposely hired at an early age, so that they will be able to withstand the fatigue of their duties; they have to be everywhere; they move about the building using routes they alone know; they climb from level to level with amazing dexterity; they are up at the top, down on the ground, in every box; they take a dive, as one might say, and disappear from view, then reappear; often they will leave the theatre, to act in a different one: one even sees some, who by a miracle—which the canes they carry would hardly allow one to hope for—are capable of walking as well as the next man. Then we move to another place, where a private play is being put on: first there are bows and curtseys; then come embraces; I am told that the slightest acquaintance gives a man the right* to smother another; apparently this place inspires tender feelings, for indeed it is said that the princesses who reign there are never cruel; if one forgets the two or three hours every day when they are rather unapproachable, one can say that the rest of the time they are very accommodating, and easily recover from their fit of disdain.

Everything I am describing to you here also takes place in much the same way in another theatre, called the Opera; the only difference is that in the one people talk, whereas in the other they sing. A few days ago a friend of mine took me into the box where one of the principal actresses was changing out of her costume; we became so well acquainted that the next day I received this letter from her:

'Monsieur
'I am the most unfortunate girl in the world; I have always been the most virtuous actress of the Opera. About seven or eight months ago I was in the box where you saw me yesterday; as I was costuming myself as a priestess to Diana, a young abbé visited me, and without the least respect for my white robes, my veil, and my virginal headband, violated my innocence: no matter how fiercely I complained to him of the sacrifice I made him,* he laughed at me, assuring me he found me very profane; however, I am so big with child that I no longer dare show myself upon the stage, for when it's a matter of honour I am fastidious to a fault; I believe that it's easier to persuade a well-born young woman to lose her virtue than her modesty; consequently, in view of my fastidiousness you will readily believe that the young abbé would never have succeeded, had he not promised to

marry me: so legitimate a motive made me bypass the customary little formalities, and begin where I should have ended; but since I have been dishonoured by his bad faith, I no longer want to stay at the Opera where, between you and me, they barely give us enough to live on, for now that my years are advancing and my charms diminishing, my income, which still remains the same, seems to grow smaller every day. I have heard, from one of your attendants, that in your country a skilled dancer is valued very highly, and that if I were in Ispahan my fortune would quickly be assured. If you were to offer me your protection and take me home with you to that place, you would have the benefit of helping a young woman who, by her virtue and her conduct would not prove herself unworthy of your kindness. I remain...'

Paris, the 2nd of the Moon of Chalval 1712

LETTER 27

Rica to Ibben, in Smyrna

The pope is the head of the Christians; he is an old idol to whom they pay homage out of habit. In the past he was feared even by kings, for he would depose them as readily as our magnificent sultans depose the kings of Irimette and Georgia; but now he is feared no longer. He claims to be successor to one of the first Christians, called St Peter, and it is unquestionably a rich inheritance, for he owns immense treasures, and has a great country under his governance.

The bishops are men of law who are subordinate to him and exercise, in his name, two very different functions. When they meet in assembly, they—like the pope—compose articles of faith. When they act individually, their sole function is to grant dispensations from observing the law. You should know that the Christian religion is burdened with an infinite number of exceedingly demanding observances; and as the Christians deemed it less easy to follow these observances than to appoint bishops who can give dispensations, the latter choice was adopted for the convenience of the public; thus, if a person prefers not to keep Ramadan, or not to conform to the required formalities for marriages, or if he wishes to break his monastic vows, or to marry in defiance of the proscriptions of the law, even sometimes to renege on an oath, he goes to the bishop, or the pope, who will immediately provide the dispensation.

The bishops do not produce articles of faith on their own initiative: there are an infinite number of scholars, for the most part dervishes, who among themselves raise thousands of new questions about religion: they are left to argue endlessly, and the war lasts until a decision is reached that concludes it.

I can consequently assure you that no kingdom has ever existed with as many civil wars as occur in the kingdom of Christ.

At first, those that produce some new proposition are called heretics. Each heresy has its own name, which is like a rallying-cry for those who support it; but no one is a heretic unless he wants to be; all that is required is to divide the point at issue into two, and provide those accusing their opponents of heresy with a *distinction*—a subtle nuance—and no matter what that *distinction* is, whether it's intelligible or not, it renders a man white as snow, and he can call himself orthodox.

What I'm telling you holds true for France and Germany: but I've heard it said that in Spain and Italy certain dervishes are very touchy on this matter, and will burn* a man to death like straw. When someone falls into the hands of such people, he's really lucky if he has always prayed to God with little wooden beads* in his hands, always carried on his person two pieces of cloth sewn to two ribbons, and if he has sometime travelled in a province called Galicia;* otherwise the poor devil's in real trouble: let him swear like a pagan that he's orthodox, they might well not agree about his qualifications, and burn him as a heretic; in vain would he present his *distinction*; no *distinction* is admitted, and he'd be reduced to ashes before anyone would even think of listening to him.

Other judges presume that an accused man is innocent, but these always presume he is guilty; if they're in doubt, they hold it a principle to come down on the side of severity, apparently because they believe that men are evil; but on the other hand, they have such a good opinion of men that they do not consider them ever capable of lying, for they admit the testimony of those who commit capital crimes, of women of ill repute, of people who exercise infamous professions. When they pass sentence, they include a little compliment to those dressed in sulphur-impregnated sanbenitos,* saying they are very distressed to see them so poorly garbed, and that they are kind

men, who hate bloodshed, and are in despair at having condemned
them: but then, to console themselves, they confiscate, for their own
profit, all the prisoner's possessions.

Happy is the country inhabited by the children of the prophets:
for there, such tragic spectacles are unknown; the holy religion which
the angels brought requires only its own truth to defend it, and has
no need of these violent means to keep it secure.

Paris, the 4th of the Moon of Chalval 1712

LETTER 28

Rica to the same, in Smyrna

The inhabitants of Paris display an excess of curiosity which verges
on the absurd. When I first arrived I was stared at as if I had been
sent from heaven: old men, young men, women, children, they all
wanted to see me; if I went out, everyone crowded at the windows;
if I went walking in the Tuileries, I would instantly find a circle
forming round me; even the ladies encircled me with a rainbow of a
thousand delicate shades; if I went to a theatre I would immediately
be conscious of a hundred lorgnettes focused on my face; in a word,
no man has ever been seen as much as me. It sometimes made me
smile, to hear people who had scarcely ever ventured from their
chambers saying to one another: 'One must admit he looks very
Persian!' Amazingly, I found portraits of me* everywhere; I saw
myself multiplied in all the shops, upon all the mantelpieces, so fearful were they of not having seen me enough!

So many honours could not fail to become burdensome: I didn't consider myself so strange, so rare a man, and although I hold a very high
opinion of myself, I'd never have imagined that I might disturb the
tranquillity of a great city where I was completely unknown.
I therefore resolved to set aside my Persian clothing and dress instead
as a European, to see whether anything in my appearance would still
astonish. From this test I learnt my true worth: stripped of my exotic
finery, I found myself appraised at my real value, and I had good reason
to complain of my tailor, through whom I'd lost, in an instant, the
attention and esteem of the public; for suddenly a dreadful void surrounded me; sometimes I'd pass an entire hour in a group of people

without anyone looking at me, or giving me an opportunity to open my mouth; but if someone in the circle happened to mention that I was Persian, I'd immediately hear a buzzing around me: 'Oh! Oh! Monsieur is Persian? That's most extraordinary! How can someone be Persian?'

Paris, the 6th of the Moon of Chalval 1712

LETTER 29

Rhedi to Usbek, in Paris

I am now in Venice, my dear Usbek; one can have seen every city in the world, and still be surprised on arriving in Venice; one will always be astonished to find a city, towers, and mosques emerging from the water, and to see innumerable people in a place where there should be only fish.

But this ungodly city lacks the most precious of all the treasures, namely, fresh water; it is impossible, in Venice, to perform a single ablution such as our law demands. It is held in abhorrence by our holy Prophet, and he never looks down upon it from the sky other than in anger.

Were that not the case, my dear Usbek, I should delight in living in a city where every day my mind is improved: I am learning about the secrets of commerce, the affairs of princes, and the form of their government; I do not even neglect the European superstitions, for I am applying myself to medicine, natural philosophy, and astronomy; I am studying the arts; in brief, I am casting off the veil that covered my eyes in the land of my birth.

Venice, the 16th of the Moon of Chalval 1712

LETTER 30

*Rica to ****

The other day I paid a visit to an establishment where some three hundred people* are being cared for in a rather modest style. I didn't stay long, since neither the church nor the buildings are worth looking at. The men living in this place seemed quite cheerful; several of them were playing cards and other games with which I am not familiar. As I was leaving, one of them, who was also leaving, heard me enquire how to get to the Marais, which is the most distant district of Paris. 'I'm going there,' he said, 'I'll take you, just follow me.' He led me very expertly, helped me out of every difficulty, and skilfully saved me from the carts and carriages; we had almost reached our destination, when, full of curiosity, I asked him: 'My friend, won't you tell me who you are?' 'I'm blind, Monsieur,' he replied. 'What,' I said, 'you're blind?* So why didn't you ask that good man who was playing cards with you to take us?' 'He's blind too,' he answered: 'for the last four hundred years there have been three hundred of us blind men living in the building where you met me; but I must leave you now; this is the street you asked for: I'm going to mingle with the crowd, and go into this church where, I assure you, I'll be more of a nuisance to other people than they'll be to me.'

Paris, the 17th of the Moon of Chalval 1712

LETTER 31
Usbek to Rhedi, in Venice

Wine is so expensive here in Paris, owing to the taxes imposed on it, that it seems the French want to implement the precept of the divine Qur'an* which forbids us to consume it.

When I reflect upon the deadly effects of this drink, I cannot help considering it the most dangerous gift nature has made to man. If anything has sullied the life and reputation of our monarchs, it has been their insobriety; it is the most poisonous source of their injustices and their cruelty.

Let me say it to the shame of men: the law forbids our princes to use wine, and they drink it to such excess as to make them less than human. Christian princes, on the other hand, are allowed wine, and it does not appear to lead them into evil ways. The human spirit is the essence of contradiction: by indulging in extreme debauchery, a man rebels against prohibitions, and the law designed to make us behave more justly frequently achieves nothing but the contrary result.

But although I object to the use of this drink, which makes men lose their reason, I do not also disapprove of those potions that raise one's spirits. Orientals have been wise enough to seek remedies for melancholy as assiduously as they have sought remedies for the most dangerous illnesses. When a European suffers some misfortune, his only resource is to read a philosopher called Seneca;* but Orientals, who are more sensible and in this regard better physicians then they, consume potions that have the capacity to make them happy, and charm away the memory of their troubles.

Nothing is as distressing as words of solace that invoke the inevitability of pain, the futility of remedies, the fatality of destiny, the determinations of providence, and the misery of the human condition; it is a mockery to attempt to alleviate suffering with the thought that we are born wretched; it is far better to banish those thoughts from the mind, and treat man as a sentient, not a rational, being.

The soul, joined to the body, is perpetually tyrannized by it: if the blood flows* too sluggishly, if the spirits are inadequately purified, if they are not sufficient in quantity, we become despondent and sad; but if we drink potions* capable of changing this balance of our body, our soul again becomes receptive to impressions which gladden it, and takes a secret delight in seeing its bodily counterpart return, as it were, to movement and to life.

Paris, the 25th of the Moon of Zilcadé 1713

LETTER 32

Rica to Ibben, in Smyrna

Persian women are more beautiful than French women; but French women are prettier. It's impossible not to love the former and not to enjoy oneself with the latter; the first are more tender and more modest; the others, livelier and more playful.

What makes women's complexions so beautiful in Persia is the orderly life that they lead there; they neither gamble nor keep late hours; they drink no wine, and almost never expose themselves to the open air. It must be admitted that the seraglio is organized with a view to health rather than to pleasure: it's a regular life, without excitement; everything speaks of subservience and duty; even the pleasures are serious, and the joys sober, and they are rarely experienced except as marks of authority and dependence.

Even the Persian men are less light-hearted than the French; one does not see, in Persians, that freedom of mind and that air of contentment that I find here in all walks of life, and in all conditions.

It's much worse in Turkey; there one could find families where, from father to son, nobody has laughed since the foundation of the monarchy.

This gravity of the Orientals comes from having little contact with one another; they meet only on ceremonial occasions, when it is required; friendship, that tender, shared commitment of the heart, which makes life here so agreeable, is almost unknown in the Orient; they keep to their own homes, where they always find company, so that each family is, as it were, isolated from the others.

One day, when I was discussing this with a Frenchman, he said to me: 'What shocks me most about your customs, is that you are obliged to live with slaves, whose heart and mind will always reflect the baseness of their condition; these ignoble people undermine the virtuous feelings that are given to you by nature, and they destroy them in childhood, when they control you.

'In short, abandon your prejudices; what can you expect of an upbringing entrusted to a wretch whose honour lies in guarding another man's wives, who takes pride in performing the vilest of human tasks, who is despicable for his very loyalty—his sole virtue—because his loyalty springs from envy, jealousy, and despair? This wretch burns to avenge himself against both sexes, of which he is the scum; he acquiesces in being tyrannized by the stronger sex, provided he can spread misery among the weaker; he draws from his imperfection, his ugliness, and his deformity all the glory of his condition, and is esteemed only because he is unworthy of esteem; in short, eternally fettered to the door where he is attached more securely than are the hinges and bolts that hold it, he boasts of spending fifty years in this shameful post, where, accountable to his master's jealousy, he has exercised all his baseness.'

Paris, the 14th of the Moon of Zilhagé 1713

LETTER 33

Usbek to his cousin Gemchid, dervish of the magnificent monastery of Tabriz

What is your opinion of Christians, noble dervish? Do you believe that at the Day of Judgement they will be condemned, like the

Turkish infidels, to serve as donkeys to the Jews, who will lead them at a rapid trot into Hell? Of course I know they will not go to the abode of the prophets, and that the great Ali did not come for them. But because they are not blessed with mosques in their country, do you think that they will be condemned to eternal retribution, and that God will punish them for not practising a religion of which he denied them knowledge? Allow me to tell you that I have frequently cross-examined these Christians, I have questioned them, to see if they had any knowledge of the great Ali, the most beautiful of men, and I have found that they had never heard of him.

They are not like the infidels that our holy prophets put to the sword because they refused to believe the miracles of Heaven; rather, they resemble those unfortunates who lived in the shadows of idolatry, before the divine light illuminated the face of our great Prophet.

Besides, if one studies their religion closely, one finds there, as it were, the seeds of our dogmas. I have often admired the secret ways of Providence, which seems to have attempted to prepare them, in this manner, for general conversion. I have heard tell of a book written by one of their scholars entitled *Polygamy Triumphant,** which proves that Christians are commanded to be polygamous: their baptism is the image of our mandatory ablutions, and the only mistake made by the Christians is in the efficacy they attribute to this first ablution, which they believe suffices for all the others; like us, their priests and monks pray seven times a day, and expect to enjoy the blessings of paradise through the resurrection of the body; like us, they keep specified fast days, and mortify the flesh, in the hope of earning the mercy of the Divine; they worship the good angels and distrust the bad; they display a saintly belief in miracles, which God performs through the ministry of his servants; like us, they recognize the inadequacy of their own merits, and their need of an intercessor on their behalf with God. I see Muhammadanism everywhere, although I do not find Muhammad here. Whatever people may do, truth will out, and shine through the shadows surrounding it. The day will come when the Eternal One will find only true believers on this earth; time, which consumes everything, will obliterate even errors, and all men will be astounded to find themselves marching beneath the same banner; everything, including the law, will come to pass: the divine volumes will be removed from the earth and carried away to the celestial archives.

Paris, the 20th of the Moon of Zilhagé 1713

LETTER 34
Usbek to Rhedi, in Venice

Coffee* is widely drunk in Paris: there are a great many public establishments where it is served. In some of these establishments news is disseminated; in others, people play chess: there is one place where coffee is prepared in such a manner as to sharpen the wits of those who drink it; at any rate, of those who emerge from there, not a single one fails to be convinced that he is four times cleverer than he was upon entering.

But what shocks me about these wits is that they give no service to their country, but fritter away their talents on childish things; for instance, when I arrived in Paris I found them all worked up over the most trivial dispute one could imagine: it concerned the reputation of an ancient Greek poet,* whose land of birth and year of death have remained a matter of conjecture for two thousand years. Both sides admitted that he was an excellent poet: it was simply a question of the degree of excellence to be attributed to him. Everyone believed his own estimate the best, but among these bestowers of reputation, some thought the poet better than did others; that was the quarrel. It was very heated, for the two parties exchanged, with great cordiality, such crude insults and acidulous witticisms that I found the style of the dispute no less amazing than its subject. If anyone, I thought to myself, were foolish enough to appear before one of these defenders of the Greek poet and attack the reputation of some worthy citizen, he would undoubtedly be challenged; and I believe that this touchy fervour over the reputation of the dead would be kindled into a real conflagration in defence of the living; be that as it may, I added, may God protect me from ever drawing upon myself the enmity of these critics of a poet whom two thousand years in the tomb have been unable to defend against such implacable hatred: at the moment they beat the air, but what would happen if their fury were fuelled by the presence of an enemy?

Those whom I have just described to you argue in the vernacular, and one should not confuse them with certain other disputants, who employ a barbaric tongue which seems somehow to add to the fury and obstinacy of the combatants; there are places where one finds a kind of dense, black confusion* of such people; they feed on fine distinctions; they live on obscure reasoning and false inferences; that occupation, whose devotees ought to be starving, does nevertheless yield a livelihood. We have seen an entire nation* expelled from its native shore and cross the sea to settle in France, bringing with it as provision for survival nothing but a formidable talent for argument. Farewell.

Paris, the last day of the Moon of Zilhagé 1713

LETTER 35

Usbek to Ibben, in Smyrna

The king of France is old;* we have no examples, in our own history, of a monarch who enjoyed such a long reign. It is said that he possesses to an extreme degree the gift of making himself obeyed, and that he displays equal genius in governing his family, his court, and his country; he has frequently been heard to remark that of all the governments in the world, that of the Turks, or that of our august sultan, would suit him best, so high is his opinion of the oriental political system.

I have studied his character and have found in it contradictions which I simply cannot understand; for example, he has a minister who is only eighteen, and a mistress who is eighty;* he loves his religion, but cannot tolerate those who declare it must be strictly observed; although he flees the tumult of cities and is by nature reserved, his principal occupation from dawn to dusk is to make people talk about him; he loves military tributes and victories, but is as frightened of seeing a good general at the head of his troops as he would be were the general and the army his enemy; he is, I believe, the only person ever to have been simultaneously possessed of greater wealth than any prince could hope for, and burdened with such extreme poverty as a private individual would find intolerable.

He likes to be generous to those who serve him, but he rewards the assiduity, or rather the idleness, of his courtiers as liberally as he does the arduous campaigns of his captains; frequently he prefers a man who disrobes him, or who hands him his napkin when he sits down to dine, to another who captures cities for him, or wins his battles; he does not believe that his royal majesty should be circumscribed in the distribution of favours, and without enquiring whether the individual upon whom he bestows his largesse is a good man, he believes that his choice will turn him into one; thus he has been known to grant a small pension to one man who had taken flight from the authorities, and a profitable command to another, even more notorious, fugitive from justice.

He is magnificent, particularly in his buildings: there are more statues in his palace gardens than there are citizens in a large city; his guards are as strong as those of the prince before whom all rulers fall defeated; his armies are as numerous, his resources as great, and his finances as inexhaustible.

Paris, the 7th of the Moon of Maharram 1713

LETTER 36

Rica to Ibben, in Smyrna

Whether it is more advantageous to grant, or to deny, their freedom to women,* is a great matter of debate among men; it seems to me that there are many arguments to be advanced on both sides. If Europeans say that it is ungenerous to make people one loves unhappy, our Orientals reply that it is contemptible for men to renounce the dominion nature gave them over women. If Europeans point out that keeping a large number of women confined is troublesome, they reply that ten obedient women are less trouble than one who does not obey. If they, in their turn, object that Europeans cannot be happy with women who are unfaithful to them, they are told that this fidelity about which Orientals love to boast does not prevent the weary distaste which invariably follows satiated passion; that our women are too exclusively ours; that so calm a possession leaves nothing to be desired or feared; that a little flirtatiousness is a spice which stimulates, and averts corruption. Perhaps someone wiser than I am would find it difficult to decide, for if Orientals are quite right to devise ways to alleviate their anxieties, Europeans are likewise quite right not to feel those anxieties.

After all, they say, even if we, as husbands, were unhappy we could always find ways, as lovers, to compensate for this; for a man to be able, rationally, to complain about his wife's infidelity, there would necessarily have to be but three people in the world; as soon as there are four, parity will be restored.

It's a different matter to know whether, according to natural law, women are subject to men. 'No,' I was told the other day by a very worldly* philosopher; 'Nature has never proclaimed such a law; the dominion we hold over them is a veritable tyranny; they only allowed us to establish it because they are much gentler than we are, and consequently more humane and more rational; these advantages, which doubtless should have established their supremacy, had we been rational, caused them to lose that position, because we are not.'

Now, if it's true that our power over women is purely tyrannical, it's no less true that women possess a natural advantage over us, that of beauty, which nothing can resist. The power we Persians enjoy does not exist in every country, whereas the power of beauty is universal: therefore why should we be privileged? Is it because we are the stronger sex? But this is a genuine injustice; we employ every kind of resource to break down their courage, but the balance between the sexes would be equal, were women's education equal to ours: let us challenge them in those talents which their education has not impaired, and we shall see if we're so strong.

However much this may shock our national character, we must admit that in the case of the most civilized races, women have always had authority over their husbands: the Egyptians established this authority by a law honouring Isis, while the Babylonians made a similar law in honour of Semiramis.* Of the Romans it was said that they held dominion over all nations, but that they obeyed their wives.* I won't cite the Sarmatians,* who were wholly ruled by women; they were too primitive for their example to be appropriate.

As you can see, my dear Ibben, I've acquired one of the tastes of this nation, whose people enjoy supporting extraordinary opinions, and reducing everything to a paradox. The Prophet decided the question,* and ruled on the rights of each sex: women, he said, must honour their husbands; their husbands must honour them; but they are superior to their wives by one degree.

Paris, the 26th of the Moon of Gemmadi 2 1713

LETTER 37

Haggi Ibbi to the Jew ben Joshua, a Muslim proselyte, in Smyrna*

It seems to me, ben Joshua, that there are always wondrous signs that herald the birth of extraordinary men; it is as if nature went through a kind of crisis, and the celestial powers could engender only with great effort.

There is nothing as marvellous as the birth of Muhammad. God who, by the decrees of his providence had, from the beginning, resolved to send mankind this great Prophet to subjugate Satan, created light two thousand years before Adam. This light passed from one to the next of God's elect, from one to the next of Muhammad's ancestors, finally passing to him, as authentic testimony that he was descended from the patriarchs.

It was also because of this same Prophet that God decreed that no child would be conceived, until the woman had ceased to be unclean and the male had been subjected to circumcision.

He came into the world circumcised, and his face shone with joy from the moment of his birth; the earth shook three times, as if it had itself given birth; all the idols prostrated themselves; the thrones of kings were overturned; Lucifer was cast into the depths of the sea, and only after swimming for forty days did he emerge from the abyss and take refuge on Mt Cabes, where in a terrible voice he summoned the angels.

That same night God established certain boundaries between man and woman which neither could cross; the art of magicians and necromancers was ineffectual; a voice was heard from Heaven uttering these words: 'I have sent my faithful friend into the world.'

According to the testimony of the Arab historian Isben Aben, generations of birds, of clouds, of winds, and all the squadrons of angels gathered together to raise this child, arguing among themselves as to whose should be the privilege. The birds declared in their twittering that it was more convenient for them to care for him, because they could more easily collect various fruits from different places. The winds, sighing, murmured: 'It is better we should do it, because we can bring him the most delightful scents from every corner of the earth.' 'No,' said the clouds, 'no; he'll be entrusted to our care, because we will bring him the coolest water at all times.' Whereupon the angels exclaimed in indignation: 'So what will there be left for us to do?' But a voice from Heaven was heard, ending all argument: 'He shall not be removed from mortal care, for blessed are the breasts that nurse him, and the hands that touch him, and the house wherein he dwells, and the bed upon which he takes his rest.'

After so much wondrous evidence, my dear Joshua, one must have a heart of stone not to believe his holy law. What more could Heaven do to authorize its divine mission, unless it were to overturn nature and kill those very humans that it wished to convince?

Paris, the 20th of the Moon of Rhegeb 1713

LETTER 38

Usbek to Ibben, in Smyrna

As soon as a great man dies, people gather in a mosque to hear his funeral oration; this is a speech in his praise, from which it would be very difficult to determine precisely the merits of the deceased.

I would like to banish funerals: we should weep for men at their birth, not at their death. Of what use are the ceremonies, and the whole lugubrious display that a dying man is exposed to in his last moments, the tears of his family, and the suffering of his friends, except to aggravate the loss he is about to experience?

We are so blind, that we do not know when we should grieve, or when we should rejoice; we hardly ever feel anything but false sorrows, or false joys.

When I see the Mogul, who every year stupidly climbs onto the scales and has himself weighed like an ox, when I see the people rejoice because their prince has become more substantial, that is to say, less capable of ruling them, I am filled with pity, Ibben, for human extravagance.

Paris, the 20th of the Moon of Rhegeb 1713

LETTER 39

The head black eunuch to Usbek

Ismael, one of your black eunuchs, has just died, Magnificent Lord, and I have no choice but to replace him. As eunuchs are extremely scarce at present, I had thought of using a black slave you have in the country, but until now I have been unable to persuade him to become a eunuch. As I can see that, after all, it's to his own advantage, I attempted the other day to use a little force with him, and, with the agreement of the keeper of your gardens, gave orders that he should, in spite of himself, be put in a condition to render you those services which are dearest to your heart, and thus be able to live, as I do, in that formidable place which now he dare not gaze upon; but he began to howl as if someone were trying to flay him, and struggled so, that he escaped from our grasp and eluded the deadly knife. I have just learnt that he wishes to write to you to beg for mercy, claiming that my actions are prompted purely by an insatiable desire for vengeance, because of certain malicious jokes he says he made about me. However, I swear to you by the hundred thousand prophets that I acted solely for the good of your service, the only thing I hold dear, and beyond which I consider nothing. I prostrate myself at your feet.

Fatmé's seraglio, the 7th of the Moon of Maharram 1713

LETTER 40

Pharan to Usbek, his Sovereign Lord

If you were here, Magnificent Lord, I would appear before you entirely covered in white paper, and even then there would not be sufficient on which to inscribe all the insults which your head black eunuch, the most evil of men, has heaped upon me since your departure.

On the pretext of certain jokes which he claims I made about the misfortune of his condition, he visits his inexhaustible vengeance upon my head; he has set against me the cruel keeper of your gardens, who since your departure forces me to undertake insuperable tasks, work which time and time again I have felt would cost me my life, but which never, for one moment, abated the ardour I feel in serving you. How many times have I said to myself, I have a master who is kindness itself, yet I am the most miserable slave living upon this earth!

I confess to you, Magnificent Lord, I did not believe myself destined for yet greater misery, but that treacherous eunuch has attempted to outdo himself in evil. Several days ago he decided, on his own authority, to condemn me to be a guard of your sacred wives; in other words, to an execution which for me would be a thousand times more cruel than death. Those who, at birth, are subjected to this by their cruel parents, may perhaps find consolation in never having known any condition different from their own; but to debase me from humanity, to deprive me of it, would make me die of misery, if I did not die from that barbarous act.

I kiss your feet, Sublime Lord, in deep humility: let me feel the effects of that widely respected virtue, let it not be said that by your order there exists upon this earth yet another miserable being.

Fatmé's gardens, the 7th of the Moon of Maharram 1713

LETTER 41

Usbek to Pharan, in Fatmé's gardens

Let joy fill your heart as you recognize these sacred characters; let them be kissed by the head eunuch, and by the keeper of my gardens; I forbid them to lay a hand upon you before my return; tell them to buy the eunuch that is required; discharge your duties as if I were always present before you, for remember that the greater my goodness, the harsher will be your punishment if you abuse it.

Paris, the 25th of the Moon of Rhegeb 1713

LETTER 42

Usbek to Rhedi, in Venice

In France there are three Estates: the church, the army, and the law. Each holds the others in supreme contempt: for example, an individual who ought to be scorned because he is a fool, is often scorned solely because he is a magistrate.

Even among the lowliest artisans there is not one who does not defend the excellence of his chosen craft;* each considers himself above someone in a different occupation, by that degree of superiority which his judgement accords to his own craft.

In varying degrees, men are like that woman from the province of Erivan who, in thanking one of our monarchs for some favour he had granted her, repeatedly called upon Heaven to bless him, by making him governor of Erivan.

I read in some account that when a French vessel put into port on the coast of Guinea, a few of the crew went ashore to buy some sheep. They were taken to the king, who was dispensing justice to his subjects under a tree; he was seated on his throne, that is, on a piece of wood, just as proudly as if he were seated upon the throne of the Grand Mogul; he had three or four guards holding wooden pikes; a canopy of leaves served as a parasol, protecting him from the sun's heat; for ornaments he and the queen his wife wore only their black skin and a few bangles. This prince, whose vanity was even greater than his poverty, enquired of the strangers whether he was much talked about in France; he believed his name should be known from one end of the world to the other; in this he was different from that conqueror* of whom it was said that he had made the whole world fall silent; it was *this* man's belief that he should cause the entire universe to talk about him.

When the Great Cham of Tartary has dined, a herald calls out that all the princes of the earth may go and dine if they so desire; that barbarian, who consumes nothing but milk, does not own a house, and lives by pillaging, considers all the kings in the world his slaves, and insults them regularly twice a day.

Paris, the 28th of the Moon of Rhegeb 1713

LETTER 43

Rhedi to Usbek, in A***

I was still in bed yesterday morning, when I heard a loud knocking at my door, which was suddenly opened, or rather battered down, by a man whom I knew slightly; he seemed quite beside himself.

His dress was barely presentable; his wig, which had not even been combed, sat askew; he had not had time to have his black doublet mended, and that morning had neglected the prudent measures with which he normally disguised the sad condition of his entire outfit.

'Get up,' he said to me, 'I need you the whole of today; I've a thousand purchases to make, and I'd love to make them in your company: first we must go to the rue St Honoré to see a notary responsible for the sale of some land costing 500,000 francs; I want him to give me first refusal. On my way here I stopped a moment in the Faubourg St Germain,* where I rented a mansion at 10,000 francs; and I hope to get the contract signed today.'

The moment I was more or less dressed, my visitor rushed me down into the street: 'Let's begin by buying a carriage and pair,' and indeed we bought not only a carriage, but also about 100,000 francs' worth of merchandise, in less than an hour; it was all done very quickly, because my man did not bargain over anything, did not keep track of his expenditures, and never moved from one spot. All this made me ponder; when I studied the man, I found in him such a strange mix of wealth and penury that I did not know what to think; but finally I broke my silence and, drawing him aside, said to him: 'Monsieur, who will pay for all this?' 'I will,' he replied; 'come to my rooms, I'll show you immense riches, treasures such as would inspire envy in the greatest of monarchs; you, however, will not be envious, for I'll always share them with you.' I followed him; we climbed up to his fifth-floor rooms, then hauled ourselves up on a ladder to the sixth floor, where a small room, open to the elements, contained nothing but two or three dozen earthenware bowls filled with various liquids. 'I rose very early,' he told me, 'and did first what I've done for the past twenty-five years, which is to go and inspect my *opus*. I realized that the great day has arrived that will make me richer than any man on this earth. Do you see this bright red liquid? It now possesses all the qualities that the philosophers specify to effect the transmutation of metals: from it I obtained these particles I have here, which are genuine gold judging by their colour, although their weight is not quite perfect. This secret, which Nicolas Flamel* discovered, but for which Raymond Lull* and a million others continued to search, has come down to me, and so today I find I have succeeded in my quest. God grant that I use the bountiful treasures bestowed upon me purely for his glory!'

I left, and walked—or rather hurled myself—down those stairs in a transport of rage, leaving that so wealthy man in his poorhouse. Goodbye, my dear Usbek, I'll come and see you tomorrow, and if you like, we'll return together to Paris.

Paris, the last day of the Moon of Rhegeb 1713

LETTER 44

Usbek to Rhedi, in Venice

I see people here arguing endlessly about religion: but at the same time they seem to be competing over who can observe it the least.

Not only are they not better Christians, they are not even better citizens, and that is what concerns me: for no matter what religion one follows, observance of the law, love of one's fellow-men, and filial devotion are always the principal results of religion.

Indeed, should not the primary object of a religious man be to please the divinity that established the religion he professes? But the surest way to do that is undoubtedly by conforming to the rules of society, and fulfilling the duties of brotherly love; for no matter what your religion may be, as soon as you assume its existence, you must assume also that God loves mankind, since he established a religion to make men happy; and that if he loves them, you are certain to please him by loving them yourself also; that is to say, by carrying out all the duties of charity and humanity towards them, and by not breaking the laws under which they live.

By so doing you are much more certain of pleasing God than by taking part in this or that ceremony, for ceremonies have absolutely no virtue in themselves, but only in relation to something, and on the assumption that God commanded them; but these issues are the subject of intense debate; you could easily err in your choice, when you have to choose the ceremonies of one religion from among those of two thousand.

Every day a certain man addressed this prayer to God: 'Lord, I don't understand any part of these disputes about you which constantly arise: I would like to serve you according to your wishes, but every man I've consulted wants me to serve you according to his wishes. When I want to pray to you, I do not know in what language I should speak to you; nor do I know what posture I should assume; one man tells me I should stand upright to pray; another wants me to be seated; a third insists that I kneel. And that's not all; some people claim that I ought to wash every morning in cold water, while others assert that you will look upon me with horror if I do not have a small piece of flesh cut off. The other day, in a caravanserai, I happened to eat some rabbit; three men sitting near me made me shake with fear. All three declared that I had grievously offended you; one, because this animal is unclean; another, because it had been killed by suffocation; and the third, because it wasn't fish. A Brahmin who was passing and whom I asked to adjudicate told me: "They are mistaken, because evidently you did not kill this animal yourself." But I did, I replied. "Then you have committed an abomination, which God will never forgive you," he said in a severe tone; "for how can you know that the soul of your father hadn't passed into that animal?" Lord, all these matters fill me with indescribable confusion: I cannot move my head without someone threatening me with offending you; yet I want to please you, and use my life, which you gave me, to that end; I don't know if I'm mistaken, but I believe that the best way to accomplish this is to live as a good citizen, in the society where you chose I should be born, and as a good father, in the family which you have given me.'

Paris, the 8th of the Moon of Chahban 1713

LETTER 45

Zachi to Usbek, in Paris

I have some great news to tell you: I've made things up with Zephis, and the seraglio, which we had divided, is now united; within these walls, where peace now reigns, only you are missing. Come back, my dear Usbek, come back and make love triumph once again.

I gave a splendid feast for Zephis, to which your mother, your wives, and your principal concubines were invited; your aunts and several of your female cousins were there as well; they came on horseback, enveloped in the shadowy clouds of their veils and robes.

The next morning we left for the country, where we hoped to find greater freedom; we mounted our camels, and travelled four to a box. As the expedition had been planned at short notice, we did not have time to announce the *courouc** to clear the way, but the head eunuch, always so industrious, took a further precaution: for he added to the drapery which prevented our being seen, a curtain so heavy as to prevent us from seeing a living soul.

On reaching the river where we cross, as usual we each climbed into a barrel which was then loaded onto the ship; they told us that the river was full of people. One inquisitive man, who approached too near to where we were imprisoned, was dealt a mortal blow that deprived him for ever of the light of day. Another, caught bathing completely nude on the riverbank, suffered the same fate; and your faithful eunuchs sacrificed those two unfortunates to your honour, and to ours.

But you must hear the rest of our adventures. When we were in the middle of the river such a fierce wind blew up, such a frightful cloud darkened the skies, that our sailors began to lose hope. Terrified by this danger, we almost all fainted. I remember I could hear the voices of our eunuchs arguing; some of them were saying that we should be warned of the danger, and let out of our prisons, but the head eunuch never wavered in declaring that he would sooner die than allow his master to be dishonoured in such a manner, and that he would plunge his dagger into the breast of anyone who made such a daring suggestion. One of my slaves, quite beside herself, with her clothing in disarray, came rushing to help me, but a black eunuch seized her brutally and forced her back to her quarters; it was then that I fainted, and only recovered my senses when the danger had passed.

How hazardous travel is for women! Men are exposed only to life-threatening perils, whereas we women are constantly in danger of losing our life, or our virtue. Farewell, my dear Usbek, I shall always adore you.

Fatmé's seraglio, the 2nd of the Moon of Rhamazan 1713

LETTER 46

Usbek to Rhedi, in Venice

Those who love acquiring knowledge are never idle; although I have
no important duties to discharge, I am nevertheless always occupied.
I spend my life observing, and in the evening I record what I have
noted, and seen, and heard, during the day; I find everything interesting, everything astonishing; I am like a child whose still-tender
organs are keenly affected by the most trivial objects.

You may not believe this, but we are warmly received in all
kinds of gatherings and social groups; I think that in this I am
much indebted to Rica's ready wit and natural good spirits, which
mean that he seeks out every type of company and is in turn equally
sought after himself; our foreignness no longer offends anyone,
and we even enjoy people's surprise when they discover we are
quite polite, for the French do not suppose that our climate can produce civilized men; however, I must admit that they are well worth
putting right.

I've been spending a few days in a country house near Paris
belonging to a gentleman of some importance, who is delighted
to have company in his home; he has a very agreeable wife whose
profound modesty is joined to that lightness of heart which our
Persian ladies invariably lose, through living in such seclusion.

Being a stranger, I had nothing better to do than to study, as is
my custom, this crowd of people who kept arriving, and whose
characters never failed to offer me something fresh. From the first
I particularly noticed a man whose simplicity pleased me; I attached
myself to him, and he to me, so that we always found we were together.

One day, in a large group, we began a private exchange, allowing
the general conversations to pass us by. 'You may find in me,' I told
him, 'more curiosity than politeness, but I beg you to permit me to
ask you some questions, for I'm growing tired of not knowing anything, and of living with people whom I am unable to sort out; my
mind has been hard at work for two days, there isn't a single one of
these men over whom I haven't been in torment countless times, yet
not in a thousand years shall I be able to fathom them; they are more
invisible to me than the wives of our great monarch.' 'You have only

to ask,' he replied, 'and I'll tell you everything you want to know, particularly as I believe you to be a discreet man, who will not abuse my trust.'

'Who is that man,' I asked him, 'who has talked so much about the splendid dinners he has hosted for men of rank, who is on so intimate a footing with your dukes, and who converses so frequently with your ministers, who are reputed to be difficult to approach? He must be a man of quality,* but his features are so coarse that he does no honour to people of quality; furthermore I find he is not an educated man. I am a foreigner, but I believe that there exists a certain level of politeness common to all nations; this seems to be absent in him: are your men of rank less well bred than other men?' 'That man', he replied with a laugh, 'is a tax farmer;* he is as superior to the others by his wealth, as he is beneath them all by his birth; he would give the best dinners in Paris, if he could only make up his mind never to dine at home; as you can see, he's a bumptious fool, but he excels in his chef, and moreover is not ungrateful, for, as you've heard, he's been praising him all day.'

'And that fat man in black,' I said to him, 'whom that lady has invited to sit beside her? How can he be dressed so lugubriously, yet have such a cheerful air and such a rubicund complexion?* He smiles graciously the instant anyone speaks to him, and his outfit is simpler, yet more carefully contrived, than a woman's.' 'He's a preacher,' he answered, 'and what's worse, a father confessor: whatever he may look like, he knows more than husbands do, he knows women's weakness; but they know that he also has his own.' 'What?' I exclaimed. 'But he talks all the time about something called grace!' 'Not all the time;' he told me, 'when he has the ear of a pretty woman he's even more eager to talk about her fall from grace; in public he thunders, but in private he's gentle as a lamb.' 'It seems to me', I then remarked, 'that people pay him a lot of attention, and he's treated with great respect.' 'What can you mean, great respect? He's an essential man; he brings sweetness to the retired life: he offers trivial advice, runs helpful little errands, pays regular visits; he cures a headache better than any living soul; he's an excellent man.'

'If I'm not being a nuisance, tell me who that man is opposite us, the one who's so badly dressed, whose expression is sometimes so affected, whose speech is so different from other people's, who doesn't let his wit shape his speech, but speaks in order to be witty?' 'That', he replied, 'is a poet, and the buffoon of the human race; such people say they were born like that; that's true, and furthermore they'll be like that their whole life, which means, almost always, that they are the most ridiculous of men; consequently they are shown no mercy, but have scorn and contempt heaped upon them; starvation has brought this one into this house; he's welcomed here by our host and hostess, whose goodness and politeness never fail; he wrote their epithalamium when they were married; it's the best thing he's ever written, for the marriage has been as happy as he predicted.'

'You may find this beyond belief,' he added, 'imbued as you are with the prejudices of the Orient, but happy marriages do exist in our society, and there are women who scrupulously protect their own virtue. The couple of whom we speak enjoy a mutual harmony which nothing can disturb; they are loved and esteemed by everybody: but there's just one thing, which is that their innate kindness makes them open their doors to all sorts of people, so that sometimes one encounters undesirable society here; it's not that I disapprove, for we have to live with one another the way we are: people who are said to be "good company" are often simply those whose vices are more refined, and perhaps it's the same as with poisons, where the most subtle are also the most dangerous.'

'And what about that old man,' I murmured, 'who looks so morose? At first I took him for a foreigner: apart from the fact that he's dressed differently from the others, he criticizes everything that's done in France, and doesn't approve of your government.'

'He's an old soldier,' he told me, 'who's made himself unforgettable to his listeners by the length of time he can spend describing his exploits. He can't bear the fact that France has won some battles where he was not present, or that a siege should be praised where he wasn't in the trenches; he believes himself to be so vital to our history that he imagines it finishes where he finished; he considers a few wounds he received as on a par with the dissolution of the monarchy; by contrast with those philosophers who say that one only enjoys the present, and that the past is nothing, he enjoys only the past, and lives only in the campaigns he fought; he breathes the air of days gone by, the way heroes live on in days that come after them.' 'But why', I asked, 'did he leave the service?' 'He didn't leave it,' he answered, 'it left him; they gave him an insignificant post where he will live out the rest of his days; he'll never advance any further; the road to glory is closed for him.' 'But why so?' 'We have a maxim in France,' he told me, 'which states that no officer should be promoted who has tolerated being kept in a low-ranking position; we see them as men whose spirit has, so to speak, grown narrower by focusing on details, and who, having accustomed themselves to small matters, have become incapable of greater things; we believe that a man who does not possess the qualities of a general at the age of thirty will never possess them; that he whose eye cannot instantly grasp all the various possibilities inherent in an extensive terrain, or who lacks that presence of mind which in victory ensures that every advantage is grasped, and in defeat every resource exploited, will never acquire those talents. That is why we keep brilliant positions for those great, exalted men upon whom Heaven has bestowed not just a heart, but a heroic genius; and subordinate positions for those whose talents also are second-rate. Among such are those soldiers who have grown old serving in an obscure war; the most they can do is what they have done all their life, and we cannot demand more of them just at the point when their powers begin to fail.'

A moment later, again filled with curiosity, I said to him: 'I promise to ask you no further questions, if you will bear with me for just one more. Who is that tall young man who has all that fancy hair,* scant wit, and great impertinence? Why does he speak louder than anyone else, and seem so pleased with himself for being alive?' 'He's a ladies' man, an adventurer,' he said. As he spoke, some people entered the room, others left it, several rose from their seats, someone approached and spoke to my companion, and I was left as ignorant as before. But soon after, I know not by what lucky chance, the young man in question found himself at my side; he addressed me: 'Monsieur, it's a fine day, would you care to take a turn round the garden?' I replied as politely as I could, and we went out together. 'I've come to the country,' he told me, 'to please the mistress of the house, with whom I'm on pretty good terms: of course a certain well-known society lady will make quite a fuss about my being here, but what is one to do? I see the prettiest women in Paris, but I don't commit myself to any, and I'm good at stringing them along; for— just between ourselves—I'm not really up to much.' 'I presume, monsieur,' I told him, 'that you hold some position, or have some employment, which prevents you from paying court to the ladies more assiduously.' 'No, monsieur, my only employment is to drive husbands wild and fathers to despair; I love alarming a woman who believes she has caught me, and making her believe that she is on the brink of losing me; there's a bunch of us young fellows who've shared out Paris between ourselves in this way, so that people are interested in the most trivial things we do.' 'As far as I can gather,' I remarked, 'you make more of a stir than the most heroic warrior, and inspire deeper respect than a solemn magistrate. If you were in Persia, you would not enjoy all these advantages; you would become more suited to guard our ladies, than to please them.' My face grew red, and I think if I had said another word I could not have avoided being uncivil.

What do you think of a country where such people are tolerated, where a man with such an occupation is allowed to live? Where infidelity, treachery, abduction, perfidy, and injustice earn respect? Where a man is esteemed because he deprives a father of his daughter, a husband of his wife, and brings trouble into the sweetest and most sacred of relationships? Happy are the children of Ali, who defend their families from dishonour and seduction: the light of the dawn is not more pure than the flame which burns in the heart of our women; our daughters tremble when they contemplate the day which will deprive them of that virtue by which they resemble the angels, and the incorporeal powers.* Land of my birth, beloved land, which the sun bathes with its first rays, you are unsullied by the horrifying crimes which force that star to hide the instant it appears in these black western skies.

Paris, the 5th of the Moon of Rhamazan 1713

LETTER 47

*Rica to Usbek, at A****

The other day I was in my room when a dervish entered, dressed in an extraordinary fashion: his beard came down to the rope girdle round his waist, his feet were bare, and his habit, of grey, coarse cloth, fell in places to a point; the whole effect was so bizarre, that my first thought was to send for a painter to make a fanciful portrait of this figure.

He began with a very fulsome compliment, in the course of which he told me he was a man of ability and, furthermore, a Capuchin friar;* 'I hear,' he added, 'that you are about to return to the court of Persia, where you hold a high rank; I have come to ask for your protection, and to beg you to obtain for us, from the king, a modest dwelling near Casbin, for two or three monks.' 'So, Father,' I replied, 'you wish to go to Persia?' 'I, monsieur? I most certainly do not; I'm the Provincial Father here, and I wouldn't exchange my situation for that of any Capuchin in the world.' 'So what the devil are you asking me for?' 'It's this: if we had this house, our Fathers in Italy would send two or three of their monks there.' 'I take it you are acquainted with these monks.' 'No, monsieur, I do not know them.' 'So why in Heaven's name do you care whether they go to Persia?' 'That's a fine project, to enable a pair of Capuchins to breathe the good air of Casbin! It will be most valuable both to Europe and to Asia! It is vital to interest monarchs in such projects! And these are what are called fine colonies! Be off with you: you and your breed are not made to be transplanted, and you'd be well advised to go on spreading in the soil where you were engendered.'

Paris, the 15th of the Moon of Rhamazan 1713

LETTER 48

Rica to ***

I have known men in whom virtue was so natural that one was not even conscious of it; they applied themselves to their duty without apparent effort, doing it as if by instinct: far from drawing attention to their rare qualities in their conversation, it seemed as if they were unaware of their own virtues. Those are the people I love, not those virtuous men who seem to be astonished at being so, and who see a good action as a marvel whose recounting should astonish.

If modesty is a virtue essential to those whom Heaven has endowed with great gifts, then what can be said of those wretches who dare to display a pride which would disgrace the greatest of men?

Everywhere, I see people who never stop talking about themselves; their conversation is a mirror that always reflects their presumptuous features: they will tell you about the most trivial things that happened to them, hoping that the interest they themselves find in this will increase their importance in your eyes; they've done everything, seen everything, said everything, thought everything; they are a universal model, an inexhaustible object of comparison, a wellspring of examples that never runs dry. Oh, how tasteless is praise, when it reflects back upon its source!

A few days ago a man of this type battered us for two hours with himself, his excellence, and his talents; but, since there is no such thing in the world as perpetual motion, he did stop talking; the conversation giving us the initiative, we grasped it.

Someone who seemed rather cross began by complaining of how boring conversations were becoming: 'Always some idiot who does nothing but talk about himself, and who works every subject round to himself.' 'You're right,' our speechifier replied quickly; 'they should do as I do. I never praise myself: I'm wealthy, well-born, a liberal spender, my friends say I'm quite witty, but I never speak of these things; if I have any good qualities, the one I value most highly is my modesty.'

This brazen braggart astounded me, and while he was holding forth I was saying to myself: happy the man who is vain enough never to praise himself, who fears his audience, and never compromises his own worth by ruffling the pride of others.

Paris, the 20th of the Moon of Rhamazan 1713

LETTER 49

Nargum, Persian envoy in Moscow, to Usbek, in Paris

I have received a letter from Ispahan saying that you have left Persia, and are now in Paris. Why must I hear your news from others, rather than from you?

Orders from the King of Kings have kept me for five years in this country, where I have concluded some important negotiations.

As you know, the tsar* is the only Christian prince whose interests coincide with those of Persia, because he is, like us, an enemy of the Turks.

His empire is greater than ours: it extends for two thousand leagues, from Moscow to the furthest outpost of his states, near China.

He is absolute master of the life and property of his subjects, who are all slaves, except for four families. The lieutenant of the prophets, the King of Kings, for whom the heavens serve as footstool, does not exercise a more awe-inspiring breadth of power.

Considering the appalling climate of Muscovy, one would never believe that it could be a punishment to be exiled from it; nevertheless, the moment a noble is disgraced, he is banished to Siberia.

Just as the law of our Prophet forbids us to drink wine, the law of the tsar forbids it to Muscovites.

They have a way of welcoming their guests which is not at all Persian. As soon as a stranger enters the house, the husband presents his wife to him; the visitor kisses her; this is considered a gesture of politeness to the husband.

When a marriage contract is drawn up, although the bride's father will normally stipulate that the husband must not whip her, nevertheless you would scarcely credit how much Muscovite women love to be beaten; a bride cannot believe that she possesses her husband's heart if he doesn't beat her in the accepted way; if his conduct were otherwise, it would be seen as an unpardonable sign of indifference. Here is a letter a married woman recently sent her mother:

'My dear Mother,
'I am the unhappiest woman in the world; there isn't a thing I haven't tried, to make my husband love me, but I've never succeeded. Yesterday I had a thousand things to see to in the house; I went out, and stayed out all day; I believed that on my return he'd give me a good beating, but he never said a single word. My sister is treated very differently, her husband beats her black and blue every day: she can't look at a man without her husband instantly striking her; therefore they love each other very much, and get on perfectly.

'That's what makes her so proud; but I'm not going to give her cause to despise me for long; I'm determined to make my husband love me, no matter what it takes; I'll get him into such a rage that he'll be forced to show me some affection; I won't have it said that I'm not beaten, and that I'm to live in this house without him caring about me: at the least little slap he gives me I'll bellow as loudly as I know how, so that people will think he's really going for me, and I believe that if a neighbour came to help me, I'd strangle him. I beg you, my dear mother, to please explain to my husband that he's treating me shamefully. My father, who's such a gentleman, did not behave like that, and I remember that when I was a little girl I sometimes thought that he loved you too well. I embrace you, my dear mother.'

The Muscovites are not permitted to leave the empire, even to travel; so that, isolated from other nations by the laws of the country, they have preserved their ancient customs all the more keenly because they do not believe anything different to be possible.

But the prince, the present ruler,* has tried to change everything; he has had some tremendous disputes with them about their beards, while the clergy and the monks have fought just as fiercely to protect their ignorance.

He is very eager to encourage the arts, and tries in every possible way to promote, across Europe and Asia, the glory of his nation, which until now has been forgotten, and, with few exceptions, known solely within its own borders.

Invariably restless and uneasy, he travels his vast territories, everywhere leaving in his wake evidence of his natural implacability.

He quits his realm as if it were unable to contain him, and seeks, in Europe, yet more provinces, and new kingdoms.*

I embrace you, my dear Usbek, send me news of yourself, I beg you.

Moscow, the 2nd of the Moon of Chalval 1713

LETTER 50

Rica to Usbek, in ***

I spent the other day with a group of people, where I greatly enjoyed myself. The party included women of all ages: one was eighty, one sixty, and there was one of forty, with a niece who must have been twenty or twenty-two. Some instinct made me approach this niece, who whispered in my ear: 'What do you think of my aunt, who at her age would like to have lovers, and still behaves as if she's pretty?' 'She's wrong,' I told her; 'that's a plan suitable only for you.' A moment later I found myself close to the aunt, who said to me: 'What do you think of that woman, who is at least sixty, and today spent more than an hour getting herself dressed?'

'She wasted her time,' I told her. 'She'd need charms like yours for it to be worthwhile.' I approached this unfortunate lady of sixty, my heart filled with pity for her, when she murmured in my ear: 'Could there be anything more ridiculous? Look at that woman, she's eighty years old, and she's wearing flame-coloured ribbons; she wants to look young, and she's succeeding, for that's almost puerile.' Dear God! I thought to myself, shall we always be conscious only of the absurdities of others? Perhaps it's a good thing, I then added, that we find consolation in our neighbours' foibles. In the meantime, I was enjoying myself, and thought: we've climbed up high enough; now let's come down, and we'll start with the old woman at the top. 'Madame, you are so very alike, that lady to whom I've been speaking and yourself, that it seems you must be sisters, and I don't believe that either of you can be older than the other.' 'Ah, truly, monsieur,' she said, 'when one of us dies the other will surely have good cause for alarm; I don't believe there's two days' difference between her age and mine.' Having caught this decrepit old woman, I approached the one of sixty. 'Madame, you must decide a wager I've made; I've bet that this lady'—indicating the forty-year-old—'and you, are the same age.' 'Upon my word,' she said, 'I don't believe there's six months' difference.' Good, I'm getting there, let's continue. I descended further, and spoke to the lady of forty. 'Madame, be so very kind as to tell me, are you joking when you refer to that young lady at the other table as your niece? You're as young as she is, indeed there's something a trifle passé about her face, which is certainly not true of yours; and then those brilliant tones of your complexion...' 'Wait' she said to me, 'I am indeed her aunt, but her mother was at least twenty-five years older than me; we had different mothers; and I heard my deceased sister say that her daughter and I were born the same year.' 'I was sure of it, madame, and I was right to be astonished.'

My dear Usbek, women who feel finished before their time because they've lost their charms, long to go back and regain their youth: how could they not attempt to deceive other people? They do everything they can to deceive themselves, and conceal from their own eyes the most distressing of all notions.

Paris, the 3rd of the Moon of Chalval 1713

LETTER 51

Zelis to Usbek, in Paris

No love can ever have been deeper or more passionate than the love the white eunuch* Cosrou feels for my slave Zelide:* he wants so desperately to marry her that I cannot refuse him. And why should I object, when her mother does not do so, and Zelide herself seems satisfied with this masquerade of a marriage, with this vain shadow she is being offered?

What does she want with this unhappy man, whose only attribute as a husband will be his jealousy; who will only abandon his frigidity for a useless despair; who will always summon the memory of what he once was, to remind her of what he no longer is; who, always yearning to give himself, but never doing so, will constantly deceive himself and her, and make her experience, at every instant, all the miseries of his condition?

And what then? A life spent eternally in the company of ideas and phantoms? A life lived only through the imagination? To be always on the brink of pleasure, and never really to know pleasure? To languish in the arms of a luckless wretch, and instead of reciprocating his sighs, only echo his laments?

Surely a man of this kind—made only to protect, and never to possess—must inspire contempt? I look for love, and find it not.

I speak to you frankly, because you love my naivety, and prefer my openness and my responsiveness to pleasure to the fake prudery of my companions.

I have heard countless times that, with women, eunuchs experience a sensual pleasure that is not known by us; that nature compensates for its losses and has resources which make up for the defect of their condition; that a man can indeed cease to be a man, without ceasing to experience pleasure; and that in this state the senses are different, and provide a different kind of pleasure.

If this were the case I would pity Zelide less; it's not without value, to live with people who are less unhappy.

Tell me your wishes on this matter, and let me know if you want the marriage to take place in the seraglio. Farewell.

The seraglio in Ispahan, the 5th of the Moon of Chalval 1713

LETTER 52

*Rica to Usbek, at ****

This morning I was in my room, which, as you know, is separated from the others by a very thin partition that is riddled with holes, so that you can hear everything being said in the adjoining room. A man was striding up and down, saying to someone: 'I don't know why it is, but everything's turning against me: it's more than three days since I've said anything to help my reputation; and I've found myself included in conversations just anyhow, without being paid the slightest attention, or spoken to more than a couple of times. I'd worked up a few sallies to enliven my talk but nobody would give me a chance to use them; I had a really lovely story all ready, but as I tried to work my way round to telling it, they managed to stop me from doing so, just as if I were trying to insert it on purpose; I've a few witticisms that for the past four days have been getting staler in my head without my being able to use them at all; if this continues, I believe eventually I'll just seem a fool; it seems to be my fate, and I can't escape it. Yesterday I had hoped to shine in the company of three or four old ladies, who naturally don't intimidate me, and I planned to say the prettiest things in the world; I spent more than a quarter of an hour trying to steer my conversation, but they never stuck to one subject and, like the Fates, cut the thread of all my speeches. I must say, the reputation of being a wit is very difficult to maintain; I don't know how you have managed it.' 'I've had an idea,' said the other man, 'let's work together on being witty; we'll team up to do it; every day we'll agree what we're going to talk about, and we'll be such a help to one another that if someone comes and interrupts us in the middle of our thoughts we'll get him to join us, and if he won't come willingly we'll make him; we'll agree on where to show approval, and where to smile; on other places where we should really laugh, laugh heartily; you'll see, we'll set the tone for all the conversations, and we'll be admired for our razor-sharp wit and the felicity of our repartee; we'll protect one another with prearranged signals; today you'll shine, tomorrow you'll support me; I'll arrive at a house with you, and exclaim, gesturing towards you: "I must tell you a very funny reply that M. just made to a man we met in the street," and I'll turn to you: "He wasn't expecting it, it certainly took him aback." I'll recite some verses of mine, and you'll say: "I was there when he composed them; it was at a supper, and he barely gave them a moment's thought;" you and I will often make fun of one another, and people will say: "Just look at how they attack each other, and defend themselves; they don't spare themselves; let's see how he'll get out of this—marvellous!— what a quick wit!" It'll be a battle royal, but they'll never guess that we've been skirmishing since the day before. We'll need to buy certain books, anthologies of witticisms for the use of those who aren't witty but would like to be thought so; it all depends on having models; I want to see us, at the end of six months, capable of holding an hour-long conversation absolutely brim-full of witty remarks. But we will have to be attentive to one thing: to making certain our witticisms stay current; it's not sufficient to say something witty, it must be published, and circulated, and disseminated everywhere; otherwise, it's a waste of time, and I must admit there's nothing so depressing as seeing a fine thing one has said expire in the ear of the fool who hears it. It's true that there is, frequently, a compensation, in that we also make stupid remarks which are likewise not recognized; that's the only thing we have to console us on such occasions. So, my friend, that's how to go about it; you do what I tell you, and I promise you a seat in the Academy* before six months are out; in other words, you won't have to work for long, because you can then abandon your study of the art; you'll be a wit no matter what you do. It's been observed that in France as soon as a man joins an association he immediately acquires what is termed *esprit de corps*; that will be your experience, and the only anxiety I feel on your behalf is that you will find the applause embarrassing.'

Paris, the 6th of the Moon of Zilcadé 1714

LETTER 53

Rica to Ibben, in Smyrna

Among the Europeans, the first few hours of marriage* smooth out all the difficulties; the ultimate favours are always of the same date as the nuptial blessing; the women do not behave in the least like our

Persian women, who sometimes defend the territory for months at a time; no victory is more complete, and if the brides do not lose anything, it's because they have nothing to lose; but—I blush to write it—the moment of their defeat is always known, and without consulting the stars, the exact hour of the birth of their children can be predicted.

Frenchmen hardly ever talk about their wives; they're afraid to speak of them in front of men who know them better than they do themselves.

There are some men here who are very unhappy, yet whom no one comforts: they are the jealous husbands; there are some whom everybody hates: they are the jealous husbands; and there are some whom all men despise: they too are the jealous husbands.

Consequently, in no country are jealous husbands rarer than in France: their tranquillity is not based upon the trust they feel for their wives, but, to the contrary, on the low opinion they hold of them; they believe that all the wise precautions of the Orientals, the veils that conceal their women, the prisons that confine them, the vigilance of the eunuchs, are more likely to encourage the ingenuity of the sex than to deter them. Here in France husbands accept things with good grace, and consider infidelities to be inevitable blows of fate. A husband who wanted to keep his wife just for himself would be seen as a disturber of public pleasure, and as a madman who wished to enjoy the light of the sun to the exclusion of all other men.

Over here, a man who loves his wife is a man who lacks the qualities to win the love of another woman; who abuses his rights under the law to compensate for the personal charms he lacks; who exploits all his advantages to the detriment of an entire society; who appropriates what he had obtained under a purely temporary agreement, behaving to the best of his ability in such a way as to overturn a tacit convention that ensured the happiness of either sex. The reputation of being the husband of a pretty woman, which in Asia is so carefully kept hidden, is here enjoyed without anxiety; a man feels free to seek entertainment everywhere. A prince consoles himself for the loss of one fortress by taking another. At the time when the Turks were taking Baghdad from us,* did we not capture the fortress of Kandahar from the Mogul?

A man who in general tolerates his wife's infidelities is not looked upon with disapproval; on the contrary, his prudence is admired; it's only in particular circumstances that dishonour is involved.

It is not the case that virtuous ladies do not exist, and one can say that they are distinguished; my guide always pointed them out to me; but they were all so ugly, that you must be a saint not to hate virtue.

After what I've told you about the customs of this country, you will easily understand that the French do not pride themselves on fidelity; they believe that it's just as ridiculous to swear to a woman that they will always love her, as it is to claim that they'll always be healthy, or always happy. When they promise a woman that they will always love her, they assume that she, for her part, is promising that they will always find her loveable, and if she does not keep her word then they no longer feel obligated to keep theirs.

Paris, the 7th of the Moon of Zilcadé 1714

LETTER 54

Usbek to Ibben, in Smyrna

Gambling is very widespread in Europe;* one can be a gambler by profession; the title alone stands in lieu of birth, wealth, and integrity; it ranks any man bearing it on a par with honest, respectable men, without further question, although everyone is well aware that, in so judging, he is very often mistaken: but everyone has agreed to remain incorrigible.

Women, especially, are addicted to it; it's true that they rarely indulge in it in their youth, unless it be in the service of a more cherished passion, but as they grow old, their passion for gambling seems to rejuvenate, and that passion completely fills the void left by the others.

They want to ruin their husbands, and to achieve this, they dispose of means common to women of all ages, from first youth to the most decrepit old age: the trouble begins with their wardrobe, their carriage and horses; then flirtations increase it, and gaming completes it.

I've often watched nine or ten women, or rather nine or ten centuries, sitting round a table; I've watched them in their hopes, in their fears, in their joys, and above all in their rages: you'd have said that they would never have time to grow calm again, and that life would abandon them before their despair did; you'd have been unsure whether those they were paying were their creditors or their heirs.

It seems that our holy Prophet was principally concerned to take from us everything which can disturb our reason: he forbade us the use of wine, which can keep our reason submerged; he forbade us, in a special precept, games of chance, and when it was impossible for him to take from us the cause of our passions, he tempered them. In our culture love brings with it neither agitation nor frenzy; it is a languid passion, which leaves the spirit calm; the plurality of our wives protects us from their power, and tempers the violence of our desires.

Paris, the 18th of the Moon of Zilhagé 1714

LETTER 55

Usbek to Rhedi, in Venice

Here in France, rakes* keep a great number of prostitutes, and religious fanatics keep a vast number of dervishes; these dervishes take three vows: of obedience, of poverty, and of chastity. It is said that the first is the best kept of them all; as to the second, I can tell you that it isn't kept at all, and you can well imagine what happens to the third.

But however wealthy these dervishes may be, they never renounce their title of 'poor'; our glorious sultan would sooner renounce his sublime and magnificent honorifics, and they are quite right, for the title of 'poor' prevents them from being so.

Physicians here, and a few dervishes known as confessors, are always either too greatly revered or too greatly despised; however, people say that the heirs put up with the physicians better than they do with the confessors.

The other day I visited a monastery belonging to these dervishes; one of them, whose white hair entitled him to great respect, welcomed me very civilly, and after showing me round the entire house, led me into the garden, where we started to converse. 'Father,' I asked him, 'what is your occupation here in the community?' 'Monsieur,' he replied, evidently delighted by my question, 'I'm a casuist.' 'Casuist?' I responded. 'I've never heard mention of such an occupation since I arrived in France.' 'What! You don't know what a casuist is! Well, listen: I'm going to give you an idea of what it is, which will explain it to your complete satisfaction. There are two kinds of sin, mortal sins, which completely exclude us from paradise, and venial sins, which do certainly offend God, but do not anger him to the point of depriving us of beatitude; well, the whole of our art consists in distinguishing clearly between these two kinds of sin; for, with the exception of a few libertines, all Christians want to attain paradise; but there's hardly anyone who does not want to attain it at the least possible cost. When one is well informed about the mortal sins, one tries not to commit those particular ones, and that's fine; but there are people who don't aim at such great perfection, and as they have no ambition, they don't care whether they are among the first to be called; consequently, they barely manage to get there, but as long as they do get in, that's good enough for them: they want to judge it exactly, with nothing to spare. They are the people who snatch, rather than attain, their salvation, and who say to God: "Lord, I've obeyed the exact letter of the law; you can't renege on your promises, and as I've done nothing more than just what you required, I acquit you of giving me more than you promised."

'Therefore, Monsieur, we casuists are indispensable. However, that's not all there is to it; there's much more, as you'll see. It isn't the action that determines the sin, it's the knowledge of the person who commits it; he who does an evil thing in the belief that it is not evil, is secure in his conscience; and as there's an infinite number of morally ambiguous actions, a casuist is able to bestow upon them a degree of goodness which they do not possess, by declaring them good; and provided that he can convince the individual that their act is untainted, his verdict clears them entirely of sin.

'I'm confiding to you the secret of an art in whose service I've grown old; I'm showing you its finer points; there's a way of interpreting everything, even matters which appear the least susceptible of interpretation.' 'Father,' I said to him, 'that's all very fine, but how do you reconcile this with Heaven? If the Great Sophy* had a man

like you in his court, who behaved towards him as you do towards
your God, who differentiated among his commands, and instructed
his subjects in which circumstances they must obey them and in
which other circumstances they may violate them, he'd have him
impaled on the spot.' Thereupon I bowed to my dervish, and
departed without awaiting his reply.

Paris, the 23rd of the Moon of Maharram 1714

LETTER 56

Rica to Rhedi, in Venice

In Paris, my dear Rhedi, there are many professions. For a trifling
sum an obliging Parisian will come and give you the secret of making
gold.

Another will promise to enable you to sleep with the ethereal
spirits, provided that you spend a mere thirty years without seeing a
woman.

Then you'll meet soothsayers so clever, that they'll recount your
entire life to you, provided that they can spend just a quarter of an
hour chatting to your servants.

There are dexterous women who can turn virginity into a flower
that dies and is reborn every day, and is plucked for the hundredth
time more painfully than the first.

There are others who repair, through the power of their art, all the
damage wrought by time, and can restore beauty to a face where it
has begun to falter; they can even recall a woman from the most
advanced old age and move her back to her most tender youth.

All these people live, or attempt to live, in a city which is the
mother of invention.

The income of the citizens is free of taxes; it consists of ideas
and ingenuity; each individual has his own which he exploits as best
he can.

Anyone trying to count all the men of religion manoeuvring for a
benefice attached to a mosque could as easily count the grains of sand
in the sea, and the slaves belonging to our monarch.

An infinite number of Masters of Languages, Arts, and Science
teach what they themselves do not know; this is quite a notable

talent, for to teach what one knows requires but little wit, whereas an infinite quantity is needed to teach what one does not know.

The only way to die here is suddenly; death cannot exercise its power in any other circumstances, for where ever you look you find people with infallible remedies for every imaginable disease.

All the shops are hung with invisible nets in which all shoppers are caught: even so you can sometimes make your escape cheaply, for a young saleswoman will cajole a man for an hour at a time, to get him to buy a packet of toothpicks.

There is not a single person who, on leaving Paris, is not more prudent than he was on his arrival; by dint of sharing one's wealth with others, one learns to conserve it; that is the sole advantage enjoyed by foreigners in this enchanting city.

Paris, the 10th of the Moon of Saphar 1714

LETTER 57

*Rica to Usbek, at ****

The other day I visited a house* where I met a very varied circle of people: I found the conversation dominated by two elderly women, who had laboured in vain the whole morning to make themselves look younger. 'One has to admit', one of them was saying, 'that the men of today are quite different from those we used to see in our youth; *they* were polite, charming, and obliging: whereas today they seem to me to be insufferably churlish.' 'It's all changed,' replied a man who appeared stricken with gout, 'things are not what they used to be forty years ago; everybody was in good health then, people could walk, their spirits were high, all they wanted was laughter and dancing; nowadays everybody is unbearably gloomy.' A moment later the conversation turned to politics; 'Upon my word,' said an old gentleman, 'the state is no longer being governed; find me a minister today like Monsieur Colbert; I knew Monsieur Colbert* well, he was one of my friends; he always saw to it that I was paid my pension before anybody else; how splendidly run the country's finances were! Everyone was well off, but today I'm ruined.' 'Monsieur,' an ecclesiastic then remarked, 'you're speaking of the most miraculous period in the reign of our invincible monarch; is there anything as great as what he did then for the destruction of heresy?' 'And what about the abolition of duels, does that count for nothing?' another man, who so far had said nothing, remarked contentedly. 'A prudent comment,' someone whispered in my ear; 'this man is delighted by the edict, and observes it so scrupulously, that six months ago he was well and truly beaten for not violating it.'

It seems to me, Usbek, that we never judge anything without secretly considering it in relation to our own self. I am not surprised that black men depict the devil as brilliantly white, and their own gods as coal-black, that the Venus of certain peoples has breasts that hang down to her thighs, and, in short, that all idolaters have depicted their gods with human faces, and have endowed them with their own propensities. It has been quite correctly observed that if triangles were to make themselves a god, they would give him three sides.

My dear Usbek, when I see men that creep about over an atom, the earth, which is simply a dot in the universe, propose themselves as models of Providence, I do not know how to reconcile such extravagance with such insignificance.

Paris, the 14th of the Moon of Saphar 1714

LETTER 58

Usbek to Ibben, in Smyrna

You ask me whether there are Jews in France?* You should know that wherever there is money, there are Jews. You ask me what they do here? Exactly what they do in Persia: nothing resembles an Oriental Jew more than a European Jew.

Among Christians, just as happens among us, they display for their religion an invincible, obstinate loyalty which borders on fanaticism.

The Jewish religion is an ancient tree, from which have sprung two branches that cover the whole earth: Muhammadanism and Christianity; or rather, it is a mother who bore two daughters who have wounded her in a thousand places: for in matters of religion, those who are closest are the bitterest enemies. But whatever cruel treatment the Jewish religion may have received from its progeny, it does not cease to take pride in having brought them into the world;

it uses them both to embrace the whole world, while at the same time embracing all the ages by virtue of its venerable life-span.

The Jews, consequently, see themselves as the source of all holiness, and the origin of all religions: they regard us, by contrast, as heretics who have changed the Law, or rather, as rebellious Jews.

Had the change occurred imperceptibly, they believe that they would easily have been seduced; but as it happened suddenly, in a violent way, as they can pinpoint the day and the hour of the birth of each religion, they are shocked to find that we claim the ages as ours, and remain faithful to a religion as ancient as the earth itself.

Jews in Europe have never before experienced such peace as they now enjoy. Christians are beginning to abandon that spirit of intolerance which formerly inspired them; the Spanish regret having banished the Jews, and the French regret having persecuted Christians whose beliefs differed slightly from those of their monarch. They have realized that zeal for the advancement of religion is different from the love one should bear it, and that in order to love it, and observe its precepts, there is no need to hate and persecute those who do not do so.

We must hope that our Muslims can think as sensibly on this subject as Christians do, and that peace may be concluded, finally and for ever, between Ali and Abu Bakr,* leaving to God the problem of deciding between the merits of these holy prophets; I would wish to see them honoured by acts of veneration and respect, rather than by vain preferences, and that people should seek to deserve their favour regardless of the place God has chosen for them, whether it be on his right hand, or beneath the footstool to his throne.

Paris, the 18th of the Moon of Saphar 1714

LETTER 59

Usbek to Rhedi, in Venice

The other day I visited a celebrated church called Notre Dame; while I was admiring that glorious building, I chanced to speak to an ecclesiastic who, like me, had been drawn there by curiosity. The conversation touched on the tranquillity of his profession. 'Most people', he told me, 'envy us the peace of our calling, and they are right; it does nevertheless have its drawbacks; we are not so isolated from the world as to preclude our being sent for in a thousand different circumstances: there, we have a very difficult role to fill.

'Society people are astounding: they cannot bear our approval, or our censure; if we try to correct them, they think us ridiculous, and if we praise them, they see us as unworthy of our calling. There's nothing as mortifying as feeling that you have shocked even the ungodly. Consequently we are forced to behave in an ambiguous way, and to fool the freethinkers; not by taking a definitive stand, but through the uncertainty they feel about our reaction to their discourse; for that you need to be very clever, because such a state of neutrality is difficult to maintain; men of the world, who will try anything, and permit themselves all their sallies, and, depending on the reception, pursue or abandon them, succeed much better.

'And that's not all; this happy, peaceful existence which is so highly vaunted, we cannot preserve it in society. As soon as we appear at a gathering, we are required to argue: we are asked, for example, to prove the utility of prayer to a man who does not believe in God; the necessity of fasting, to someone else who has, all his life, denied the immortality of the soul; such enterprises are difficult, and the mockers are not on our side. In addition, a certain desire to persuade others to share our beliefs torments us constantly and is, so to speak, integral to our profession. That is as ridiculous as if Europeans were to labour, on behalf of mankind, to whiten the faces of Africans. We disturb the state, and we torture ourselves, to force acceptance of points of religious doctrine which are not fundamental; we are like that conqueror of China* who spurred his subjects to general rebellion by obliging them to gnaw their hair or their nails.

'Our very zeal in ensuring that those for whom we are responsible fulfil the obligations of our holy religion is often dangerous; it cannot be accompanied by too much discretion. An emperor called Theodosius* put to the sword all the inhabitants of a town, even the women and young children, and then presented himself at the entrance to a church; a bishop, Ambrose by name, ordered the doors to be shut in his face, as if before a murderer and sacrilegious man; in this, he committed a heroic deed. The emperor, having completed the penance that such a crime demanded, and being then admitted into the church, went and took his place among the priests; the same bishop made him move away, and in this he acted like a fanatic and a madman: so true is it that we must beware of our zeal. What did it matter to religion, or to the state, whether the emperor did, or did not, stand among the priests?'

Paris, the 1st of the Moon of Rebiab 1 1714

LETTER 60
Zelis to Usbek, in Paris

Your daughter has reached her seventh birthday, so I thought it time to have her transferred to the inner apartments of the seraglio, and not wait until she was ten before entrusting her to the black eunuchs. One cannot too soon deprive a young person of the freedom of childhood, and give her a holy education within the sacred walls where modesty dwells.

I cannot share the opinion of those mothers who only confine their daughters when they are on the point of giving them a husband, who condemn them rather than consecrate them to the seraglio, and who force them into accepting a way of life that they should have shown them as an inspiration. Must one expect everything from the power of reason, and nothing from the ease of habit?

It is useless to talk to us about the subordinate role nature has given us; it's not sufficient to make us feel it, we must be made to practise it, so that it will sustain us at that critical stage when the passions begin to emerge and encourage us to be independent.

If we were bound to you only by duty, we could sometimes forget it; if we were drawn to you only by preference, a stronger preference could perhaps weaken it. But when the Law gives us to a man, it takes us from all others, placing us as far from them as if we were 100,000 leagues away.

Nature, ever industrious on behalf of men, did not stop at inspiring desires in them, but determined that we women should also have desires, and be the living instruments of men's felicity; nature gave us the fire of passion so that they could live in peace; if they should lose their insensibility, she has destined us to ensure they can regain it, without our ever being able to share in that state of bliss which we enable them to enjoy.

Nevertheless, Usbek, do not imagine that your situation is happier than mine; here in the seraglio I have tasted a thousand pleasures unknown to you; my imagination has worked unceasingly to make me appreciate their value; I have lived, whereas you have barely existed.

In this very prison where you keep me confined, I am freer than you: you cannot redouble your measures to guard me, without my taking pleasure in your misgivings; your suspicions, your jealousy, and your unhappiness are all signs of your dependence.

Do not stop, my dear Usbek, having me guarded night and day; do not even rely on ordinary precautions: increase my happiness by ensuring your own, and know that I fear nothing but your indifference.

The seraglio in Ispahan, the 2nd of the Moon of Rebiab 1 1714

LETTER 61

*Rica to Usbek, in ****

I believe that you mean to spend your entire life in the country; at first I was only going to lose you for two or three days, and now it's two weeks since I've seen you; of course I know you're staying in a charming house, that you've found company to your taste and can discuss things to your heart's content; that's enough to make you forget the entire universe.

As for me, I'm leading much the same kind of life that you saw me leading before you left; I go about in society, and attempt to understand it; my mind is gradually shedding what little it still retained of the Oriental, and adapting effortlessly to European ways. I am no longer so astonished to find, in a house, five or six women together with five or six men, and I begin to think that this is not a bad idea.

I can say this: I've only come to know women since I've been here; in one month I've learnt more than I would have learnt in thirty years, in a seraglio.

In Persia, all characters are identical because they are forced; we never see people as they are, but as they are constrained to be; in that enslavement of the heart and mind you hear nothing but the voice of fear, which speaks only one language, and not the voice of nature, which expresses itself in such different ways and assumes such different forms.

Dissimulation, among us so widespread and so essential an art, is here unknown; all is said, all is seen, all is heard; the heart, like the face, reveals itself; in customs, in virtue, and even in vice, you are always conscious of something artless.

In order to please women, a particular talent (which differs from that which pleases them even more) is required; this consists in a kind of banter, a playfulness of mind, which amuses them, in that it seems at every instant to promise something that can only be fulfilled, alas, at too infrequent intervals.

This banter, which is perfectly suited to informal morning visits, seems to have become part of the general character of the nation; there is banter at the council, among military leaders, in conversation with an ambassador; the professions only appear ridiculous when they are pursued with gravity; a physician would no longer be ridiculous if his costume were less lugubrious, and he indulged in banter while killing off his patients.

Paris, the 10th of the Moon of Rebiab 1 1714

LETTER 62

The head black eunuch to Usbek, in Paris

I find myself in difficulties which I know not how to describe to you, Magnificent Lord: the seraglio is in an appalling state of chaos and confusion; war rages between your wives; your eunuchs are divided; one hears nothing but recriminations, complaints, and reproaches; my remonstrances are scorned, nothing seems too brazen in this hour of licence, and my position in the seraglio is now meaningless.

There is not a single one of your wives who does not believe herself superior to the rest by her birth, her beauty, her wealth, her wit, and by the love you bear her; not a single one who does not believe herself entitled to preferential treatment by virtue of some of these claims; these days, I constantly lose control of that boundless patience by which I nevertheless have had the misfortune to anger them all; my prudence, my very kindness—so rare and foreign a quality in this post of mine—have been to no avail.

Do you wish me to reveal to you, Magnificent Lord, the cause of all this disorder? It lies entirely in your heart, and in the warm regard that you feel for your wives. If you did not stay my hand, if instead of rebuking you allowed me to punish, if, without letting yourself be moved by their moans and tears, you sent them to weep in my presence, I, who am never softened, would soon bend them to the yoke they must bear, and wear down their imperious, independent spirit.

Abducted at the age of fifteen from my homeland in the heart of Africa, I was first sold to a master who had more than twenty wives or concubines. Because of my serious, taciturn manner, my master judged me suitable for the seraglio, and ordered that I should be rendered fit for it; I underwent an operation that at first I found hard to bear, but which I eventually realized was to my advantage, because it gave me the ear, and the trust, of my masters. I entered the seraglio, which for me was a new world: the chief eunuch, the sternest man I have ever known, ruled it as absolute master. There, divisions or quarrels were unknown; complete silence reigned throughout it; all the women retired to bed, and got up, at the same hour year in, year out; they went in turn to the bath, and came out at the smallest signal we made to them; the rest of the time, they were almost always shut into their rooms. There was a rule which stipulated that they must be always scrupulously clean, and an extraordinary degree of care was taken to ensure that this rule was observed; the least refusal to obey was punished unmercifully. 'I am', the head eunuch would say, 'a slave, but I am slave of a man who is your master and mine; I use the power over you which he has given me; it is he who chastises you, not I; I am simply his instrument.' Those women never entered into my master's bedroom unless they were summoned; they would welcome this favour with joy, and did not complain if they were deprived of it; I was the lowest of the black slaves in that peaceful seraglio, yet I was a thousand times more respected there than I am here in yours, where I rule over everyone.

As soon as that chief eunuch understood my true gifts, he watched me attentively, and spoke to my master about me, as a man capable of working in accordance with his views, and of succeeding him in the post he filled; my extreme youth did not alarm him; he thought my attentiveness would make up for my lack of experience. What can I say? I made such progress in gaining his confidence, that he no longer felt any hesitation in handing over the keys of those redoubtable portals which he had guarded for so long. It was under that great mentor that I learnt the difficult art of command, and that I assimilated the maxims of an inflexible form of government; beneath his guidance I studied the hearts of women; he taught me to exploit their weaknesses and not be dismayed by their arrogance. Often he would take pleasure in letting me put them to the test, and force them to obey the most extreme demands; he would then, by imperceptible degrees, make them feel better, and would make me seem to bend a little myself. But you should have seen him in those moments when the women were close to despair, alternating between prayers and reproaches; he watched them weep without a flicker of emotion. 'Now that', he would say in a pleased tone, 'is how women should be controlled; the fact that they are many doesn't trouble me, I'd deal exactly the same way with all the wives of our great monarch. How can a man hope to capture a woman's heart, if his faithful eunuchs haven't begun by subduing her spirit?'

Not only was he firm, he was perceptive; he could read their minds and see through their dissimulation; their studied gestures and deceptive looks concealed nothing from him; he knew all their most surreptitious actions and their most secret words; he would use one woman to learn about another, and take pleasure in recompensing the most trifling confidence. As they never approached their husband except when summoned to him, the eunuch would send for whomever he chose, and induce his master to favour the one he had selected; this distinction would be her reward for revealing some secret; he had persuaded his master that it was a good method to leave this choice to him, in order to give him greater authority. That was the way matters were organized, Magnificent Lord, in a seraglio which was, I believe, the best run in all of Persia.

Give me a free hand; allow me to make myself obeyed; a week will see order replace disorder; that is what your honour demands, and your safety requires.

The seraglio at Ispahan, the 9th of the Moon of Rebiab 1 1714

LETTER 63

Usbek to his wives, in the seraglio at Ispahan

I have learnt that disorder reigns in the seraglio, and that it is full of quarrels and domestic discord. When I departed, did I not urge you to live peacefully, on good terms with one another? When you promised that you would do so, did you mean to deceive me?

You would be the ones deceived, were I to take the advice of the chief eunuch, and use my authority to force you to live as my injunctions required of you.

I cannot resort to those violent methods until I have tried all others; so do, for your own sakes, what you would not do for mine.

The head eunuch is entirely justified in his complaints; he says you show him no respect. How can you reconcile such conduct with the modesty of your condition? During my absence, is it not to him that your virtue is entrusted? It is a sacred treasure which he holds in trust; but this contempt you show him is a sign that you find irksome those whose duty it is to keep you true to the laws of honour.

Therefore, I beg you, change your behaviour, and so conduct yourselves that I may once more reject the suggestions I have received, which would jeopardize your freedom and your comfort.

For I would like to make you forget that I am your master, so that I need remember only that I am your husband.

Paris, the 5th of the Moon of Chahban 1714

LETTER 64

*Rica to ****

People here are very keen on the sciences, but I am not sure whether they are truly learned. The man who, as a philosopher, doubts everything, dare not, as a theologian, deny anything: this contradictory individual is invariably pleased with himself, provided everyone agrees on the *qualities* of the matter under discussion.

Most Frenchmen are desperately eager to be thought witty and, of those who seek to be witty, most are desperately eager to write a book.

No plan, however, could be less well conceived; nature in her wisdom seems to have arranged for man's follies to be short-lived, and books render them immortal. A fool ought to be satisfied with having bored all his own contemporaries, but he also seeks to torment those as yet unborn; he wants his stupidity to triumph over oblivion, which he might, like the tomb, have enjoyed; but no, he wants posterity to be notified that he has lived, and he wants her to know, for all eternity, that he was an idiot.

Of all authors, I despise none more than the compilers, who go off in all directions looking for bits and pieces of other writers' works, which they then stick into their own, like pieces of turf into a lawn; they're in no way superior to those printer's typesetters, who arrange letters which, combined together, make a book, to which they contributed only the manual labour. I would like the original texts to be respected; I feel it's a kind of profanation, to extract the pieces which make them up from the sanctuary where they belong, and expose them to a contempt they do not deserve.

When a man has nothing new to say, why does he not keep silent? Why use something twice over? Ah, but I intend to order everything differently. You're a clever man; that is, you come into my library, and you transfer the books that are higher up to a place lower down, and you move the books that are low down higher up; you've created a masterpiece.

I'm writing to you about this, ***, because I'm outraged by a book I've just put aside, which is so fat that it seemed to contain all the knowledge of the universe; but it wore me out without teaching me a thing. Farewell.

Paris, the 8th of the Moon of Chahban 1714

LETTER 65

Ibben to Usbek, in Paris

Three vessels have arrived here without bringing me any word of you. Are you ill, or do you enjoy worrying me?

If you feel no affection for me while in a country where you have no ties, what will happen when you are settled back in Persia, in the bosom of your family? But perhaps I'm wrong; you are amiable enough to make friends everywhere: the heart is a citizen of every country; how could someone with a pure heart prevent himself from making friends? I must admit that although I respect old friendships, I'm not reluctant to make new ones wherever I go.

No matter which country I've visited, I've lived in it as if I were going to spend my entire life there; I've been drawn just as eagerly to virtuous people; I've felt just as compassionate, or rather tender, to the unfortunate; I've felt the same esteem for anyone not blinded by prosperity. Such is my character, Usbek: wherever I encounter men, I shall choose friends.

There is a Zoroastrian* here who, after you, I hold dearest in my heart: he is probity personified; special circumstances have obliged him to retire to this town, where he lives peacefully on the proceeds of an honest trade, with a wife he loves. His entire life is distinguished by acts of generosity; and although he seeks obscurity, there is more heroism in his heart than in the heart of the greatest monarchs.

I have spoken to him of you time and time again; I show him all your letters, and it's clear to me that this gives him pleasure; so you already have a friend, although you do not know him.

You will find his principal adventures described here: however averse he was to writing them, he could not refuse it of my friendship, and I now entrust them to yours.

THE STORY OF APHERIDON AND ASTARTE

'I was born among the Zoroastrians, a religion which may well be the most ancient in the world. I had the misfortune to fall in love before I had attained the age of reason. When I was scarcely six years old, I found I could bear to live only with my sister; my eyes would never leave her; if she absented herself for a moment, on her return she would find me in tears: every passing day increased my love faster than it increased my age. My father, amazed at such a powerful bond of feeling, would happily have married us, according to the ancient custom of the Zoroastrians, introduced by King Cambyses;* but fear of the Muslims, beneath whose yoke we live, prevents our people from contemplating these holy alliances which our religion does not merely permit, but prescribes, and which are such naive reflections of the union already established by nature.

'My father, therefore, realizing that it would have been dangerous to gratify the wish I and he both cherished, resolved to stifle a passion which he believed to be at its birth; but it had already reached full maturity; he thought up a reason to travel, and took me with him, leaving my sister in the care of one of his relatives, for my mother had died two years earlier. I shall say nothing of the despair this separation occasioned; my sister was bathed in tears as I kissed her, but I did not weep, for pain had made me numb. We reached Tiflis, where my father, having entrusted my upbringing to one of our relatives, left me and returned home

'Some time later I heard that, through the influence of a friend, he had arranged for my sister to enter the harem of the king, where she was in the service of a sultana. If I had been told of her death it could not have been a greater shock; her entrance into the harem had made her a Muslim, and, according to the prejudices of that religion, she could not now look upon me with anything other than horror. Meanwhile, unable to stay any longer in Tiflis, weary of myself and of life, I returned to Ispahan. My first words to my father were bitter: I reproached him for having placed his daughter in a position which required a person to change their religion. "You have brought down upon your family", I told him, "the anger of God, and of the sun which gives you light; you have done worse than if you had sullied the elements, for you have sullied the soul of your daughter, which is no less pure; I shall die of love and anguish because of this, but may my death be the only pain that God inflicts upon you!" With these words I left and, for the next two years, I spent my time gazing at the walls of the harem and contemplating the building where my sister dwelt; repeatedly running the risk, every day, of having my throat cut by the eunuchs who guarded that fearsome place.

'Eventually my father died, and the sultana whom my sister attended, seeing her beauty increase with every passing day, grew jealous of her, and married her to a eunuch who loved her passionately. By this means my sister left the seraglio and, with her eunuch, took a house in Ispahan.

'It was more than three months before I managed to speak to her, for the eunuch—of all men the most jealous—kept finding different excuses to put me off. Finally I was admitted to his harem, and he arranged that I speak to her through a screen; even the eyes of a lynx would not have been capable of seeing her, so enveloped was she in garments and veils; I could recognize her only by the sound of her voice. How deeply was I moved, at finding myself so near and yet so distant from her! I controlled myself, for I was being closely watched. As for her, I thought she shed some tears. Her husband tried to offer some lame excuse, but I treated him as the most despicable of slaves. He was very nonplussed when he saw that I was addressing my sister in a language he did not know, ancient Persian, which is our sacred language. "Can it be, sister," I asked her, "that you have abandoned the religion of your ancestors? I know that when you entered the harem you were obliged to profess yourself a Muslim; but tell me, did you consent with your heart as well as with your lips, to relinquish a religion which permits me to love you? And for whom are you relinquishing this religion which should be so dear to us? For a wretched man who still carries the ignominy of the chains he wore, and who, were he really a man, would be the lowest of them all?" "Brother," she replied, "this man of whom you speak is my husband; I must honour him, however unworthy he may seem to be to you, and I too would be the basest of women if..." "Ah! My sister, you're a Zoroastrian; he is not your husband nor could he be; if you are as faithful as were your forebears, you ought not to consider him as anything but a monster." "Alas," she said, "how indistinct is my memory of that religion! I had barely learnt its precepts when I had to forget them. You can see that I'm no longer familiar with this language I'm speaking to you, and that I'm finding it extremely hard to express myself; but you may be sure that the remembrance of our childhood still delights me; that since that time I've known no true joy; that not a day has passed without my thinking of you, and that you played a greater part in my marriage than you may think; the only reason I was persuaded to agree to it was the hope that I might see you again; but this day, which has cost me so much, will cost me still more dearly! I can see that you're distraught; my husband is trembling with fury and jealousy; I shall not see you again, and I'm probably speaking to you for the very last time in my life; if that is so, brother, then my life will soon be over." Overcome by emotion as she said this, she walked away, unable to pursue the conversation, and left me the most despairing man in the world.

'Three or four days later I asked to see my sister; the brutish eunuch would have been delighted to prevent me from doing so, but, besides the fact that husbands like him do not have the authority over their wives that other husbands enjoy, he loved my sister so desperately that he could not refuse her anything. I saw her again in the same place, and with the same garments and veils, attended by two slaves; because of this, I used our special language. "Sister," I said, "why is it that I can't see you except in these dreadful surroundings? These walls that imprison you, these bolts and bars, these wretched guards who watch you, fill me with rage; how have you managed to lose the sweet liberty that your ancestors enjoyed? Your mother, who was so chaste, gave her husband no guarantee of her virtue other than her virtue itself; they both lived happily in mutual trust, and the simplicity of their way of life was for them a treasure infinitely more precious than the counterfeit glitter which you seem to enjoy in this luxurious house. In losing your religion, you have lost your liberty, your happiness, and that precious equality which is the honour of your sex. But what is even worse is that you are not even a wife, because you cannot be one, but the slave of a slave who has lost his humanity." "Oh please, brother, respect my husband," she replied; "respect the religion which I have embraced, and according to which I cannot listen to you, or speak to you, without crime." "What, sister!" I exclaimed, quite beside myself, "so you believe that religion is true!" "Ah!" she sighed, "how fortunate for me were it not so! I am sacrificing too much for it, not to believe in it, and if my doubts…" With these words she fell silent. "Yes, sister, your doubts, whatever they may be, are well founded. What do you expect of a religion which makes you unhappy in this world, and leaves you with no hope for the other? Remember that our religion is the oldest in the world; that it has always prospered in Persia; that it has no other origin than this empire, whose beginnings are lost in time; that it is only chance which introduced Muhammadanism to Persia, and that the sect was established here, not through persuasion, but by conquest; if our rightful princes had not been weak you would still see the religion of those ancient Magi flourishing here. Take yourself far, far back to much earlier centuries; everything will bear witness to the presence of Magism, and nothing to that of the Muslim religion which, thousands of years later, had not even reached its childhood." "But," she replied, "even if my religion is more modern than yours, it is at least more pure, for it worships God alone, whereas you also worship the sun, the stars, fire, and even the elements." "I can see, sister, that by living among Muslims you've learnt to slander our holy religion. We do not worship the stars or the elements, and our forefathers never worshipped them; never did they build temples in their honour, nor did they offer up sacrifices to them; rather, they venerated them as holy, but lesser, works and testimony of the Divine. Please, sister, in the name of God who illuminates our path, take this sacred book that I have brought you; it is the book of our legislator Zoroaster;* read it with an open mind and accept into your heart the light which will instruct you as you read it; remember your forefathers, who for so long honoured the sun in the holy city of Balq,* and, finally, remember me, whose only hope of peace, fortune, and life depends on your conversion." In this exalted state, I left her by herself, to decide the most important question of my whole life.

'Two days later I returned there; I did not speak to her, but awaited in silence the verdict that would determine whether I lived or died. "You are loved, brother," she told me, "and by a Zoroastrian; I have long struggled but, thank the Gods! How many difficulties love overcomes! How relieved I feel! I am no longer afraid that I love you too well, I need no longer restrain my love; to love you to excess is now right and proper. Oh, how well this accords with the feelings in my heart! But you, who have been capable of breaking the chains that bound my spirit, when will you break those which bind my hands? From this moment I give myself to you; show me, by your speed in accepting me, how much you treasure this gift. Brother, the first time that I am able to kiss you, I believe I shall die in your arms." I shall never be able adequately to express the joy I felt at these sweet words; I thought myself, and indeed actually found myself, in an instant, the happiest of men; I saw as near fulfilment every desire that I had formed in twenty-five years of life, and all the troubles vanish that had made that life such a burden; but when I had become a little accustomed to these delightful thoughts, I realized that my happiness was not so close at hand as I had first imagined, although I had overcome the greatest of all the obstacles. I had to outwit the vigilance of her guards; I dared not share with anyone the secret of my life; we—she and I—would have to do everything; if I missed my opportunity and was caught, I risked being impaled, but I could imagine no torture more cruel than missing my opportunity. We agreed that she would send me a note asking for a clock that her father had left her, and that I would put inside it a file to cut through the bars of her window which gave onto the street, as well as a knotted cord for climbing down to it. We agreed also that I would not visit her again, but would wait every night under her window for her to be able to put her plan into execution.

I passed fifteen entire nights without seeing a soul, because no favourable opportunity presented itself. Finally, on the sixteenth night, I heard the sound of a saw at work; from time to time the sound would stop, and I spent those intervals in an indescribable state of terror. Finally, after waiting while she worked for an hour, I saw her tying on the rope; she let herself go and slid down into my arms; I thought no more of the danger, and for a long time remained rooted to the spot; then I led her out of the city where I had a horse standing ready; I seated her on it behind me, and rode as fast as I could away from a place which could be so fatal to us. We arrived before dawn at the home of a Zoroastrian who had chosen as his retreat an unfrequented spot, where he lived frugally on what he himself could grow; but we did not think it wise to remain with him; we followed his advice and took refuge in a dense forest, where we hid in the hollow trunk of an old oak until the excitement over our escape had died down. The two of us lived completely alone in this seclusion, constantly telling one another that our love would be eternal, and awaiting the opportunity when some Zoroastrian priest could conduct the marriage ceremony prescribed by our holy books. "Sister," I would tell her, "our union is holy; nature had already united us, and our holy Law shall unite us yet more closely." Finally, we found a priest to calm our amorous impatience, and, at the home of the peasant, he performed all the marriage rites; he blessed us, and wished us a thousand times the strength of Gushtasp and the holiness of Hohoraspe. Shortly thereafter we left Persia, where we were not safe, and travelled to Georgia. For a year we lived there, each day more delighted with one another, but as my money was running out and I feared poverty, not on my own account, but for my sister, I left her in order to go and seek help from our family. No parting could have been more loving, but my journey was not only of no use to me, it was fatal; for, in addition to my discovering that all our property had been confiscated, I found that my relatives were unable to offer me any substantive help. I had brought only sufficient money for my return home, where, to my indescribable despair, I no longer found my sister. A few days before my return, a band of Tartars* had raided the town where she was living; and, as they thought her beautiful, they took her, and sold her to some Jews who were going into Turkey, leaving behind a little girl she had given birth to a few months earlier. I followed the Jews, and caught up with them about three leagues from there; my tears and prayers were in vain: they demanded thirty tomans for her and adamantly refused to lower the price by even one toman. After begging everyone to help me, and imploring the protection of the Turkish and the Christian priests, I turned to an Armenian merchant, to whom I sold my daughter and myself for thirty-five tomans; I then went to the Jews, gave them thirty tomans, and took the remaining five to my sister, whom I had not yet seen.

'"You are free, sister," I told her, "here are five tomans; I'm sorry they didn't pay a better price for me." "What, you have sold yourself?" "Yes," I replied. "Oh, what have you done, you wretched man! Wasn't I already sufficiently unfortunate without your adding to my troubles? Your freedom consoled me; your servitude will bring me to my grave. Ah, brother, how cruel is your love! And I don't see my daughter, where is she?" "I have sold her as well," I told her. We both burst into tears, and were quite unable to say anything more to one another. Eventually I went to find my master, and my sister followed close behind me. She threw herself down on her knees. "I implore you," she said, "to make me a slave, as others implore you for their liberty; take me, you can sell me for a better price than my husband." The duel that ensued drew tears from the eyes of my master. "Unhappy man," she said, "did you suppose that I could accept my freedom at the price of yours? My Lord, you see before you two wretches who will die if we are separated; I give myself to you; pay me, and perhaps one day that money and my work will buy of you what I dare not ask: it is in your own interest not to separate us; please believe that I hold his life in my hands." The Armenian was a kind man, whose heart was touched by our misfortunes. "If you both serve me with loyalty and zeal, I promise that in a year I will give you your liberty; I can see that neither of you deserves the adversities of your present state; when you are free, if you are as happy as you deserve, and fortune smiles upon you, I am certain that you will compensate me for the loss I shall suffer." We both embraced his knees, and followed him on his travels. We comforted one another while serving as his slaves, and I was delighted whenever I was able to relieve my sister of duties which fell to her lot.

'When the year came to an end, our master kept his word and gave us our freedom. We returned to Tiflis, where I found a former friend of my father's who was a successful physician in that city; he lent me money, which I used to do some trading. Then, having gone to Smyrna on business, I settled there; I've been living there for six years, enjoying the company of the most pleasant, amiable friends imaginable; we are a most united family, and I wouldn't change my condition for that of all the kings in the world. I was lucky enough to find the Armenian merchant to whom I owe everything, and was able to help him in significant ways.'

Smyrna, the 27th of the Moon of Gemmadi 2 1714

LETTER 66

Rica to Usbek, at ***

The other day I dined at the home of a man of law, who had invited me on several occasions. After conversing about many things, I said to him: 'Monsieur, it seems to me that your calling is a most arduous one.' 'Not as arduous as you imagine,' he replied: 'the way we manage it, it's simply a pastime.' 'How can that be? Isn't your head always full of other people's affairs? Aren't you always busy with things that are not interesting?' 'You're quite right, those things are not interesting; for we hardly take any interest whatever in them, and because of that, the profession is not as arduous as you say.' When I saw that he was treating the matter in such an offhand manner, I went on: 'Monsieur, I've never seen your office.' 'I believe you, for I do not have one. When I accepted this appointment I needed money to pay for the necessary letters patent, so I sold my library, and the bookseller who took my books—of which there were an astonishing number—left me only my family record book; it's not that I miss them; we judges don't cram ourselves with useless knowledge; why should we bother with all those law books? Almost all the cases are problematical, and deviate from the general rule.' 'But might that not be, monsieur,' I asked him, 'because you decide that they deviate? After all, why would almost all the nations of the world have laws, if they never applied? And how can you apply them, if you don't know what they are?' 'If you were familiar with the Palace of Justice,' replied the magistrate, 'you wouldn't be saying these things; we have living books, which are the lawyers; they work for us and make it their business to instruct us.' 'And do they not also make it their business, sometimes, to deceive you?' I responded. 'So it wouldn't be a bad idea for you to protect yourself from their traps; they have weapons with which to attack your justice, and it would be a good idea for you to have weapons with which to defend it, rather than joining in the fray, inadequately protected, against fighting men who are armed to the teeth.'

Paris, the 13th of the Moon of Chahban 1714

LETTER 67

Usbek to Rhedi, in Venice

I am sure that you never supposed that I could become more of a metaphysician than I already was, but such is the case; you will be convinced of it when you've endured this flood of philosophy.

The most sensible philosophers who have reflected upon the nature of God, have said that he is a consummately perfect being; but they have overworked this idea to an extreme degree, enumerating all the different kinds of perfection that man is capable of possessing or imagining, and then conferring them upon the concept of divinity, without realizing that frequently these attributes are mutually exclusive, and cannot coexist in the same subject without destroying themselves.

The poets of the West relate how a painter,* wishing to paint the portrait of the goddess of beauty, gathered together the most beautiful women of Greece, and from each one copied her most attractive feature, making of these a whole which, he believed, resembled the loveliest of all goddesses. If a man had described this goddess as both fair and dark, with eyes which were both blue and black, and said that she was both gentle and proud, he would have been thought ridiculous.

Often, God lacks one attribute of perfection which might produce a grave imperfection: but he is never limited* except by himself; he is his own necessity; thus, although God is all-powerful, he cannot break his own promises nor deceive man. Often, indeed, the lack of power is not in him, but in related things; that is the reason why he cannot change their essences.

Consequently it is hardly astonishing that some of our learned men have dared to deny the infinite prescience of God, on the grounds that it is incompatible with his justice.

However bold this idea may be, metaphysics finds absolutely no difficulty with it. According to metaphysical principals, it is not possible for God to foresee things which are determined by free causation, because that which has not happened, is not, and therefore cannot be known; a non-existent thing which has no properties cannot be perceived; God cannot read an intention which has no existence, or see in the soul something which is not there; for until it is decided upon, the action that gives rise to it has no existence in the soul.

The soul is the agent of its own determination; but there are occasions when it is so indecisive that it cannot decide which choice to make. Often, indeed, it only chooses in order to make use of its freedom, so that God cannot see this decision in advance, either in the action of the soul, or in the way other objects act upon it.

How could God foresee things which depend on the outcome of free choices? He could only foresee them in two ways: by conjecture, which is inconsistent with his infinite prescience, or else by seeing them as necessary effects infallibly resulting from a cause which produced them; this last is even more contradictory, for the freedom of the soul is assumed, whereas in actual fact the soul would be no freer than is a billiard ball, which is only free to move when pushed by someone else.

Do not imagine, however, that I wish to set limits to God's knowledge. Just as he can make all his creatures act as he desires, he knows everything that he wishes to know; but, although he can see everything, he does not always make use of this faculty: usually he lets his creatures act or not act, so as to let them deserve or not deserve merit. It is then that he renounces his right to control and determine the actions of his creatures; but when he wishes to know something, he always knows it, because he has only to intend that something should happen as he proposes, and determine his creatures to act according to his will. This is how he can identify what *will* happen from among all the events that simply *might* happen, by directing, through his decrees, the future decisions of human souls, and depriving them of the power he gave them to act or not to act.

If one might use a comparison to clarify a matter which is above such comparisons: a monarch does not know what his ambassador will do in an important matter; if he wants to know, then all he need do is order him to behave in such and such a manner, and he can be certain that it will happen as he predicts.

The Qur'an and the Jews' holy books continually refute the dogma of absolute prescience: throughout, God appears to be ignorant of how souls will act, and it seems that this was the first truth which Moses taught mankind.

God puts Adam on earth, in paradise, on condition that he not eat a certain fruit: an absurd precept in a Being who knows all the future choices of souls; for could such a Being attach conditions to his Grace, without making it derisory? It's as if a man who had learnt of the fall of Baghdad had said to another: 'I'll give you a thousand crowns if Baghdad doesn't fall.' Wouldn't that be a very nasty joke?

Paris, the last day of the Moon of Chahban 1714

LETTER 68

Zelis to Usbek, in Paris

Soliman, of whom you are fond, is in great despair over an insult he has just received. For the last three months a young fool named Suphis had been asking for his daughter in marriage; he seemed to like the girl's face, from the account and description of her he was given by women who had seen her in her childhood; the dowry had been agreed upon and everything arranged without any trouble. Yesterday, after the first ceremonies, the girl left on horseback accompanied by her eunuch, covered up from head to foot as is our custom: but as soon as she reached her prospective husband's house he had the door slammed in her face, and swore that he would never receive her unless the dowry was increased. The relatives hurriedly gathered together from all sides to arrange the affair, and with considerable difficulty persuaded Soliman to make his son-in-law a small present. Eventually, the ceremonies were concluded, and the girl taken forcibly to the bed; but an hour later the idiot got up in a rage; he cut her face in several places, and returned her to her father, claiming she was not a virgin. No one could be more upset than Soliman by this insult: there are some people who claim the girl is innocent. Fathers are indeed very unfortunate to be exposed to such insults; if my daughter were treated like that, I think the pain of it would kill me. Farewell.

Fatmé's seraglio, the 9th of the Moon of Gemmadi I 1714

LETTER 69

Usbek to Zelis

I pity Soliman, all the more so because there is nothing to be done; his son-in-law has simply taken advantage of the freedom the law grants him. I consider this law a very harsh one, in that it exposes the honour of a family to the caprice of an irresponsible fool; in spite of what people still believe—that there are indisputable ways of determining the truth—that is an ancient error which has now been disproved here, and our physicians give overwhelming reasons why those proofs are unreliable. Even the Christians regard them as delusory, although they are clearly set forth in their sacred books, and their ancient legislator* uses them to determine the innocence, or the guilt, of all young girls.

It pleases me to hear of the care you bestow upon the upbringing of your own daughter: God grant that her husband find her as beautiful and as pure as Fatima; let her have ten eunuchs to guard her and may she be the honour and the ornament of the seraglio for which she is destined; may her head always be sheltered by golden canopies and her feet tread only upon magnificent carpets, and, to crown my wishes, may my eyes look upon her in all her glory!

Paris, the 5th of the Moon of Chalval 1714

LETTER 70

Rica to Usbek, at ***

A few days ago, at a social gathering, I encountered a man who was quite delighted with himself. In a quarter of an hour he

pronounced upon three ethical points, four historical problems, and
five questions of physics; I have never seen such a universal
pronouncer, his mind never hesitated over the smallest uncertainty.
The conversation abandoned the sciences and turned to the latest
news: he pronounced upon the latest news. Wanting to catch him
out I said to myself: I must be very sure of my ground, I'll take
refuge in my own country. I addressed him on the subject of Persia,
but barely had I spoken four words to him than he contradicted
me twice, basing his authority on Messrs Tavernier and Chardin.*
Good God, I thought to myself, whatever sort of man is this? He'll
soon know the streets of Ispahan better than I do myself! I didn't take
long to decide what to do: I kept silent, I let him talk, and he's still
pronouncing.

Paris, the 8th of the Moon of Zilcadé 1715

LETTER 71
Rica to ***

I've heard talk of a kind of tribunal called the French Academy;*
nothing in the world can be held in less respect, for they say that as
soon as it has decided a matter the people nullify its decrees, and
impose upon it laws which it is obliged to obey.

Some time ago, to consolidate its authority, the Academy
published a Code of its decrees;* this child of many fathers was
almost an old man when it was born, and although it was legitimate,
it was nearly stifled at birth by a bastard* who had already made his
appearance.

The sole duty of those who belong to the Academy is to babble
incessantly: the eulogy seems to sprout of its own accord from their
eternal jabbering, and as soon as they are initiated into the mysteries
of this form, the members are overtaken by a frenzy for eulogizing
which never abandons them.

This body is composed of forty heads stuffed full of figures of
speech, metaphors, and antitheses: as many mouths that do almost
nothing but exclaim, while the ears yearn constantly to be struck by
cadences and harmonies. As for the eyes, they're not of any importance, it appears that the Academy is designed for speaking, and not

for seeing. It is shaky on its feet, because time, its scourge, is every moment weakening it, and destroying all it has accomplished. It used to be said that the hands of this body were rapacious; I shall not comment, but leave those better informed than I to decide this matter.

Such aberrations do not exist in our land of Persia; our minds do not lean towards peculiar, bizarre institutions; we invariably seek nature in our simple customs and unaffected manners.

Paris, the 27th of the Moon of Zilhagé 1715

LETTER 72

Rica to Usbek, in ***

Some days past an acquaintance of mine said to me: 'I promised to introduce you into the best houses in Paris; I'm taking you now to visit a great noble, one of the most impressive presences in the kingdom.'

'What does that mean, monsieur? Is he more polite, more affable than the next man?' 'No, it's not that,' he replied. 'Ah! I understand; he constantly makes it clear how much he is superior to those who approach him; if that's the case, there's no point in my going, I accept my fate and willingly admit his superiority!'

We were obliged to go, however; I saw a little man with such a lordly air, who took a pinch of snuff so haughtily, blew his nose so mercilessly, spat with such icy self-possession, and stroked his dogs in a manner so offensive to people that I could not stop gazing upon him in wonder. Good God, I said to myself, if I appeared at the court of Persia with manners like his, I would appear a terrible fool! My dear Usbek, we would have had to have really unpleasant natures for us to insult, in those countless tiny ways, people who came to see us every day to demonstrate their friendship; they were quite aware that we were their superiors, and if they had not known it, every day our kindness would have proved that it was so. Not having to do anything to make ourselves respected, we did everything we could to be agreeable; we talked to the least important among them; amid all that grandeur, which invariably makes people insensitive, they found us to be responsive; they saw only that our hearts were greater than theirs, for we listened as equals to their needs. But when we were called upon to support his majesty the prince in public ceremonies; when we were called upon to ensure that our nation was respected by foreigners, and finally when, in moments of danger, we were called upon to inspire and lead our soldiers, we ascended a thousand times higher than we had ever descended; our reanimated pride energized our features, and people sometimes thought us men of quite impressive presence.

Paris, the 10th of the Moon of Saphar 1715

LETTER 73
Usbek to Rhedi, in Venice

I must admit to you that I have not observed, in Christians, the intense belief in their religion that is apparent in Muslims; for Christians there exists a great distance from profession to belief, from belief to conviction, from conviction to practice. Religion is less a subject of sanctification than a subject of disputation in which anybody may participate: the courtiers, the military, even the women raise their voices against the ecclesiastics, demanding that they prove to them what they have resolved not to believe. It is not the case that they have made up their minds on a rational basis, and that they have taken pains to examine the truth or falsity of this religion that they reject; no, they are rebels who have felt the yoke and cast it off before knowing it. Therefore they are no firmer in their incredulity than in their faith; they live in a state of perpetual flux, ceaselessly carried back and forth from one to the other. The other day one of them said to me: 'I believe in the immortality of the soul by semester; my opinions depend entirely on the constitution of my body; according to whether I have more or less animal spirits, whether my stomach is digesting well or badly, whether the air I breathe is pure or impure, whether the food I take as nourishment is light or heavy, I am a Spinozist, a Socinian, Catholic, ungodly, or devout. When the physician stands at my bedside, the confessor has me at a disadvantage. I'm good at stopping religion from troubling me when I'm well, but I allow it to console me when I'm sick; when I've nothing more to hope for on one side, religion presents itself and wins me over with its promises; I'm very ready to give in to it, and die with something to hope for.'

It is many years since the Christian monarchs freed all the slaves in their lands, because, they said, for Christians all men are equal. It's true that this religious act was extremely useful to them, because they thereby lessened the power of the feudal lords, from whose control they freed the peasants; later, in wars of conquest, they realized that it was advantageous to own slaves, and they permitted them to be bought and sold, forgetting that religious principle about which they felt so strongly. What can I say? Yesterday's truth is tomorrow's lie. Why don't we do as the Christians do? We are very foolish to refuse to settle in places where the climate is good, which are easy to conquer, because the water there is not pure enough for our ablutions according to the principles of the holy Qur'an.

I give thanks to almighty God, who has sent his great prophet Ali, for the fact that I profess a religion which is superior to any human interest, and which is as pure as the heavens, whence it came.

Paris, the 13th of the Moon of Saphar 1715

LETTER 74

Usbek to his friend Ibben, in Smyrna

In Europe the laws deal extremely harshly with those who kill themselves;* suicides are, as it were, put to death a second time: they are dragged ignominiously through the streets, declared infamous, and all their goods confiscated.

It seems to me, Ibben, that these laws are most unjust. When I am crushed by physical pain, by poverty, by scorn, why should anyone wish to prevent me from ending my suffering, and cruelly deprive me of a remedy which lies in my own hands?

Why should I be required to work for a society to which I no longer wish to belong? Why should I have to accept, against my will, a covenant which I had no part in making? Society is based on mutual advantage: but when it becomes a burden to me, why should I not renounce it? Life was accorded me as a favour; I can therefore give it back when it is no longer such; the cause ceases to be and consequently the effect ceases also.

Is it the prince's will that I be his subject when I do not receive the advantages of that condition? Can my fellow-citizens demand such an iniquitous distribution—their benefit and my despair? Does God, unlike all other benefactors, want to condemn me to receive blessings which oppress me?

I am bound to obey laws when I am living under those laws, but when I am no longer living under them, can they still bind me?

But, people will say, you are interfering with the order of Providence. God has united your soul with your body, and you are separating them; you are therefore opposing his purposes, you are resisting him.

What does that mean? Do I interfere with the order of Providence when I modify matter, and make square a sphere that the first laws of movement, that is to say the laws of creation and of conservation, had declared to be round? Obviously not; I am simply using a right I have been given, and in this sense I can interfere to my heart's content with the whole of nature, without anyone being able to claim that I am opposing the purposes of Providence.

When my soul is separated from my body, will there be any less order, any less organization, in the universe? Do you believe that this new arrangement will be less perfect, and less dependent on general laws? That the world will be somehow diminished, and the works of God less grand, or rather less vast?

Do you believe that when my body has become an ear of corn, a worm, or a sod of turf, it will have become any less worthy to be called a work of nature? And that my soul, freed from everything about it that was earthly, will have become less sublime?

All these ideas, my dear Ibben, spring from nothing but our own pride; we are not conscious of our insignificance; and despite everything, we want to count for something in the universe, be a part of it, be of importance in it. We imagine that the annihilation of a being as perfect as we are would degrade the whole of nature, and we cannot conceive that one man less or more in the world—what am I saying?—that all men taken together, a hundred million earths like ours, are nothing but a delicate, tiny atom that God sees only because of the immensity of his knowledge.

Paris, the 15th of the Moon of Saphar 1715

LETTER 75

Rica to Usbek, in ***

I am sending you a copy of a letter which arrived here from a Frenchman living in Spain: I believe you'll be delighted with it:

'I have been travelling for the last six months in Spain and Portugal, and living among people who, while they despise everyone else, pay no one but the French the compliment of loathing them.

'The striking characteristic of both nations is gravity, which reveals itself principally in two ways: by spectacles, and by moustaches.

'The spectacles prove conclusively that he who wears them is a man totally engrossed in learning, and so preoccupied by deep intellectual reading that his sight has been impaired; any nose that is adorned, or encumbered, by spectacles may be considered as the nose of an unquestionably learned man.

'As for the moustaches, they are respectable in themselves, independently of any consequences; however, they have been used to great advantage in the service of the prince, and for the honour of the nation; as was definitively proved by a famous Portuguese general in the Indies, who, finding himself short of funds, cut off one of his moustaches, and on this security demanded 20,000 gold coins from the inhabitants of Goa; this sum was immediately advanced, and, subsequently, he honourably retrieved his moustache.

'It is easy to imagine that people as grave and imperturbable as these may also be vain; and indeed such is the case. As a rule their vanity is grounded in two rather significant facts. Those who live in continental Spain and Portugal feel enormous pride if they are what are called old Christians; that is to say, that they are not descended from those who, over the course of the last two centuries, were persuaded by the Inquisition to embrace the Christian religion. Those who live in the Indies feel no less gratification in reflecting that they can claim the sublime virtue of being, as they put it, white-skinned. No sultana living in the seraglio of the great lord has ever taken such pride in her beauty, to equal the pride that the oldest and ugliest rogue in a Mexican town takes in his olive-white skin, as he sits in his doorway with folded arms. A man of such consequence, a creature of such perfection, would not work for all the gold in the world; he would never bring himself to compromise the honour and dignity of his skin with any base, mechanical labour.

'For you must understand that when a man enjoys a certain standing in Spain, for example, when he can claim, in addition to the qualities I have just described, to possess a large sword, or to have learnt from his father the art of making discordant sounds on an out-of-tune guitar, he no longer works; his honour demands the repose of his limbs. The man who remains seated for ten hours in the day is esteemed exactly twice as much as his neighbour who remains seated for merely five, for it is upon chairs that nobility is acquired.

'But although these obdurate enemies of toil seem to display a philosophical serenity, they are not serene in their hearts, for they are always in love; they are unrivalled in the art of dying of love beneath their mistress's window; any Spaniard who does not suffer from a chest cold would endanger his reputation as a ladies' man.

'First and foremost they are pious, and secondly, jealous. Never would they risk exposing their wife to the attentions of a badly wounded soldier, or of a decrepit magistrate, but they will confine her with a fervent novice who lowers his eyes, or a stalwart Franciscan, who raises his.

'They are more aware of women's weakness than are other men: they cannot allow anyone a glimpse of a woman's heel, and they fear the worst from the exposure of a toe; they know that the imagination always moves on, that nothing can distract it from its path; it reaches its destination, and sometimes finds itself expected.

'It is widely asserted that the hardships of love are cruel; for Spaniards they are even more so; in alleviating their pain the women simply replace it with a different kind of suffering, and the men are always left with a lasting and troublesome remembrance of an extinguished passion.

'They have their little courteous ways which in France would seem inappropriate; for example, a captain never flogs his soldier without asking his permission, and the Inquisition never condemns a Jew to be burnt at the stake without apologizing to him.

'Spaniards who are not burnt at the stake seem to be so fond of the Inquisition, that it would seem peevish to deprive them of it; I only wish that another Inquisition could be established, not against heretics, but against heresiarchs, who attribute the same efficacy to trivial monastic practices as they do to the seven sacraments, who worship everything they venerate, and are so pious that they are barely Christians.

'You can find wit and common sense among Spaniards, but do not seek these in their books; take a look at a Spaniard's library: one half novels, and the other half works of scholasticism; you'd say that the parts had been chosen and the whole thing put together by some secret enemy of human reason.

'The only one of their books* that is good, is the one that makes fun of all the others.

'They have made vast discoveries in the New World, and they don't yet know their own continent; they have rivers with ports that have not yet been discovered, and peoples living in their mountains about whom they know nothing.

'They say that the sun rises and sets in their kingdom, but one should add that in the course of its journey the sun encounters only devastated lands and deserted countryside.'

I would not be displeased, Usbek, to see a letter written to someone in Madrid by a Spaniard travelling in France; I believe he would avenge his nation very thoroughly: what a vast field for a dispassionate, thoughtful man! I imagine he'd begin the description of Paris like this:

'There's a house here where mad people are confined: at first you'd believe that it's the largest house in the city but no—the remedy is very small, considering the disease. No doubt the French, who enjoy such a deplorable reputation among their neighbours, have imprisoned some lunatics in a house, in order to persuade people that those remaining outside are not so afflicted.'

And there I leave my Spaniard. Farewell, my dear Usbek.

Paris, the 17th of the Moon of Saphar 1715

LETTER 76

Usbek to Rhedi, in Venice

The majority of legislators have been men of narrow views, whom chance has placed in positions of authority, and who have been guided by little other than their own prejudices and whims.

It seems that they failed to grasp the greatness or even the dignity of their work; they wasted their time creating puerile institutions, with which they did indeed conform to the wishes of the small-minded, but they discredited themselves among those of good sense.

They immersed themselves in useless details and seized upon particular cases, tendencies which indicate limited minds, that see things only one part at a time, and never grasp the significance of the whole.

Some affected to use a language other than the vernacular, an absurd notion for a lawmaker, for how can people obey laws if they do not know what they say?

Often, they needlessly abolished already established laws, that is, they plunged people into the confusion which inevitably follows change.

It is true that owing to a bizarre quality in the nature, rather than the mind, of man, sometimes it is necessary to change certain laws. But such cases are rare, and when they do occur, they should only be approached with trembling hands; so many procedures should be required, and such precautions taken, that the common people will naturally conclude that laws are most sacred, since so many formalities are needed to abrogate them.

Frequently, they made laws that were too subtle, and were based on the ideas of logicism rather than on ideas of natural equity. Later, these laws were found to be too harsh, and in a spirit of equity people believed they should not be observed, but this remedy was a fresh evil. Whatever the laws may be, they should always be obeyed and regarded as the public conscience, to which the conscience of individuals must always conform.

We must, however, admit that some legislators displayed a degree of care that demonstrates considerable wisdom; this is evident in the great authority they gave fathers over their children; nothing is more helpful to magistrates, nothing so effectively reduces the work of the courts; in a word, nothing spreads greater tranquillity in a state, where standards of behaviour always produce better citizens than does the law.

Of all authoritative powers, paternal authority is the one which is least abused; it is the most sacred of all magistratures; it is the only one which does not depend upon conventions, and which even preceded them.

It has been observed that in those countries where paternal hands wield greater powers of reward and punishment, family life is more orderly: the father is in the image of the Creator of the universe, who, although he may guide men by his love, always binds them by hope and fear as well.

I will not conclude this letter without remarking upon the oddity of the French mind. People say that they have retained from Roman law an infinite number of things that are useless or worse than useless, yet they did not keep paternal power, which the Romans established as the first legitimate authority.

Paris, the 18th of the Moon of Saphar 1715

LETTER 77

The head black eunuch to Usbek, in Paris

Yesterday some Armenians brought to the seraglio a young Circassian slave whom they wished to sell. I took her into the secret apartments, where I undressed her and examined her with the eyes of a judge; the more I examined her, the more charms I discovered in her. A virginal modesty seemed to incline her to conceal those charms from my sight; I saw how hard she found it to obey me; she blushed at seeing herself naked even in front of me who, exempt from those passions which alarm the bashful, remain unmoved by the power of her sex, and who, ministering to modesty even in its most immodest moments, turn upon it a purely chaste gaze, capable of inspiring nothing but innocent thoughts.

As soon as I had judged her to be worthy of you, I lowered my eyes; I covered her with a scarlet cloak and placed upon her finger a ring of gold; I prostrated myself at her feet and adored her as the queen of your heart; I paid the Armenians and concealed her from all eyes. Fortunate Usbek, you possess more beauties than are confined in all the palaces of the Orient. What pleasure for you to find, upon your return, all that is most exquisite in Persia, and to watch, in your seraglio, charms being reborn, while time and possession are working to destroy them!

Fatmé's seraglio, the 1st of the Moon of Rebiab I 1715

LETTER 78

Usbek to Rhedi, in Venice

Since coming to Europe, my dear Rhedi, I have seen a great many governments; it's not like in Asia, where the rules of politics are everywhere the same.

I have often asked myself which of all types of government* conforms the most closely to the dictates of reason. It seems to me that the most perfect government is that which fulfils its purpose at the lowest cost, and therefore, that the government which controls men in the manner most appropriate to their proclivities and desires is the most perfect.

If, under a tolerant government, the people are as obedient as they are under a harsh government, then the former is preferable, since it conforms better to reason, whereas harshness is alien to it.

You can be certain, Rhedi, that in any state the degree of severity of a punishment does not make people observe the law any better. In countries where punishments are moderate, these are feared exactly as they are in countries where penalties are tyrannical and horrifying.

Whether the government be tolerant or harsh, punishment is always meted out by degrees; a lesser or greater punishment is inflicted for a lesser or greater crime. The imagination adapts itself automatically to the customs of the country one inhabits; a week in prison or a small fine weigh as heavily on the mind of a European raised in a moderate society, as the loss of an arm intimidates an Oriental. People associate a certain level of fear with a certain level of punishment, and everyone feels it in his own way; despair at the idea of disgrace will oppress a Frenchman sentenced to a penalty that would not deprive a Turk of a quarter of an hour's sleep.

Furthermore I have not noticed that order, justice, and equity are better observed in Turkey, in Persia, or under the Mogul than in the republics of Holland and of Venice, or even in England; I do not see that less crimes are committed there, and that men, intimidated by the severity of the punishments, are more subservient to the law.

On the contrary, I observe a source of injustice and oppression in these same states.

I think that the prince himself, the very embodiment of the law, is less in control there than anywhere else.

I see that during periods of harshness, there are always rebellious stirrings where nobody is in control: and when once despotic power has been flouted, no one is left with sufficient authority to restore it.

I believe that despair, born of hopelessness, sanctions disorder and renders it greater.

I believe that in such states trivial uprisings do not ever occur, and that there is never any interval between grievance and rebellion.

I believe that events of great significance do not necessarily spring from great causes; on the contrary, the smallest incident may provoke a great revolution, often as unforeseen by those who are its agents as it is by those who are its victims.

When the Turkish emperor Osman was deposed,* not one of those who committed this act had planned it beforehand; they were only appealing, as supplicants, for justice regarding some grievance; a voice—never since identified—happened to arise from the crowd, calling the name of Mustapha, and suddenly, Mustapha was emperor.

Paris, the 2nd of the Moon of Rebiab 1 1715

LETTER 79

Nargum, Persian envoy in Moscow, to Usbek, in Paris

Among all the nations of the world, my dear Usbek, not one has surpassed the Tartars, neither in reputation, nor in the extent of their conquests. This nation is the true master of the universe; all others seem created to serve it; it is at once the founder and the destroyer of empires; in every age it has left behind it upon the earth evidence of its power; in every age it has been the scourge of other nations.

The Tartars have twice conquered China, and she is still bound to them in obedience.

They control the vast lands that form the empire of the Mogul.*

Masters of Persia, they sit on the throne of Cyrus and of Gushtasp. They have conquered Muscovy.* As Turks, they have made immense conquests in Europe, Asia, and Africa; they rule over three-quarters of the universe.

And, if we look at earlier times, it is from them that almost all the peoples who overpowered the Roman Empire are descended.

What are the conquests of Alexander, compared with those of Genghis Khan?

The only thing lacking to that victorious nation was historians to celebrate the memory of its marvellous achievements.

How many immortal exploits have vanished into oblivion! How many empires were founded by them, of whose origin we know nothing? That bellicose nation, concerned solely with its fame today, certain of conquering in every age, has given no thought to assuring its future reputation by recording its past conquests.

Moscow, the 4th of the Moon of Rebiab 1 1715

LETTER 80

Rica to Ibben, in Smyrna

Although the French are great talkers, there exists among them a taciturn kind of dervish called a Carthusian; it's said that these men cut off their tongues* when they enter the convent; it would be eminently desirable if all other dervishes would likewise cut off everything that their profession renders useless to them.

On the subject of taciturnity, there are some individuals, vastly more peculiar than the Carthusians, who possess a most extraordinary talent. I refer to those who are able to talk without saying anything, and who can drag out a conversation for two hours, without it being possible to determine anything about them or their thoughts, or to plagiarize them, or to retain one single word of what they have said.

Women adore men of that type, although not as much as they adore some others whom nature has blessed with the pleasing talent of smiling at the right moment, in other words, all the time; and who greet with joyful approbation every word uttered by the ladies. But they attain the pinnacle of wit when they detect witticisms in everything, and point to countless ingenious little subtleties in the most ordinary remarks.

There are others I know who have hit upon the happy idea of introducing inanimate objects into the conversation, and letting their embroidered coat, their blonde wig, their snuffbox, cane, and gloves speak for them. It's wise to begin to make oneself heard out in the street, with the noise of the carriage and the sharp rap of the door-knocker; this preface forewarns about the rest of the speech, and when the exordium is a fine one, it makes bearable all the idiocies that follow, but which, mercifully, come too late.

I give you my word that these little talents, which in Persia we do not value at all, are of great service here to those fortunate enough to possess them, and that a man of good sense rarely shines among people such as these.

Paris, the 6th of the Moon of Rebiab 2 1715

LETTER 81

Usbek to Rhedi, in Venice

If there is a God, my dear Rhedi, he must necessarily be just; for if he were not so, he would be the most evil and most imperfect of all beings.

Justice is a relationship of accepted values and common interests between two entities; this relationship is always the same, regardless of who is considering it, whether it be God, or an angel, or indeed a man.

It is true that men do not always see these relationships; even when they do see them, they often distance themselves from them; their own interest is always what they see best. Justice raises her voice, but she has difficulty making herself heard amid the tumult of the passions.

Men can commit injustices, because it is in their interest to do so, and they would rather satisfy themselves than others. It is always through thinking of themselves that they act unjustly; no one is gratuitously bad, there must be a reason which determines the act, and that reason is invariably one of self-interest.

But it is impossible for God ever to act unjustly; once we assume that he is aware of justice, it is necessary that he should act according to it, for since he needs nothing, and is sufficient unto himself, he would be the most evil of all beings were he evil without the motivation of self-interest.

So, even if there were no God, we should always love justice, that is, try hard to resemble that being of whom we hold so perfect an idea, and who, if he existed, would necessarily be just. Although we would be free of the bonds of religion, we ought not to be free of the bonds of justice.

Such, Rhedi, are my reasons for thinking that justice is eternal,* and independent of human conventions; if it were to depend upon them, that would be a terrible truth which we would have to conceal from ourselves.

We are surrounded by men who are stronger than us; they can hurt us in a thousand different ways; three-quarters of the time they can do so with impunity. What a comfort to know that deep in the hearts of all men lies a principle which fights on our behalf, and protects us from their schemes!

Otherwise, we would live in a state of perpetual fear; we would walk among men as among lions, and we would never know a moment's security about our life, our possessions, or our honour.

All these thoughts fill me with anger against those scholars who portray God as a being that uses his power tyrannically; who show him acting in a manner that we ourselves would avoid, for fear of offending him; who endow him with all the imperfections he punishes in us, and who, in their contradictory pronouncements, represent him now as an evil being, and now as a being that detests and punishes evil.

When a man searches his own heart, what satisfaction for him to find that it is just! This pleasure, for all its austerity, must fill him with delight: he sees himself fully as superior to the unjust as he is superior to tigers and bears. Yes, Rhedi, if I were certain of invariably, inviolably, obeying the dictates of that justice that I see clearly in my mind, I would believe myself to be the best of men.

Paris, the 1st of the Moon of Gemmadi 1 1715

LETTER 82

Rica to ***

Yesterday I visited the Invalides;* I would be as pleased to have built that institution, were I the king, as I would be to have won three battles. Everywhere you look, you find evidence of the hand of a great monarch. I believe it is the most impressive place in the world.

What a spectacle it is to see, assembled together in one place, all those that suffered for their homeland, and live solely to defend it; who, feeling themselves as strong as ever in courage, but no longer so in body, lament only their inability to sacrifice themselves once more for France!

What could be more admirable than seeing how, in this retreat, these enfeebled warriors observe as strict a discipline as if they were constrained to do so by the presence of an enemy, and how they seek their final satisfaction in this simulacrum of war, where they divide their feelings and thoughts between the duties of religion and those of military science!

I would like the names of those who die for their country to be recorded and preserved in churches, in registers that would serve as a wellspring of pride and nobility.

Paris, the 15th of the Moon of Gemmadi 1 1715

LETTER 83

Usbek to Mirza, in Ispahan

As you know, Mirza, some of Shah Soliman's* ministers made a plan to force all the Armenians in Persia either to leave the kingdom or to become Muslims, in the belief that our empire would always be defiled as long as it harboured infidels within its borders.

Persia's greatness would have become a thing of the past if, on that occasion, the voice of blind piety had been heard.

No one knows how the plan came to fail; neither the men who proposed it nor those who rejected it had thought out what would be its consequences; chance did the work of reason and politics, and saved the empire from a danger greater than it would have faced through three defeats in battle, and the loss of two cities.

By banishing the Armenians,* they planned to destroy, in a single day, all the merchants and almost all the craftsmen of the kingdom. I am convinced that the great Shah Abas* would have done better to cut off both his arms than to sign such an order, and that in sending to the Mogul, or to the other kings of the Indies, his most industrious subjects, he would have felt he was giving them half his kingdom.

The persecutions to which our fervent Muslims have subjected Parsees forced great numbers of them to flee to the Indies, thereby depriving Persia of that hard-working race, which is so addicted to farming the land that they alone, with their labour, were capable of overcoming the sterility of our fields.

All that remained for piety to do was to ruin industry, and then the empire would have fallen on its own, and with the empire, as a natural consequence, this same religion that piety was so eager to preserve and promote.

If I think this question through without prejudice, Mirza, then it is unclear to me whether having several religions is not a good thing for a state.

It has been pointed out that those who practise a religion tolerated by the state make themselves, as a rule, more valuable to their homeland than do those who belong to the state's dominant religion; barred from consideration for public honours, and able to achieve distinction only by an affluent lifestyle and their own prosperity, they tend to acquire wealth by hard work, and to seek out the most arduous occupations in a society.

Besides, because every religion contains precepts that are useful to society, it is good that these should be zealously observed. Now, what is better at inspiring this zeal than a multiplicity of religions?

These different religions are rivals, which forgive one another nothing. Jealous competition extends even over the details; everyone is on his guard, fearful of doing something that would dishonour his own side and expose it to the unpardonable scorn and criticisms of the adversary.

Indeed, observers have always noted that the introduction of a new sect into a society was the surest way of correcting all the abuses of the old one.

It is useless to claim that it is not in the prince's interest to permit several religions to coexist in his realm. If every sect in the world assembled there together, it would in no way harm the prince, because there is not a single religion that does not prescribe obedience, and preach submission.

I admit that history is full of wars of religion; but on this point we must be very careful; it is not the multiplicity of religions that produced these wars, but the spirit of intolerance animating the religion that believed itself to be dominant.

It is this spirit of proselytism that the Jews picked up from the Egyptians, and then passed on, like a common epidemic, to the Muslims and the Christians.

In short, it is a kind of vertigo, whose progress can only be considered as a total eclipse of human reason.

In fact, even were it not inhuman to trouble another man's conscience, even were there none of the bad effects that spring up by the thousands, one would have to be deranged to engage in such a purpose. He who tries to make me change my religion only does so, presumably, because he would never change his own, even were someone to try to force him to do so; so how can he find it strange that I should refuse to do something that he himself would not do, even perhaps were he offered the world as his empire?

Paris, the 26th of the Moon of Gemmadi 1 1715

LETTER 84

Rica to ***

It appears that here nobody is in control in a family; the husband has only a semblance of authority over his wife, the father over his children, the master over his slaves; and you may be sure that justice will always side against the jealous husband, the angry father, and the troublesome master.

The other day I visited the halls of justice. Before reaching it, I had to run the gauntlet of a countless number of young merchants, who call out to you in a blandishing voice. This is quite a cheerful spectacle at first, but it grows lugubrious when you walk into the great halls full of men whose garments are even gloomier than their faces. Finally, you enter the hallowed chamber where all the secrets of families are revealed and the most hidden acts are exposed to the light of day.

There, a modest young girl will admit to the torments of a too-long preserved virginity, and tell of her struggles and her painful resistance; so far is she from feeling pride in her victory, that she threatens soon to accept defeat, and, in order to force her father to recognize her needs, she exposes them to the whole world.

Next, a brazen wife divulges the flagrant offences she has committed against her husband, citing them as a reason for being separated from him.

With similar modesty, another then declares that she is weary of bearing the title of wife without enjoying its rights, and goes on to reveal the mysteries of the bridal night; she demands to be examined by the most skilful experts, so that their opinion may restore to her the rights of virginity. There are even some wives who defy their husbands and demand a public test that witnesses render so problematic; a test as sullying for the wife, who demands the test, as for the husband, who doesn't.

Endless numbers of violated or seduced young girls depict men as far worse than they are. This lawcourt reverberates with the vocabulary of love. You hear of nothing but angry fathers, deceived young girls, faithless lovers, and embittered husbands.

According to the law which is followed here, any child born of a marriage is assumed to be the husband's; whatever good reasons he may adduce for not believing the child his, those reasons are unavailing; the law believes for him, and relieves him of both enquiry and scruples.

In this court decisions are made by majority vote; however, experience has shown it is better to go by the opinion of the minority, which is perfectly natural, for the number of righteous judges is very small, and every one agrees that those with poor judgement are too numerous to count.

Paris, the 1st of the Moon of Gemmadi 2 1715

LETTER 85

*Rica to ****

Man is said to be a sociable animal.* Seen in that light, a Frenchman, I feel, is more man than the rest of us; he is the ultimate man, for he appears to be made purely for society.

However, I've noticed some individuals among them who are not only sociable, but who constitute, all on their own, a universal society. They multiply in every corner, and in an instant populate the four quarters of a city; a hundred men of this type are more numerous than two thousand citizens; to the eyes of outsiders they could make up for the ravages of a plague, or a famine. Universities debate the problem of whether a body can be in several different places at the same instant; these men provide proof of what philosophers challenge.

They are always in a rush, because they have the important responsibility of asking every man they meet where he is going, and where he has been.

It is impossible to expunge from their mind the conviction that etiquette requires them to visit everybody every day; that's not including the visits they pay in groups, at large assemblies, but since such events are too easily reached they count for nothing in the rules of their ceremonial.

With their hammering upon the knocker they wear out the front door of a house faster than the wind and rain can do. If you were to examine every porter's list, you would find their name there every day, misspelled in a thousand different ways by the porter's illiterate hand. They spend their life following funeral processions, paying visits of condolence, or attending celebrations of forthcoming marriages. The king never confers an honour upon one of his subjects without it costing them the price of a cab, so that they may express their joy in person. Finally, utterly exhausted, they return home to rest, so that they can again take up their heavy tasks the following day.

Some days ago one of them died of weariness, and the following epitaph was inscribed upon his tomb: 'He who now rests here, was never before at rest. He followed the coffin at 530 funerals. He celebrated the birth of 2,680 children. The total sum of the pensions upon which he congratulated his friends—expressing himself differently each time—amounts to 2,600,000 livres. The total distance he covered in the city streets, to 9,600 stades, and in the country, to 36 stades. His conversation was entertaining; he had a ready-made supply of 365 anecdotes; from early youth he could quote 118 apophthegms drawn from the classics, which he employed on special occasions. He died, finally, in the sixtieth year of his life. Passer-by, I fall silent; for how can I ever do justice to all he did, and all he saw?'

Paris, the 3rd of the Moon of Gemmadi 2 1715

LETTER 86

Usbek to Rhedi, in Venice

In Paris, liberty and equality reign. Birth, virtue, or even a reputation won, no matter how brilliantly, in war, do not exempt a man from being lost in the crowd. Jealousy over rank is unknown here. It is said that the greatest man in Paris is the one with the best horses to draw his carriage.

A great noble is a man who sees the king, speaks to the ministers, and can lay claim to ancestors, debts, and pensions. If, in addition, he is able to conceal his idleness with a busy air, or a simulated appetite for pleasure, he believes himself the happiest of men.

In Persia there are no great men except those to whom the monarch entrusts an office in the government. Here, there are men who are great by birth, but they are without influence. Kings are like those clever workers who, to produce their works, always use the simplest machines.

Favour is the great deity of the French. The minister is its high priest, who supplies it with sacrificial offerings in abundance. Those who attend him are not clad in white; by turn sacrificers and sacrificed, they immolate themselves to their idol, as does the entire nation.

Paris, the 9th of the Moon of Gemmadi 2 1715

LETTER 87

Usbek to Ibben, in Smyrna

The desire for glory* is no different from that instinct for preservation that is common to all creatures. It is as if we enhance our being if we can gain a place in the memory of others; it is a new life that we acquire, which becomes as precious to us as the one we received from Heaven.

However, just as not all men are equally attached to life, they are not all equally responsive to glory. That noble passion is certainly always imprinted in their heart, but imagination and education modify it in a thousand ways.

This difference, which exists between one man and another, is even more apparent between one nation and another.

One can posit the maxim that, in every state, the desire for glory increases in proportion to the liberty of the subjects, and decreases in similar fashion; it is never the companion of servitude.

A man of good sense remarked to me the other day: 'In many regards, one is much freer in France than in Persia; consequently, here men love glory much more. That delightful illusion induces a Frenchman to find pleasure and joy in doing things which your sultan can only obtain from his subjects by constantly confronting them with punishments and rewards.

'Furthermore, here in France the monarch watches over the honour of the humblest of his subjects. To defend it there are respected tribunals, the nation's sacred treasure, the only one which the sovereign does not control; he cannot do so without hurting his own interests. Thus, if a subject believes his honour to have been injured by his king, either by a preference shown to someone else, or the smallest hint of contempt, he promptly abandons the court, his position, his service, and retires to his own estates.

'The difference between the French army and your own, is that the one is composed of slaves who are cowardly by nature, and can only overcome their fear of death with the fear of punishment; this creates in the soul a new kind of terror that stupefies it, whereas the French army marches eagerly into battle, banishing fear with a sense of fulfilment which is far superior.

'But the sanctuary of honour, fame, and virtue seems to be in republics, and in countries where there is a deep sense of patriotism. In Rome, in Athens, in Sparta, honour was the sole reward for the most signal services. A garland of oak or laurel leaves, a statue, or a eulogy were an immense recompense for a battle won or a city taken.

'There, a man who had performed an outstanding feat, considered himself sufficiently rewarded by the action itself. He could not look upon one of his compatriots without feeling pleasure at being his benefactor; he reckoned the number of his services by the number of his fellow-citizens. Every man is capable of doing good to another, but to contribute to the happiness of an entire society is to become akin to the gods.

'But is not this noble emulation completely stifled in the heart of your Persians, for whom high offices and prestigious posts are conferred solely at the whim of the sovereign? In Persia fame and virtue are thought imaginary, unless they are accompanied by the favour of the prince, where they are born and where they also die. A man who enjoys the esteem of the public is never certain that the next day will not find him disgraced; today he is a general in the army; it may be that the prince will appoint him as his cook, and the only praise he can ever again expect will be that of having made a tasty stew.'

Paris, the 15th of the Moon of Gemmadi 2 1715

LETTER 88

Usbek to same, in Smyrna

This general passion for glory, common to the entire French nation, has evolved, in the mind of particular Frenchmen, into a certain *je ne sais quoi*, which they call 'point of honour'; strictly speaking, it is a characteristic of every profession, but it is more evident among the military; there you find the point of honour in its purest form. It would be very difficult for me to convey to you precisely what it is, because we Persians do not have an exactly equivalent concept.

In the past the French, especially the nobility, rarely heeded any laws other than those of this point of honour; these laws governed the entire conduct of their lives, and were so severe that men risked a penalty harsher than death, not in breaking them, but even in simply circumventing them to the slightest degree.

When it came to settling disputes, these laws prescribed only one way of doing so: by the duel; duels solved every problem.* But the evil of this practice lay in the fact that frequently the settling was done by parties other than the principals involved.

Even if a man barely knew one of the parties to the quarrel, he would be obliged to side with his acquaintance, and pay, with his own life, as though he himself had been offended. A man would always feel honoured and flattered at being chosen as a second; and someone who would not have parted with a few crowns to save a man and all his family from the gallows, saw no problem whatever in risking his own life a thousand times for the sake of that same individual.

This fashion of settling differences was rather ill conceived; for it does not follow, because one man is more adroit or stronger than another, that his reasons are the best.

Therefore, monarchs have forbidden duels under pain of severe penalties, but in vain: honour, resolutely determined to reign supreme, refuses to submit and recognize any other law.

So the French find themselves in a most dire situation: for those same laws of honour oblige a gentleman to avenge himself if he has been offended, but, on the other hand, the forces of justice punish him in the harshest manner when he does take his revenge. If he obeys the laws of honour, he dies upon the scaffold; if he obeys the laws of the land, he is banished for ever from the society of men. All he can do, then, is choose between these cruel alternatives: to die, or to be unworthy of living.

Paris, the 18th of the Moon of Gemmadi 2 1715

[SUPPLEMENTARY LETTER 4]

LETTER 89

Usbek to Rhedi, in Venice

The monarch who reigned for so long is dead.* He caused a lot of talk while he was alive; at his death, everyone fell silent. Steadfast and brave at the end, he seemed to submit only to destiny. The great Shah Abas died in such a manner, after making his name known throughout the world.

Do not imagine that, here in France, this great event has prompted purely moral considerations. Everyone has thought of his own interests, and how this change may be used to his own advantage. Since the king, the great-grandson of the late monarch, is only five years old, his uncle the prince has been appointed regent of the kingdom.

The late king had made a will limiting the authority of the Regent. This clever prince went to the Parlement, where he enumerated his rights by birth, and managed to overturn the stipulations of the monarch, who, attempting to outlive himself, seems to have intended to go on governing after his own death.

The Parlements resemble those ruins we trample underfoot, but which invariably evoke the memory of some temple celebrated in a religion of ancient times. Today they concern themselves with little other than administering justice, and their authority is always weak, unless some unforeseen conjuncture arises to restore them to vigour and to life. These great corporate bodies have followed the destiny of things human: they have yielded to time, which destroys everything; to social corruption, which weakens everything; to supreme authority, which overturns everything.

But, intending to ingratiate himself with the people, the regent seemed at first to respect this symbol of public liberty; and, as if to rebuild both the temple and the idol from the ground, he wanted the Parlements to be seen as the mainstay of the monarchy, and the foundation of all legitimate authority.

Paris, the 4th of the Moon of Rhegeb 1715

LETTER 90

Usbek to his brother, a santon* at the Monastery in Casbin

I humble myself before you, holy santon, I prostrate myself: your footprint is dearer to me than the dearest of my wives. Your saintliness is so great that it seems as if you have the heart of our sacred Prophet; your ascetic practices astonish Heaven itself; the angels have looked upon you from the heights of their glory and said: 'How can he still be upon earth, when his spirit is with us, hovering about the throne which the clouds support?'

And how could I not honour you, I who have been taught by our learned men that even unfaithful dervishes still bear the stamp of saintliness, which makes them worthy of the respect of true believers, and that God has chosen, from every corner of the earth, souls that are purer than the rest, and has separated them from the ungodly world, so that their mortifications and their fervent prayers might arrest his rage, which otherwise would be about to thunder down upon so many rebel peoples.

The Christians say marvellous things about their first santons, who took refuge by the thousand in the terrible deserts of Thebaid, under the leadership of Paul, Anthony, and Pachomius.* If what they say about them is true, their lives were as full of wonders as are those of our most holy imams. They sometimes spent as many as ten whole years without seeing a single person, but they lived day and night with demons, and were constantly tormented by those evil spirits; they found them in their bed, at their table; they knew no refuge from them. If all this is true, venerable santon, one would have to admit that nobody could ever have lived in worse company.

Sensible Christians regard all these stories as a very natural allegory, which serves to heighten our awareness of the misery of the human condition. In vain do we seek tranquillity in the desert; temptations are always with us; our passions, represented by the demons, never let us alone: those monsters created by the heart, those illusions produced by the mind, those vain spectres that are our errors and our lies always appear before us to seduce us; they attack us even in our fasting or our mortifications, in other words, in our very strength.

For my part, santon, I know that God's emissary bound Satan in chains and cast him into the abyss; that he purified the earth which had been, until then, filled with Satan's power, and rendered it worthy to be the dwelling-place of angels and of prophets.

Paris, the 9th of the Moon of Chahban 1715

LETTER 91

Usbek to Rhedi, in Venice

I have never heard a discussion of public law* which did not begin with a careful examination of the origin of societies; this seems to me ridiculous. If men did not form societies, if they sought solitude and shunned one another, one would want to discover the reason for this and find out why they lived in isolation; but they are all born connected to one another; a son is born close to his father, and remains with him: there we have a society, and also its origin.

Public law is better known in Europe than in Asia; however, it can be said that the passions of princes, the patience of the common people, and the flattery of writers have corrupted all its principles.

This law, as it stands today, is a science which teaches princes how far they may contravene justice, without running counter to their own interests. What a project, Rhedi, to plan to inure their own conscience by systematizing iniquity, giving it rules and principles, and then drawing conclusions from the results!

The unlimited power of our sublime sultans, which recognizes no rule but itself, does not produce more monstrosities than does this shameful art, which seeks to bend justice, despite justice's reputed inflexibility.

One might suppose, Rhedi, that there are two quite different kinds of justice: one, that regulates the affairs of individuals, and governs civil law; and the other, that regulates differences arising between peoples, and tyrannizes over public and international law; as though public and international law were not themselves part of civil law, not, indeed, the civil law of a particular country, but of the whole world.

I'll explain my thoughts on this subject in another letter to you.

Paris, the 1st of the Moon of Zilhagé 1716

LETTER 92

Usbek to same

Magistrates are responsible for ensuring that justice prevails between individual citizens; each nation must itself ensure that justice prevails between itself and another nation. This second dispensing of justice must be governed by exactly the same maxims as the first.

From nation to nation, there is rarely a need for adjudication by a third party, because the subjects of disagreement are almost always clear-cut and easy to settle. The interests of the two nations are usually so separate, that one need only love justice to be able to perceive where it lies; one cannot let oneself be influenced by one's own interests.

The same is not true of disagreements between individuals. Because they live in society, their interests are so intermingled and tangled together, and are so diverse in nature, that a third party is needed to clarify what the greed of the parties involved tries to obscure.

There are only two types of just war: those which are undertaken to defend one's country against an enemy on the attack, and those undertaken to help an ally who is under attack.

It would not be just to go to war over a private quarrel of the prince's, unless the case were so serious that it would result either in the death of the prince or the destruction of the nation that had committed the offence. Furthermore, a prince may not go to war because he has been refused an honour to which he is entitled, or because his ambassadors have been slighted in some fashion, or for any reason of that kind, any more than an individual may kill a man who has refused to allow him precedence. The reason for this is that a declaration of war must be an act of justice, where the penalty is proportionate to the crime, and one must be sure that the party against whom war is declared deserves to die. For to make war against someone is to sentence him to death.

In international law the most extreme resource of justice is war, since its purpose is the destruction of society.

Reprisals are a resource of second degree, after war. The courts are obliged to observe the law that metes out penalties in proportion to the crime.

A third resource of justice is to deprive a prince of the advantages he may enjoy over us, always in proportion to the offence.

The fourth resource of justice, which should be the most common, is to repudiate the alliance with the offending nation. This penalty is equivalent to banishment, whereby the civil courts exile guilty parties from society. In similar fashion, a prince whose alliance we repudiate is cut off from our society, and is no longer one of our members.

There is no greater insult to a prince than to repudiate his alliance, nor can there be any greater honour paid him than to form an alliance with him. Among men there is nothing that reflects greater glory upon them, and even nothing that is of greater service to them, than to have others always attentive to their protection and support.

But in order for an alliance to bind us together, it must be just; thus, an alliance between two nations to oppress a third is not legitimate, and can be violated without crime.

Similarly, it goes against the honour and dignity of a prince to ally himself to a tyrant. It is said that an Egyptian monarch* had a warning delivered to the king of Samos about his cruelty and tyranny, demanding that he change his ways; when the king did not do so, the Egyptian ruler sent him word that he renounced his friendship and his alliance.

The right of conquest is not a right. A society cannot be founded other than upon the will of its members; if it is destroyed by conquest, then the people become free and no new society exists; if the conqueror tries to form one, that is an act of tyranny.

As to peace treaties, they are never legitimate when they mandate cession of territory, or compensation greater than the damage caused; in such an event the treaty is a product of brute force, and can always be broken; except that when reclaiming what was lost involves such violent means that they result in an evil greater than the good they sought to attain.

Such, dear Rhedi, is what I call public law; such is the law of humankind, or rather the law of reason.

Paris, the 4th of the Moon of Zilhagé 1716

LETTER 93

The head eunuch to Usbek, in Paris

A great many golden-skinned women have arrived here from the kingdom of Visapor; I have bought one for your brother the governor of Mazandran, who sent me his sublime orders a month ago, together with 100 tomans.

I am expert at selecting women, the more so because I am not affected by them, and my eyes are not influenced by the emotions of my heart.

I have never seen such regular, such perfect beauty; her brilliant eyes give life to her face, and enhance the radiance of a colour that could efface all the charms of Circassia.

The head eunuch of an Ispahan trader was vying with me to buy her, but she concealed herself disdainfully from his glances, and seemed to seek mine, as if she were trying to tell me that a base merchant was not worthy of her, and she was destined for a more illustrious husband.

I must confess that I feel a secret joy in my heart when I think of the charms of that beautiful creature; it is as if I can see her entering your brother's seraglio; it pleases me to imagine the astonishment of all those women, the haughty anguish of some, and the mute but deeper sorrow of others; the malicious consolation offered by those who no longer hope, and the angry ambition of those who do still cherish hope.

I travel from end to end of the kingdom to transform a seraglio: what passions I shall arouse! What fears, what suffering I am setting in motion!

Nevertheless, despite the turmoil within, the surface will reveal nothing but tranquillity; fierce rebellion will lie buried deep within the heart, misery stifled and joy repressed; and from the very blackest despair a mask of studied sweetness will emerge.

We have observed that the more women we have to choose among, the less trouble they are. A greater need to please; less opportunity to unite; more examples of submission: all these forge their chains; some women perpetually watch what the others are doing, it is as if they were working with us to make themselves more dependent; they do half our work for us, and alert us to open our eyes when we close them. Indeed, they constantly arouse the master's anger against their rivals, and do not see how close they themselves are to those being punished.

But all of this, Magnificent Lord, all of this is nothing without the presence of the master. What can we achieve with this futile ghost of an authority that is never completely present? We can only weakly represent one half of you; all we can show them is a hateful severity. But you temper fear with hope; and your rule is more absolute when you caress, than when you threaten.

So return to us, Magnificent Lord, return to this place and fill it with the evidence of your sovereignty. Return and soothe passions that despair; return and banish all pretext for weakness; return to comfort the laments of love and make duty pleasurable; and finally, Magnificent Lord, return to relieve your faithful eunuchs of a burden which every day grows heavier.

The seraglio at Ispahan, the 8th of the Moon of Zilhagé 1716

LETTER 94

Usbek to Hassein, dervish of the mountain of Jaron

Wise dervish, you whose enquiring mind shines with so much learning, listen to what I am about to tell you.

There are philosophers here who, it is true, have never attained the heights of oriental wisdom; they have never been exalted to the luminous throne, nor heard the ineffable words with which the concert of angels resounds, nor known the fearsome experience of a divine ecstasy; but on their own, deprived of any knowledge of holy marvels, they follow in silence the path of human reason.

You would never believe how far this guide has taken them. They have unravelled the mystery of the primal chaos and have explained, by means of a simple mechanism, the order of divine architecture. The Creator of Nature set matter in motion,* which was all that was required to produce the miraculous variety that we see in the universe.

We have so many ordinary legislators, who give us laws that regulate human societies; these laws are as subject to change as are the minds of the men who propose them, and the minds of those who observe them; but philosophers tell us of laws that are universal, immutable, and eternal, and which are observed, without any exception,* in an infinitely orderly, regular, and immediate manner, in the immensity of space.

And what do you suppose, holy dervish, these laws are about? Perhaps you imagine that when you are privy to the counsels of the Eternal One, you will be overwhelmed by the sublimity of the mysteries; you abandon, ahead of time, the thought of understanding; you mean only to marvel.

But you will quickly change your mind; these laws do not blind us with misleading veneration; their simplicity has meant that they have long been disregarded, and it is only after much reflection that the full extent of their fecundity and reach has become known.

The first law is: that every body tends to describe a straight line unless it encounters some obstacle that deflects it; and the second,* which is a corollary of the first, that every body that circles round a central point tends to move away from it, because the further it gets from the centre, the straighter will be the line it describes.

And that, sublime dervish, is the key to nature. These are fertile principles, from which one may draw an infinite number of consequences, as I shall demonstrate to you in a special letter.

The grasp of five or six truths has resulted in their philosophy being rich in miracles,* and has enabled philosophers to perform more prodigies and marvels than all of those told about our holy prophets.

For indeed, I am convinced that there is not one of our learned scholars who would not have been perplexed had he been told to weigh, on a scale, all the air surrounding the Earth, or to measure all the water which falls each year upon its surface; and that he would have had to think it through time and time again, before declaring how many leagues sound covers in an hour, and how long a ray of light takes to travel from the sun to us. How far is it from here to Saturn? What is the ideal curve for building the keel of a boat, so that it sails as well as possible?

Perhaps if some divine writer had adorned these philosophers' treatises with elevated and sublime language, if he had woven some bold images and mysterious allegories into them, he would have created a beautiful work which would have been transcended only by the holy Qur'an.

However, if you press me, I will tell you that I do not really like the highly wrought style. Our Qur'an contains a great number of puerile passages which I still see as such, even though they are enhanced by the vigour and vitality of their expression; it seems at first as if inspired writings are simply divine ideas expressed in human language: on the contrary, in our holy books we find the words of God and the ideas of men, as if by some extraordinary caprice God had dictated the words, and man had provided the thought.

Perhaps you will say that I speak too freely of what is most sacred to us Persians, and will think this the fruit of the independence we enjoy here in France. No, thanks be to Heaven, the mind has not corrupted the heart, and as long as I live, Ali shall be my prophet.

Paris, the 15th of the Moon of Chahban 1716

LETTER 95

Usbek to Ibben, in Smyrna

There is no country in the world where fortune is as fickle as she is in France. Every ten years there are revolutions, which precipitate the rich into the deepest poverty and raise up the poor, on rapid wings, to the greatest wealth. The first is astonished by his penury, the second, by his plenty. The upstart is amazed by the wisdom of Providence, the newly poor by the blind reversals of Destiny.

Tax farmers luxuriate in opulence: rarely will you see Tantalus among their number. However, when they begin this work they are the poorest of the poor; they are despised and treated like dirt while they still remain poor; when they become rich they are respected somewhat, and consequently they are determined to gain respect at any cost.

At present their situation is dire. Recently a body has been established, entitled a Chamber of Justice,* its purpose being to expropriate all the tax farmers' wealth. They cannot abstract or conceal their possessions, for they are required to declare them accurately, on pain of death; thus they are being forced to make a very difficult choice: that is, between their life and their money. And to crown it all, there's a minister, well known for his quick wit, who honours them with his witticisms, and jokes through all the deliberations of the Council. It's not every day you encounter ministers who are prepared to make the common people laugh, and you have to like this one for having decided to do so.

The corps of footmen is more respectable in France than elsewhere; it's a training-ground for noblemen, and fills in the gaps between the other estates. Those who belong to it stand in for luckless noblemen, disgraced magistrates, and gentlemen killed in the heat of war; and when they are unable to fill this role themselves, they raise up all the great families by means of their daughters, who are like a kind of manure that enriches rocky and arid soils.

I think, Ibben, that Providence is admirable in the way she has shared out wealth: if she had given it only to good people we would not have distinguished it clearly enough from virtue, and we would no longer have been aware of the utter nothingness of wealth. But when we examine which people are burdened with the greatest wealth, by dint of despising rich people, we come to despise riches.

Paris, the 26th of the Moon of Maharram 1717

LETTER 96

Rica to Rhedi, in Venice

I'm dumbfounded by the caprices of French fashion.* They've forgotten what they were wearing this summer; even less do they know what they'll be wearing this coming winter; but, above all, it's hard to believe how much it costs a husband to keep his wife in fashion.

What would be the use of my giving you an exact description of their clothing and their hair-pieces? A new fashion would appear and destroy all my efforts, along with those of their seamstresses; and before my letter had reached you everything would have changed.

A woman who leaves Paris to spend six months in the country returns as antiquated as if she had sequestered herself there for thirty years. The son fails to recognize the portrait of his mother, so outlandish does the outfit in which she is painted seem to him; he imagines that it's a painting of some Amerindian woman, or that the painter was attempting to portray one of his fantasies.

At times, little by little, the coiffures* grow taller and taller, and then quite suddenly a revolution brings them all down; there was a period when, because of their colossal height, a woman's face seemed to be in her own middle. At another time it was the feet that occupied this central spot: the high heels formed a pedestal which held the feet in the air. Who would credit it? Architects have frequently been obliged to raise, lower, and widen doors, according to whether female fashion required these changes; the rules of their art have been governed by such whims. Occasionally one observes an astonishing number of beauty-spots upon a face, and the following day they have all vanished. In the past women had waists, women had teeth; nowadays there's no question of such things. In this changeable nation, whatever a critic may say on the subject, young girls discover that they are made differently from their mothers.

What can be said of fashion can be said also of manners, and of lifestyles: the French change their ways according to the age of their king. The monarch could even succeed in making the nation serious, if he attempted it. The prince imprints his kind of disposition on the court, the court on the town, the town on the provinces. The soul of the sovereign is a mould that determines the shape of all the others.

Paris, the 8th of the Moon of Saphar 1717

LETTER 97

Rica to the same

I was telling you the other day about the extraordinary inconstancy of the French with regard to fashion. The extent of their obstinacy about it, however, goes beyond belief; it is the rule by which they judge everything that happens in other nations, they gauge everything by it: all things foreign invariably strike them as ridiculous. I confess that I cannot quite see how to reconcile this passion for their own customs with the inconstancy they demonstrate in changing these customs every day.

When I tell you that they despise everything foreign, I speak purely of trivialities. When it comes to important matters, they seem to distrust themselves to the point of disparagement. They cheerfully admit that other nations are wiser, as long as you agree that they, the French, are better dressed. They are willing to be subject to the laws of a rival nation, as long as French wig-makers can legislate on the style of foreign wigs. They think nothing could be more splendid than to see the taste of their chefs prevail from north to south, and the ordinances of their hairdressers be displayed on all the well-dressed heads of Europe.

With these noble advantages, why should they care that they have to look outside their borders for common sense, and that they have taken everything relating to political and civil government from their neighbours?

Who can believe that the most ancient and powerful kingdom in Europe has been governed, for more than the last ten centuries, by laws which were not created for it? If the French had been conquered this would not be hard to understand. But they are the conquerors.

They abandoned the ancient laws made by their first kings in national general assemblies; and the odd thing is that the Roman laws* they adopted in their stead were, in part, made and written by emperors who were the contemporaries of their own legislators.

In order that the acquisition might be complete, and that all their good sense might come from elsewhere, they adopted all the Papal Bulls, and have based a new part of their law on them: a new kind of servitude.

It is true that recently some statutes concerning cities and provinces have been composed and written into law; but they are almost all taken from Roman law.

This abundance of laws adopted and, as it were, naturalized, is so vast that it is equally burdensome to justice and to judges. But these volumes of laws are nothing compared with the dreadful army of glossarists, commentators, and compilers; men as weak in their want of judgement as they are powerful by virtue of their huge numbers.

That is not all. These alien laws have introduced formal procedures which are a disgrace to human reason. It would be quite difficult
to decide if these formalities have been more pernicious in their
effect on jurisprudence or on the practice of medicine; if they have
caused more harm garbed in the robes of a lawyer or under the wide-
brimmed hat of a physician, and if more people have been ruined by
the one than have been killed by the other.

Paris, the 12th of the Moon of Saphar 1717

LETTER 98

Usbek to ***

People here talk constantly about the Papal Bull.* The other day
I visited a house where I encountered a fat man with a red face, who
was saying in a loud voice: 'I've written my pastoral letter, so I'm not
going to reply to everything you're saying: but you should read my
letter and you'll see that in it I settle all your doubts. Composing
it was really hard work,' he said, wiping his brow with his hand,
'I needed all my doctrinal knowledge, and I had to read a great many
Latin scholars.' 'I believe you,' said a man standing nearby, 'because
it's a fine work, and I defy that Jesuit who is always visiting you to
write a better one.' 'So just read it,' continued the bishop, 'and you'll
be better informed about this subject in fifteen minutes, than if I'd
talked to you for two hours.' Thus he avoided involving himself in
the conversation and compromising his self-importance. But, as
people were pressing him, he was forced to abandon his defences,
and embark on a series of theologically idiotic declarations, supported by a dervish who echoed them most respectfully. When two
of the men present denied some principle he would promptly
respond: 'It's beyond question, that is our judgement, and we are
infallible judges.' 'And how does it come about,' I then asked him,
'that you are infallible judges?' 'Don't you understand,' he replied,
'that the Holy Spirit enlightens us?' 'How fortunate,' I responded,
'for judging by the way you have been talking all day, I see that you
are in great need of enlightenment.'

Paris, the 18th of the Moon of Rebiab 1 1717

LETTER 99

Usbek to Ibben, in Smyrna

The most powerful states of Europe are those belonging to the emperor, and to the kings of France, Spain, and England. Italy, and a large part of Germany, are divided into an infinite number of small states, ruled by princes who are, in reality, martyrs to sovereignty. Our glorious sultans have more wives than most of those princes have subjects. The princes of Italy, who are not very united, are the most to be pitied: their states are as open as caravanserais, to which they are forced to welcome all comers; out of necessity, then, they attach themselves to princes that are powerful, and offer them a share of their fears, rather than their friendship.

Most European governments are monarchical, or rather bear that label; for I do not know whether such governments have ever actually existed: at any rate, it is impossible that they should last long: such states are unstable, and invariably degenerate into despotism or republicanism. Power can never be shared equally between the people and the prince; the balance is too difficult to maintain, power necessarily always diminishing on the one side while increasing on the other; as a rule, however, the advantage is to the prince, who heads the armies.

The European kings, therefore, enjoy great power, and one can say that they exercise it as they choose; but they do not exercise it as broadly as do our sultans; first, because they do not want to offend against the customs and religion of their subject peoples; and secondly, it is not in their best interests to take it to such extremes.

Nothing brings princes so close to the condition of their subjects as does this immense power they hold over them, for nothing makes them more vulnerable to the reversals and caprices of destiny.

The practice of some rulers of putting to death, for the slightest offence, all those who displease them reverses the proportion which should exist between the offence and the penalty, a proportion that gives a state its soul, an empire its harmony; Christian princes, who scrupulously preserve this proportion, hold an infinite advantage over our sultans.

A Persian who, through imprudence or ill luck, has fallen out of favour with the sultan, is certain to die: the smallest slip, or the slightest whim, will render this inevitable. But had he made an attempt on his sovereign's life, or intended to deliver up his fortresses to the enemy, he would also forfeit his life; consequently he incurs no greater risk in the second situation than in the first.

Therefore, in the slightest disgrace, realizing death is certain and that no further action can be taken against him, he is naturally impelled to trouble the state and conspire against the sovereign; it is his sole remaining resource.

European noblemen are in a different situation: for them disgrace deprives them of nothing but goodwill and favour; they retire from court, and expect only to enjoy a peaceful life and the advantages of their birth. As they are rarely put to death except for the crime of high treason, they are wary of committing this, when they weigh what they have to lose against how little they would gain; consequently, one sees here few rebellions, and few princes who die a violent death.

If our princes in Persia, with the limitless power they enjoy, did not take so many precautions to safeguard their own life, they would not live a day; nor, if they did not keep a vast number of troops in their pay to tyrannize over their subjects, would their empire last a month.

It is a mere four or five centuries ago that a king of France, contrary to the custom of the times, created a guard* to protect his person against some assassins that an insignificant Asian prince had sent to kill him; until then the kings had lived peacefully among their subjects, like fathers among their children.

Far from being empowered, as are our sultans, to order a subject put to death if they so desire, the kings of France have, by contrast, a permanent right to pardon criminals; it is enough that a man be fortunate enough to look upon the august features of his prince, to cease to be unworthy of life. These monarchs are like the sun, they bestow warmth and life everywhere.

Paris, the 8th of the Moon of Rebiab 2 1717

LETTER 100

Usbek to the same

To return to the topic of my last letter, here, more or less, is what quite a sensible European said to me the other day:

'The worst strategy oriental princes could adopt is to hide themselves away, as is their wont. Their intention is to make themselves more respected, but they inspire respect for royalty, rather than for the king, and attach the minds of their subjects to a particular throne, rather than to a particular person.

'For the common people, this invisible power governing them always remains the same. Even if ten kings, whom they knew only by name, were to be slaughtered one after another, they would experience no difference; it would be as if they had been governed by a succession of ghosts.

'If the abhorrent parricide of our great King Henri IV* had committed his act against a king of the Indies, the criminal, possessor of the Royal Seal and of an immense treasure apparently amassed for his benefit, would calmly have taken up the reins of government, without a single person thinking of protesting on behalf of his king, or his king's family, or his king's children.

'People find it astonishing that they so rarely see any changes in the government of an oriental prince. Why should that be the case, unless because that government is tyrannical and appalling?

'Changes can be made only by the prince, or by the people; but princes are very careful not to make any changes, because, since they wield such immense power, they already have everything possible; if they were to change anything, it would only be to their own detriment.

'As for their subjects, if one of them were to resolve on some scheme, he could not implement it against the state: he would have to be capable of instantly neutralizing a formidable and unique power; he has neither time nor means; but he need only go to the source of that power; all he requires is an arm, and an instant.

'The murderer ascends the throne as the monarch falls from it and expires at his feet.

'A malcontent in Europe thinks of setting up a secret correspondence; of going over to the enemy; of capturing a fortress; of stirring up vain grievances among the people. A malcontent in Asia goes straight to the prince, surprises, strikes, and overcomes; he obliterates the very idea of that person; at one moment he is slave, then master, and the next moment usurper, then lawful ruler.

'Unhappy the king who has only one head: he seems to unite all his power upon it, simply to signal to the first opportunist where to find that power entire and undivided.'

Paris, the 17th of the Moon of Rebiab 2 1717

LETTER 101

Usbek to the same

Not all the nations of Europe are equally submissive to the control of their prince; for example, the impatient temper of the English rarely leaves their king time to make his authority felt: submission and obedience* are the virtues on which the English pride themselves the least. On that subject they say some extraordinary things. According to them, there is only one bond which is capable of ensuring a man's devotion, and that is gratitude; a husband, a wife, a father, a son are united solely by the love they feel for one another or by the benefits they provide for one another: and these various grounds for gratitude form the basis of all kingdoms and all societies.

But if a prince, far from wishing to ensure that his subjects live happily, tries to subjugate and destroy them, the reasons for obedience cease to exist; nothing binds the subjects, nothing attaches them to him, and they regain their natural freedom. The English believe that no unlimited power can be legitimate, because it can never have been legitimate in origin. For we are not able, they say, to bestow upon another more power over us than we ourselves possess; and since we do not possess unlimited power over ourselves, being unable, for example, to deprive ourselves of life, nobody upon the earth, they conclude, possesses such a power.

According to the English, the crime of high treason is simply the offence the weaker party commits against the more powerful, in disobeying him, regardless of the nature of the disobedience. So the people of England, finding that they were stronger than one of their kings,* declared this king guilty of high treason for having made war against his subjects. They are, therefore, entirely correct when they say that the precept in their Qur'an, exhorting them to submit to those in power, is not really difficult to obey, since it is impossible for them not to obey it, in that it is not to the most virtuous that they are obliged to submit, but to the most powerful.

The English record that one of their kings, having vanquished and captured a prince* who had taken up arms against him, and disputed his right to the crown, reproached the latter for his perfidy and treachery. 'It is barely a moment', replied the luckless prince, 'since it was decided which one of us is the traitor.'

A usurper will declare that all those who have not oppressed their homeland, as he has done, are rebels; and, believing that there is no law where he sees no judges, he rules that the caprices of chance and of fortune be revered as if they were decrees of Heaven.

Paris, the 20th of the Moon of Rebiab 2 1717

LETTER 102

Rhedi to Usbek, in Paris

You wrote to me at length, in one of your letters, about the sciences and the arts that are cultivated in the West; you will think me a barbarian, but I'm not convinced that the benefits they bestow compensate man for the evil purposes to which they are turned every day.

I've heard it said that the invention of bombs alone had deprived all the peoples of Europe of their freedom. Monarchs, no longer able to entrust the defence of fortified towns to the local inhabitants, who would have surrendered at the first bomb, had an excuse for creating large bodies of regular troops, which they subsequently used to oppress their subjects.

As you know, since the invention of gunpowder no fortification is impregnable; in other words, Usbek, there no longer exists, anywhere on earth, any asylum from injustice and violence.

I live in fear that men of science will eventually discover some secret which would offer a faster way to kill people, destroy races, and wipe out entire nations.

You have read the historians; think carefully about what they say: almost all monarchies were founded upon ignorance of the arts, and were destroyed only because they cultivated them too assiduously. We have a domestic example of this in the ancient Persian Empire.

I have not been long in Europe, but I have heard sensible people talk of the ravages of chemistry; it seems to be a fourth plague, which ruins men's health and destroys them one by one, but continuously, whereas war, pestilence, and famine destroy them *en masse*, but intermittently.

Of what value to us has been the invention of the compass, and the discovery of so many different peoples, other than to give us their diseases rather than their wealth? A commonly accepted convention had established gold and silver as the price of all merchandise and a symbol of their value, because they are rare metals, and unsuitable for any other purpose; therefore why did it matter to us that they should become more common? And that to indicate the value of a product, we had to use two or three figures, instead of one? It was just more inconvenient.

But, on the other hand, the invention of the compass has been very harmful to the countries discovered. Entire nations have been destroyed; and those men who escaped death were reduced to such harsh servitude that the accounts alone have made Muslims tremble.

Blessed ignorance of the children of Muhammad! Gracious simplicity so beloved of our holy Prophet, you remind me always of the innocence of ancient times, and the peace that reigned in the hearts of our first fathers!

Venice, the 2nd of the Moon of Rhamazan 1717

LETTER 103

Usbek to Rhedi, in Venice

Either you don't believe what you're saying, or you're saying more than you realize. You left your homeland to learn, and you despise all learning; you seek to educate yourself in a country where the fine arts flourish, and you consider them pernicious. Shall I tell you something, Rhedi? I am more in agreement with you than you are with yourself.

Have you thought carefully about the miserable, brutish conditions that would follow the loss of all branches of human knowledge?

You need not imagine it, you can see it. There still exist peoples on the earth among whom a fairly well-educated monkey could live and be respected; he would be more or less on an equal footing with the other inhabitants; no one would think his mind unusual, or his character strange; he would be like anybody else, and would even stand out on account of his kindness.

You say that the founders of empires have almost all been unenlightened. I do not deny that barbarian peoples managed to spread across the earth like raging torrents, and overwhelmed the best-run kingdoms with their fierce armies; but be careful, they did study the different arts, and ensure that these were practised by those they had conquered; otherwise their power would have passed, like the sound of thunder and of tempest.

You are afraid, you say, that someone may invent a means of destruction crueller than what is currently in use. No; if such a fatal invention were discovered it would soon be prohibited by international public law, and the nations would unanimously agree to bury this discovery; it is not in the interests of monarchs to make conquests by such means; they want subjects, not land.

You complain about the invention of gunpowder and bombs, and think it strange that there are no more impregnable strongholds: in other words, you think it strange that nowadays wars end sooner than they did in the past.

You have surely noticed, when reading historical accounts, that since the invention of gunpowder battles have been much less bloody than formerly, because there is now almost no hand-to-hand fighting.

And supposing there were a particular case where the pursuit of a branch of learning had harmful consequences; is that a reason to reject it? Do you think, Rhedi, that the religion our holy Prophet brought from Heaven is pernicious, because it will serve one day to bring down the perfidious Christians?

You believe that the pursuit of the arts emasculates nations, and hence brings about the downfall of empires. You mention the ruin of the ancient Persian Empire, caused by indolence: but this is far from being a conclusive example, since the Greeks, who subjugated them, cultivated all the arts far more exhaustively than they did.

When people say that the arts make men effeminate, they are not, at any rate, referring to those who pursue them, for they are never idle, and of all the vices it is idleness that saps willpower the most.

It is, therefore, a matter of those who take pleasure in them; but since, in a well-regulated country, he that enjoys the amenities provided by a particular form of art must dedicate himself to some other branch, assuming he wishes to avoid the disgrace of penury, it follows that idleness and effeminacy are incompatible with the pursuit of the arts.

Paris is, perhaps, the most sensual city in the world, the city where pleasures are most highly refined and cultivated; but it is also, perhaps, the one where life is hardest. For one man to lead an epicurean life, it is necessary for a hundred others to work unremittingly. A woman has decided that she must appear at a gathering wearing a particular style of finery: consequently, from that moment, fifty artisans can no longer sleep, nor have time to eat or drink; she commands, and is obeyed, more promptly than our monarch would be, because self-interest is the greatest monarch on earth.

This passion for work, this passion to acquire wealth, affects people of every condition, from the artisan to the nobleman; nobody wants to be poorer than the man he's just seen, whose situation is by a mere hair's breadth inferior to his own. In Paris one encounters men with enough to live on until the Day of Judgement, who toil incessantly and risk cutting short their life in order to store up, they say, sufficient to live on.

The same spirit is spreading throughout the whole country: all you see is work and activity: so where is this effeminate nation you talk about so much?

If, Rhedi, I imagine a kingdom where the only occupations permitted were those essential to the cultivation of the land (and indeed these are very numerous), and where all those were banished that merely provided pleasure or nourished the imagination, I am convinced that that nation would be the most miserable in the world.

Even if the inhabitants had sufficient fortitude to deprive themselves of so many things they needed, the population would every day decline, and the state would become so enfeebled that there would exist no power, however insignificant, that was incapable of conquering it.

Here I could enter into endless detail and show you that the revenues of individuals would dwindle away almost to nothing, and that consequently the same would be true of the revenues of the monarch; there would be almost no commercial exchange between citizens, and that circulation of wealth, that increase of revenues which flow from the interdependence of the different occupations, professions, and crafts in the arts would cease absolutely; an individual's sole revenue would come from his land, and he would only draw from it precisely enough to keep him from dying of hunger; but as that constitutes merely one hundredth part of the revenue of a kingdom, the number of inhabitants would necessarily diminish in proportion, leaving only one hundredth part remaining.

Think carefully about what happens to the revenue from an industry. The investment made by an owner gives him an annual return of a mere 5 per cent of its value; but with a pistole's worth of paints, a painter can create a picture that will earn him fifty. The same can be said of goldsmiths, of wool- and silk-workers, and of every type of craftsman.

All this leads to the conclusion, Rhedi, that for a monarch to be powerful it is necessary that his subjects live a pleasurable life; he must be just as vigilant in ensuring that every kind of luxury is available to them as he is in ensuring they have the necessities of life.

Paris, the 14th of the Moon of Chalval 1717

LETTER 104

Rica to Ibben, in Smyrna

I have seen the young king; his life is very precious to his subjects, and no less so to all of Europe, because of the terrible turmoil that could ensue from his death. But kings are like the gods; while they live one must think of them as immortal. His face is dignified, but charming; a fine education seems to combine with a happy nature, and already promises a great monarch.

People say that one can never know the character of a western king until he has undergone the two important tests of his mistress and his confessor; we shall soon be watching those two struggling for control of the king's mind; then there will be some great battles! For, when the king is young these two powers are always rivals, although when he is old they become reconciled, and join their forces. Under a young king the role of the dervish is particularly difficult; the strength of the king is the measure of the dervish's weakness, but the other triumphs equally in the king's weakness and in his strength.

When I arrived in France, I found the late king* completely under the control of women, and yet, considering the age he had reached, I believe he had less need of women than any other monarch on this earth. One day I overheard a woman saying: 'Something must be done for that young colonel; I know what an admirable man he is; I'll speak to the minister about him.' Another said: 'It's surprising that that young abbé should have been passed over; he ought to be a bishop; he's a man of good family, and I can vouch for his morals.' You should not, however, imagine that these women were favourites of the king; they might perhaps have spoken to him a couple of times in their entire life, although it is very easy, at European courts, to speak to the king. The fact is, everyone that holds a position at court, whether in Paris or the provinces, has a wife or lady friend through whose hands passes every favour and, sometimes, every injustice he may dispense. These women are all acquainted with one another and form a sort of government, whose ever-busy members assist and oblige one another; it's like a new state within a state; and the bystander at the court in Paris or the provinces, who watches ministers and magistrates and prelates carrying out their duties, unless he knows the women who control them, is like a man watching a machine function without being aware of the springs that drive it.

Do you believe, Ibben, that a woman decides to become a minister's mistress in order to sleep with him? What a notion! It's so that she can present him with half-a-dozen petitions every morning; and her natural goodness can be seen in her eagerness to help a vast number of unfortunate people, who procure her an income of 100,000 francs.

People in Persia complain that the kingdom is governed by two or three women; it's far worse here in France, where women in general govern, and seize the authority not just to make decisions wholesale, but even to apply them retail.

Paris, the last day of the Moon of Chalval 1717

LETTER 105
Usbek to ***

There's a type of book* which we do not have in Persia, and which I find is very fashionable here; I refer to the periodical.

These publications pamper laziness; the indolent are overjoyed to be able to skim thirty volumes in a quarter of an hour.

With the average book, the reader has barely read past the author's usual prefatory compliments than he begins to feel desperate; he is obliged to half drown in a sea of words before he arrives at the subject matter. This writer wants to immortalize himself with a duodecimo edition, that one with a quarto, another, with more aesthetic leanings, aspires to a folio: he is therefore obliged to stretch out his material accordingly; this he does mercilessly, never heeding the suffering of his poor reader, who exhausts himself condensing what the author has taken so much trouble to expand.

I do not know where the merit lies in writing such works; that is precisely what I would do, if I wished to ruin my health, and my bookseller.

The great mistake made by the writers of periodicals is that they write only about new books, as if the truth were ever new. It seems to me that until a man has read all the ancient books he has no reason to prefer the new ones to them.

But, when they make it a rule to discuss only works that are hot off the press, they also make themselves another rule, which is to be very boring. They are careful not to criticize the books from which the extracts are taken, however good their reasons for doing so; and indeed, what man is bold enough to want to make himself ten or twelve enemies every month?

The majority of authors are like poets, who would endure a beating without complaint, but who, unconcerned about their own skin, are so touchy about the reputation of their works that they cannot tolerate the smallest adverse criticism; one must therefore be extremely careful not to attack them on such sensitive ground, and reviewers are well aware of this; consequently they do the exact opposite, and begin by praising the subject-matter treated; here begin the yawns also; then they continue by praising the author, but their praise is forced, for they are dealing with men who are on the watch for any offence, ready to demand satisfaction, and lambaste a rash reviewer with their pen.

Paris, the 5th of the Moon of Zilcadé 1718

LETTER 106

Rica to ***

The University of Paris* is the eldest, and very elderly, daughter of the kings of France, for she is more than nine hundred years old; consequently, she is occasionally confused.

I've been told that some time ago she had a tremendous dispute with some scholars over the letter *Q*, which she wanted them to pronounce like a *K*.* The dispute became so extremely heated that some people were stripped of their possessions; the Parlement had to settle the argument; it issued a solemn decree granting permission to all subjects of the king of France to pronounce that letter as they preferred. It was a fine thing to see the two most respected assemblies in Europe occupied in deciding the fate of a letter of the alphabet.

It seems, my dear friend, that the brains of the greatest men contract when they are gathered together, and that where there are more wise men, there you will also find less wisdom. The great assemblies are so preoccupied with minutiae, with formalities, and with empty orthodoxies, that essential issues are always relegated to the end. I have heard tell that when a king of Aragon convened the assemblies of Aragon and Catalonia, the first sessions were spent in deciding in which language the deliberations would take place; the dispute was impassioned, and the assemblies would have broken up a thousand times if someone had not suggested an expedient, namely, that the questions be asked in Catalan and the replies made in Aragonese.

Paris, the 25th of the Moon of Zilhagé 1718

LETTER 107

Rica to ***

The role of a pretty woman is a much more serious one than people suppose; nothing could be more serious than what takes place every morning when she dresses, surrounded by her servants; an army general does not give more thought to positioning his right flank or his reserves than she gives to placing a beauty-spot, which may miss its target, but which she hopes, or expects, will be a hit.

Under what constraint of spirit does she live! With what vigilance must she constantly reconcile the interests of two rivals, so as to appear to both to be impartial, while actually yielding to each of them, and acting as mediator for all the complaints she inspires.

How hard she must work, in perpetually setting up parties and outings, in ensuring that these follow one upon another in an endless succession, and in forestalling all the hazards that might make them miscarry!

And on top of all that her gravest concern is not to have a good time, but to look as if she's having a good time; you may bore them as much as you like, they'll forgive you as long as you can believe that they've had a wonderful time.

A few days ago I attended a supper party in the country, given by some women. On the way they kept repeating: 'At least we'll laugh our heads off, we'll have a really great time.'

As a group we were somewhat mismatched, and consequently rather solemn. 'You must admit,' said one of the women, 'that we're having tremendous fun; in the whole of Paris there isn't another party today as lively as ours.' Boredom was overtaking me when a woman gave me a nudge, saying: 'Well, aren't we in a happy mood?' 'Yes,' I replied with a yawn, 'I think I'm going to die from laughing.' Gloom, however, invariably prevailed over these observations, and for my part I was drawn, by dint of yawning, into a lethargic doze which put an end to all my pleasures.

Paris, the 11th of the Moon of Maharram 1718

[SUPPLEMENTARY LETTER 5]

LETTER 108

Rhedi to Usbek, in Paris

During my stay in Europe I'm reading both the ancient and the modern historians; I'm comparing all the ages, and enjoy seeing them pass, as it were, before my eyes; I'm concentrating particularly on those tremendous changes which made some ages so different from others, and the earth so very unlike itself.

You may never have noticed something that surprises me every day. How has it come about that the world is so sparsely populated, compared with former ages?* How has it come about that Nature has lost that miraculous fecundity of earlier times? Might she already have reached old age? Could she be losing her vitality?

I've spent more than a year in Italy, and I've seen only the debris of that ancient Italy which was so famous in the past. Although everybody lives in cities, these are quite empty and depopulated; it's as if they only survive today to mark the place where long ago there stood one of those powerful cities so celebrated by history.

There are men who claim that the city of Rome alone once contained more inhabitants than the greatest kingdom in Europe does today; a citizen of Rome might have ten, even twenty thousand slaves, not counting those that worked on his country estates; and as it was estimated that there were four or five hundred thousand citizens, the number of its inhabitants cannot be estimated without the imagination rebelling.

Sicily, in the past, contained powerful kingdoms and a large population which have now disappeared; the only remaining thing of note about this island today is its volcanoes.

Greece is so deserted that it does not comprise even a hundredth part of its former population.

Spain, once so densely populated, offers today's travellers uninhabited countryside; and France is nothing compared with that ancient Gaul described by Caesar.

The countries of the north are so badly reduced in population that they are far from being forced, as was once the case, to divide up and expel, like swarms of bees, colonies and entire peoples to seek new homes.

Poland and the European part of Turkey are almost denuded of inhabitants.

In America, you cannot find one-fiftieth part of the inhabitants who once formed such great empires there.

Asia is hardly in a better state. Asia Minor, where formerly there were such powerful monarchies and such a prodigious number of great cities, no longer has more than two or three. In Asia itself, the part under Turkish rule is no better populated; and as for the part ruled by our kings, a comparison with the flourishing populations of former ages shows that there now exists no more than a small proportion of the inhabitants who, in the days of the Xerxes and Darius dynasties, were myriad.

The small states neighbouring these great empires are truly deserted; take, for example, the kingdoms of Irimette, Circassia, and Guriel.* Those monarchs, all with vast realms, can lay claim to barely fifty thousand subjects.

Egypt is no less lacking in population than the other countries.

In brief, I travel the world and everywhere find rack and ruin; it's as if I am witnessing the aftermath of plague, and of famine.

Africa has always been so little known that one cannot speak as precisely about it as about other parts of the world; but even considering only the Mediterranean coast, which was discovered in early times, it's clear that there has been a great decline from its former state as a Roman province. Today its kings are so weak that they are the most insignificant powers in the world.

After doing calculations as exact as is possible in matters of this kind, I have concluded that the earth supports barely a fiftieth of the population that it had in Caesar's day. What is astonishing is that the population continues to diminish daily, and if this trend persists, within ten centuries the earth will be nothing but an uninhabited desert.

We see here, my dear Usbek, the most terrible catastrophe the world has ever experienced; but people have barely noticed it, because it has occurred so gradually, and over the course of a great many centuries; this points to an internal defect, a secret, hidden poison, a decline afflicting the human race.

Venice, the 10th of the Moon of Rhegeb 1718

LETTER 109

Usbek to Rhedi, in Venice

The world, my dear Rhedi, is not proof against decay; the heavens themselves are not; astronomers are eyewitnesses to all the changes that follow quite naturally upon the universal movement of matter.

The earth, like the other planets, is subject to these same laws of movement; it endures a perpetual, internal struggle between its basic elements: the sea and the land seem to be eternally at war, and each instant produces fresh combinations.

Human beings, dwelling in a place so subject to change, are in an equally uncertain state; a hundred thousand causes may be at play, the least of which can destroy, increase, or lessen their number.

I shall not dwell on those isolated catastrophes so common in historians' accounts, which destroyed entire cities and even kingdoms, but on those universal catastrophes which so often brought humankind within a hair's breadth of extinction.

History is full of those universal pestilences which by turn devastated the universe. They speak of one in particular,* which was so violent that it burned even the roots of the plants, and spread throughout the known world, as far as the Empire of Cathay; had it been one degree more virulent, it might perhaps have destroyed the entire human race in a single day.

Barely two centuries have passed since the most shameful of all maladies* appeared in Europe, in Asia, and in Africa; it caused unparalleled harm in a very short time; had it continued to rage at that rate, man would have been doomed. Worn out by afflictions from the moment of his birth, incapable of bearing the burden of his responsibilities to society, he would have perished miserably.

What if the poison had been a little more virulent? And it would undoubtedly have become so, had someone not had the good fortune to find a remedy as powerful as the one discovered. Perhaps this disease, which attacks the organs of generation, would have attacked reproductive capacity itself.

But why speak of something that might have wiped out the human race? Did that not actually occur, did the Flood not reduce humanity to one single family?

Can those people who have studied nature, and have a rational concept of God, comprehend that matter, and all of creation, are only six thousand years old? That God postponed his works throughout eternity, and only yesterday made use of his creative power? Might this have been because he could not, or because he would not use them? But if at one time he could not use them, then he could not use them at another; therefore, it must have been because he would not; however, since time does not exist for God, if we agree that he willed a thing once, then he has always willed it, and from the beginning.

Therefore, the years the world has existed must not be counted; the number of grains of sand in the sea is not more comparable to them than is an instant of time.

All historians, however, tell us of a first father, and paint for us a picture of the birth of humanity. Is it not natural to think that Adam was saved from a world-wide disaster, just as Noah was saved from the Flood, and that such cataclysms* have occurred frequently on earth, ever since the creation of the world?

I have enjoyed outlining these general ideas for you, before replying more specifically to your letter on the decline in population that has been evident over the last seventeen or eighteen centuries; I plan to show you, in my next letter, that apart from physical causes there are also moral causes that have produced this result.

Paris, the 8th of the Moon of Chahban 1718

LETTER 110

Usbek to the same

You ask the reason why the earth is less populated than in the past; if you consider the question carefully, you will see that this great difference results from the difference in the way people live.

Ever since the Christian and the Muslim religions divided up the Roman world, enormous changes have occurred; these two religions are far from being as favourable to the propagation of mankind as was that of the masters of the universe.

The religion of the Romans forbade polygamy, and in this enjoyed a huge advantage over the Islamic religion; divorce was permitted, which gave it another, no less significant advantage over Christianity.

I find nothing as contradictory as the plurality of wives permitted by the holy Qur'an, and the command to satisfy them decreed by the same work. 'Look to your wives,' says the Prophet, 'because you are as necessary to them as their garments, and they are as necessary to you as are yours.'* That is a precept which makes the life of a true Muslim very laborious. A man with the four wives prescribed by the Law, and only an equal number of concubines and slaves, must he not be weighed down by so many garments?

The Prophet says also: 'Your wives are the fields where you labour, therefore frequent them, for the good of your souls, and one day you will find Heaven.'*

I think of a good Muslim as an athlete destined to strive without respite, but who, too soon debilitated, and stricken with untimely fatigue, lies exhausted upon the very field of victory, and is buried, as it were, beneath his own triumphs.

Nature always works slowly, and so to speak thriftily; her operations are never violent; even in her productions she seeks moderation, she never acts other than with regularity and restraint; if you hurry her, she quickly wearies, and uses all her remaining strength to conserve herself, losing her productive energy and generative power.

Such is the debilitated state which we reach because of this multiplicity of wives, who are more likely to exhaust than to satisfy us; it is commonplace, in our society, to see a man with a vast seraglio and a very small number of children; these same children are generally weak and sickly, and reflect the enfeeblement of their father.

That is not all: these women, subjected to compulsory continence, require men to guard them who must necessarily be eunuchs; religion, jealousy, even reason cannot permit other men to approach them; these guards must be very numerous, both to maintain peace inside, amid the conflicts that these women constantly provoke among themselves, or to prevent ventures from outside the seraglio. Thus, a man with ten wives or concubines would need at least as many eunuchs to guard them. But what a loss to society, that so large a number of men are dead from the day of their birth! What a decline in population must be its consequence!

There are a great many female slaves who live, like the eunuchs, as servants in the seraglio, and almost invariably preserve a burdensome virginity into old age; they cannot marry while they remain in the seraglio, and their mistresses, once they become accustomed to them, rarely allow them to leave.

This is how just one man alone can employ so many subjects of both sexes for his own pleasures, can nullify their value to the state, and render them useless for the propagation of the species.

Constantinople and Ispahan are the capitals of the two greatest empires in the world; it is in those cities that everything should converge, and to them that all peoples, drawn there from all sides, and for a thousand reasons, should come. But these cities are dying, and would soon be destroyed if their sovereigns did not bring in entire populaces to inhabit them. I shall conclude this topic in another letter.

Paris, the 13th of the Moon of Chahban 1718

LETTER 111

Usbek to the same

The Romans did not have fewer slaves than we do, they actually had more, but they made better use of them.

Far from forcibly preventing their slaves from multiplying, on the contrary, they actually encouraged them in every way they could; they united them as much as possible in a kind of marriage; by this means filling their houses with domestic servants of both sexes and all ages, and the state with a vast population.

These children, who in the long run constituted the fortune of their master, were born in large numbers under his roof; he alone was responsible for their food and their education, so that their fathers, relieved of this burden, were entirely free to follow their natural instinct, and reproduced without fear of fathering too large a family.

I have already pointed out that, in our case, all our slaves are occupied in guarding our women, and do nothing else; from the state's point of view they live in perpetual lethargy, so that the cultivation of the arts and sciences, and of the land, falls upon just a few free men and a few heads of families, who actually do as little as possible in those domains.

It was not so with the Romans; the Republic employed its slave population to infinite advantage. Every slave had his *peculium*,* which he owned subject to conditions imposed by his master; with this he worked, applying himself to whatever occupation he felt suited his skills. This one ran a bank, that one concentrated on maritime trade; one sold merchandise retail while another applied himself to some mechanical art, or perhaps leased some land and developed it; there was not one who did not work as hard as he could to make a profit with his money, which gave him both an easier life in his present servitude, and hope of future liberty; this produced an industrious populace and energized the arts and sciences, as well as industry.

Those slaves who, thanks to their own conscientiousness and hard work, grew rich, bought their freedom and became citizens. The Republic renewed itself continuously, welcoming new families into its bosom as the old families brought about their own annihilation.

I may perhaps have occasion, in a future letter, to prove to you that the larger a nation's population, the better does its commerce flourish; I shall prove just as easily that the more commerce flourishes, the more the population increases; these two things assist one another and are, inevitably, mutually favourable

If that is the case, consider how much that vast number of invariably hard-working slaves must have multiplied and increased! Industry and abundance produced them; and they in their turn produced abundance, and industry.

Paris, the 16th of the Moon of Chahban 1718

LETTER 112

Usbek to the same

Until now, we have only discussed Muslim countries, and sought the reason why they are less populated than were those under Roman rule; let us now examine what has produced this effect in Christian countries.

Divorce was permitted by the pagan religion, and forbidden to Christians. This change, which at first seemed to be of such trivial importance, very gradually came to have terrible consequences, consequences of a kind that almost defy belief.

Not only did it rob marriage of all its sweetness, it also attacked its purpose; in attempting to strengthen its bonds, it weakened them; and instead of uniting hearts, as was the intention, it divided them for ever.

Constraint, necessity, even the fatality of destiny became part of a transaction which ought to be freely engaged in, and where the heart ought to play so significant a part. No allowance was made for dislike, or caprice, or incompatibility of temper; the intention was to permanently secure the heart, the heart which is the most variable, the most inconstant of nature's creations; two people, almost invariably ill-matched, were burdened with each other, bound together without recourse and without hope; it was like those tyrants who chained living men to corpses.

Nothing was more conducive to mutual attachment than the freedom to divorce; a husband and wife were inclined to bear their domestic difficulties with patience, knowing that they had the power to end them; and frequently that power remained unused throughout their lives, only because they were free to invoke it.

Such is not the case with the Christians, whose present troubles make them despair of the future; all they see, in the disadvantages of marriage, is their duration for, as it were, eternity; from this come dislike, discord, and contempt, and posterity suffers. Couples married for barely three years will already be neglecting the essential, and spend the next thirty at arm's length from one another; private separations occur that are as powerful, and perhaps more pernicious, than if they were public; each partner lives, and remains, on his or her own, and all this to the detriment of future generations. Soon, weary of the same eternal wife, a man will turn to prostitutes, a shameful trade, most injurious to society, in that, without fulfilling the purpose of marriage, it represents at best only its pleasures.

If one of the two people thus bound together is not fitted, either by temperament or by age, to nature's purpose, and to the propagation of the species, that individual buries the partner also, rendering each as useless as the other.

It is not, therefore, astonishing that we should see such a large number of Christian marriages produce such a small number of citizens; divorce is abolished; there is no longer any remedy for an incompatible marriage; wives can no longer, as was the case under the Romans, be passed along by several successive husbands, each of whom could use her to his best advantage.

I dare to say that if, in a republic like Sparta, where the citizens were constantly hindered by peculiar, cunning laws, and where there was only one family, namely the republic, a law had been passed requiring husbands to change wives every year, the birth-rate would have been incalculably large.

It is quite difficult to satisfactorily explain the reason that induced Christians to abolish divorce. In every nation of the world marriage is a contract open to a wide range of stipulations, so all that was necessary was to exclude those that weakened its purpose; but Christians do not regard marriage in that light; they are, however, hard pressed to define what it actually is. They do not think it consists in sensual pleasure; on the contrary, as I have said, it seems that they want to banish sensuality from marriage as much as they are able; no, it is an idea, a representation, something mysterious that I do not understand.

Paris, the 19th of the Moon of Chahban 1718

LETTER 113

Usbek to the same

The prohibition of divorce is not the only cause of the depopulation of the Christian countries; the great number of eunuchs they have is of equal importance.

I refer to the priests and dervishes of either sex, who vow to remain eternally chaste; for Christians, chastity is the supreme virtue,* and this I cannot understand, not knowing what a virtue is from which nothing results.

I believe that their learned men blatantly contradict themselves when they declare that marriage is holy, and that celibacy, its opposite, is even holier; quite apart from the fact that when it comes to precepts, and basic dogma, what is good is always the best.

The number of those people who take vows of celibacy is extraordinary; in the past fathers condemned their children to it from the cradle; today the children themselves embrace it at the age of fourteen, which amounts to much the same thing.

The profession of celibacy has destroyed more men than the plague and the bloodiest wars have ever done. In every house of religion you find an everlasting family, into which no one is ever born, and which supports itself at the expense of everyone else; these houses are always open, like so many pits where future races are entombed.

This policy differs greatly from that of the Romans, who made laws imposing penalties on those who refused to obey the marriage laws,* and wished to enjoy a freedom that was so contrary to the public good.

I refer here only to Catholic countries. In the Protestant religion everybody has the right to have children; this religion tolerates neither priests nor dervishes; and if, when Protestantism, which referred everything back to the earliest authorities,* was being established, its founders had not constantly been accused of intemperance, there is no doubt that after making the practice of marriage universal they would also have slackened its chains, and finally removed the barrier that on this matter divides the Nazarene and Muhammad.

However that may be, it is unquestionable that their religion gives Protestants an infinite advantage over Catholics.

I dare to assert that, given the current state of Europe, it is impossible for the Catholic religion to persist there for five hundred years.

Before the power of Spain was brought low, the Catholics were much stronger than the Protestants; little by little the latter have attained an equilibrium, and today the balance is beginning to shift to their side; this superiority will grow greater every day; the Protestants will become richer and more powerful, and the Catholics weaker.

The Protestant countries should be, and in fact are, more heavily populated than the Catholic ones; the first consequence of this is that the tax revenue is larger, because it increases in proportion to the number of people paying taxes.

The second consequence is that the land is better cultivated. Finally, commerce thrives better, because there are more people who want to make money, and because when there is more demand, people seek more resources to supply those needs. When the population is only sufficient to cultivate the land, commerce will inevitably die away; and when there is only sufficient population to keep commerce going, the cultivation of land will deteriorate, that is to say, both will fail simultaneously, because people can never dedicate themselves to one of the two without it being at the expense of the other.

As far as the Catholic countries are concerned, not only has the cultivation of the land been abandoned, but even such work as is undertaken is pernicious; it consists solely in learning five or six words of a dead language; as soon as a man has committed these to memory, he need concern himself no longer with his fortune; in the cloister he finds a life of tranquillity, that in the world outside he would have paid for in sweat and toil.

That is not all; the dervishes own and control almost all the state's wealth; they are a company of misers, who perpetually take and never return; they continually accumulate revenue in order to acquire capital; all this wealth becomes, as it were, paralysed; no longer is there any circulation, or any commerce, or any arts and science, or any manufacturing.

There is no Protestant monarch who does not impose upon his people ten times the amount in taxes that the pope levies upon his subjects; nevertheless the latter live in misery while the former live in opulence; in the one case commerce brings everything back to life, whereas in the other monasticism spreads death over everything.

Paris, the 26th of the Moon of Chahban 1718

LETTER 114

Usbek to the same

There is nothing more to say about Asia and Europe; let us turn to Africa. We can speak only of its coast, because the interior remains unknown.

The coast of Barbary, where the Muslim religion is established, is no longer as populous as it was in Roman times, for reasons I have already discussed. As for the coast of Guinea, its population must have become extraordinarily depleted over the past two hundred years, during which the little kings, or village chiefs, have been selling their subjects to the rulers of Europe for them to transport to their colonies in America.*

What is so strange is that this same America, which every year receives so many new inhabitants, is itself unpopulated, and does not profit from Africa's relentless losses. The slaves, transported into a different climate, die there by the thousand: the work in the mines, where both natives and foreigners are employed, the pestilential gases emanating from the mines, and mercury, which the miners are obliged to use all the time, destroy them beyond hope.

Nothing can be more outrageous than to cause the death of an incalculable number of men in order to remove gold and silver from the depths of the earth; these metals are in themselves completely useless, and are only seen as wealth because they have been chosen as its symbols.

Paris, the last day of the Moon of Chahban 1718

LETTER 115

Usbek to the same

The fertility of a nation sometimes depends on the most trivial circumstances in the world, so that frequently all that is required to bring about a large increase in a population* is a fresh way of looking at the problem.

The Jews, who are constantly wiped out and constantly reborn, have counterbalanced the continual losses and destruction of their race by the single hope all Jewish families cherish, that into their midst may be born a powerful king who will become master of the earth.

The only reason why the ancient kings of Persia had so many thousands of subjects was the dogma of the Religion of the Sages, which held that the acts most pleasing to God in which a man could engage were to make a child, cultivate a field, or plant a tree.

If China fosters such an amazingly large population, it is due simply to a certain way of thinking; for, since children look upon their parents as gods, respect them as such in this life, and honour them after their death with sacrifices in which, they believe, their souls, annihilated in the T'ien,* are reborn into a new life, everybody is induced to increase a family which in this life is so submissive, and in the next so necessary.

Muslim countries, on the other hand, become every day less populated, because of an idea which, holy as it is, does nevertheless have most pernicious consequences when it is entrenched in people's minds. We see ourselves as travellers, who should think only of another homeland; any useful, lasting work, any care given to ensuring the fortunes of our children, any projects that require longer than the span of a brief and fleeting life seem to us foolish extravagances. Easy in our minds about the present, and unconcerned about the future, we do not trouble to repair public buildings, or to clear uncultivated fields, or to cultivate those that are in a condition to benefit from our work; we live in a state of general indifference, and leave everything in the hands of Providence.

It is a spirit of vanity that led Europeans to establish the unjust law of primogeniture, which is so detrimental to procreation in that it focuses the attentions of the father upon a single child and turns his eyes away from all the others; this law forces the father, in order to assure the fortune of one child, to oppose the establishment of several; in short, it does away with the equality of citizens, which constitutes their greatest wealth.

Paris, the 4th of the Moon of Rhamazan 1718

LETTER 116

Usbek to the same

The countries inhabited by savages are sparsely populated, owing to the dislike the inhabitants almost all have for work, and for cultivating the land. This unfortunate aversion is so strong that, when they curse one of their enemies, they wish him nothing less than to be reduced to cultivating a field, believing that the only activities that are noble, and worthy of them, are hunting and fishing.

But, as there are many years when hunting and fishing yield very little, they are devastated by frequent famines; quite apart from the fact that no country is sufficiently rich in game and fish to support a large population, since animals always flee areas which are too densely inhabited.

Besides, the larger native villages, numbering two or three hundred inhabitants, isolated one from another and with interests as divergent as those of two great empires, cannot support themselves; they lack the resources of large countries, whose different regions all cooperate and help one another.

The savages have another custom, which is no less pernicious than the first; I mean the brutal habit among the women of having abortions, so that pregnancy may not render them unappealing to their husbands.

Here, there are terrible laws against this iniquity; they verge on the fanatical. Any unmarried woman who has not reported her pregnancy before a magistrate is punished by death if her offspring dies; modesty, shame, even accidents or miscarriages never excuse her.

Paris, the 9th of the Moon of Rhamazan 1718

LETTER 117
Usbek to the same

The usual effect of colonies is to weaken the countries from which inhabitants are removed, without populating the countries to which they are sent.

Men should remain where they are; some maladies are caused by changing from good air to bad, others are directly caused by the very fact of changing.

When a country is uninhabited, that is evidence of some particular defect in the nature of its climate; when we remove people from a benign climate and transport them to such a country, we are doing the exact opposite of what we intended.

The Romans knew this from experience; they sent all criminals to Sardinia, and they sent Jews there as well; they had to reconcile themselves to the loss of the Jews, a circumstance which the contempt they felt for that unfortunate people made very easy.

The great Shah Abas, intending to deprive the Turks of their ability to maintain large armies on the frontier, transported almost all the Armenians out of their country, and sent more than twenty thousand families into the province of Gilan, where practically all of them very soon perished.

Not one of the attempts to repopulate Constantinople by transporting people there has been successful.

The vast number of blacks already mentioned did not populate America.

Ever since the Jews were wiped out* under Hadrian, Palestine has been uninhabited.

It must be acknowledged, therefore, that the great massacres of peoples are almost irreparable, because once a race is too small, it remains so; and if by chance it re-establishes itself, this can only occur after many centuries have passed.

We must also recognize that if, while the race is in this weak condition, the least of the circumstances already mentioned comes into play, then not only does this people not re-establish itself, it declines further every day, tending towards its own annihilation.

The effects of the expulsion of the Moors* from Spain are still as evident as they were at the very start; the vacuum, far from being filled up, grows greater every day.

Ever since the devastation of America, the Spaniards who replaced its former inhabitants have not managed to repopulate it; on the contrary, owing to a misfortune that would be more appropriately called divine justice, the destroyers are destroying themselves, and decaying further every day.

So monarchs should not think of populating large countries by means of their colonies; I do not say that there are no examples of this policy succeeding, for there are some climates so benign that human reproduction always flourishes in them; witness those islands populated by sick people who had been abandoned there by their ships, and who immediately recovered their health.*

But, if such colonies were successful, instead of increasing the might of the mother country they would simply share it, unless they were very small indeed, as are those that are occupied for the purpose of commerce.

The Carthaginians, like the Spaniards, had discovered America, or at any rate some large islands where they engaged in commerce with extraordinary success; but when they found that the population was decreasing, that wise republic forbade its subjects to transact any business with the islands or to sail there.

I venture to assert that, instead of sending Spaniards to the Indies, all Indians and mestizos should be sent to Spain; the Spanish throne needs the return of all its scattered subjects; if it preserved only half of its great colonies Spain would become the most formidable power in Europe.

You can compare empires to a tree, whose overlong branches draw away all the sap from the trunk, and serve only to give shade.

Nothing should be as effective as the examples of Spain and Portugal in counteracting the frenzy that drives monarchs to make distant conquests.

These two nations, after conquering vast realms with unimaginable speed, were more amazed by their victories than were the vanquished peoples by their defeat; they then considered ways to preserve their conquests, and each chose a different method to accomplish this.

The Spaniards, seeing no hope that the conquered peoples would remain loyal, decided to exterminate them* and send trusted Spaniards in their place; never was a horrible plan more faithfully executed. We saw a people as numerous as the entire population of Europe vanish from the earth at the arrival of those barbarians, who seemed to intend, on discovering the Indies, to reveal also to mankind the most extreme degree of cruelty possible.

By their barbaric act the Spaniards retained their dominion over America. Reflect upon these consequences of conquest, and by them measure its deadly nature. For indeed this horrifying remedy was unique; how could they have ensured the obedience of so many million men and women? How could a civil war waged at such a distance be sustained? What would have happened to the Spanish if they had given those people time to recover from the state of wonderment that beset them at the arrival of these new gods, and their terror of their thunderbolts?

As for the Portuguese, they chose a completely opposite approach, never employing any cruelty, and were, consequently, rapidly driven out of all the countries they had discovered; the Dutch fostered the rebellion of those peoples, and used them to their own advantage.

What ruler would envy the fate of those conquerors? Who would desire conquests at such a price? The Portuguese were promptly driven out, the others turned their conquered lands into deserts, and did the same to their own country.

It is the fate of heroes to ruin themselves conquering countries that they immediately lose, or to subdue nations that they themselves are then forced to destroy: like that maniac who wore himself out buying statues that he cast into the sea, and mirrors that he immediately smashed.

Paris, the 18th of the Moon of Rhamazan 1718

LETTER 118

Usbek to the same

Tolerance in government encourages, to an astonishing degree, the propagation of the species. All republics offer constant proof of this, above all Switzerland and Holland; judged by the nature of their terrain these two countries are the worst in Europe yet they have the largest populations.

Nothing is more attractive to foreigners than liberty and affluence, freedom's invariable companion; the first is sought for its own sake, while deprivation draws people to those countries where affluence reigns.

The human species multiplies in countries where abundance supplies the needs of the children, without in any way infringing upon the resources of the fathers.

The very equality of the citizens, which generally produces equality in their fortunes, brings to each part of the body politic abundance and vitality, disseminating these everywhere.

Such is not the case in countries subject to an arbitrary power; there, the monarch, the courtiers, and a few private individuals own all the wealth, while everyone else endures terrible poverty.

If a man is not securely situated, and feels that children fathered by him will be worse off than he is, he will not marry; or if he does marry, he will be afraid of begetting too many children, who would complete his financial ruin and live more poorly than their father.

I admit that the peasant and the common labourer, once married, will breed without a thought, whether he be rich or poor; the above considerations do not concern him, he always has an indisputable legacy to bequeath to his children, that is, his hoe; and nothing ever prevents him from blindly following the instinct nature gave him.

But of what use to the state are so many children that exist in dire poverty? They almost all perish as fast as they are born; they never do well; weak and debilitated, they die, individually, in a thousand ways, or are killed off in great numbers by the common diseases that are the inevitable consequence of poverty and malnourishment; those that escape attain manhood without developing a man's vigour, and are sickly for the remainder of their days.

Humans are like plants, which never prosper if they are not properly cultivated; among the poor our species loses ground, and sometimes actually degenerates.

France gives us an excellent example of this. In past wars, fear of being enrolled in the militia forced the young men of a family to marry, at too young an age, while they were still very poor. A multitude of children were born of these numerous marriages, children who are now needed in France, but who vanished because of poverty, famine, and disease.

If, in such a beneficent climate, in a kingdom as well organized as France, such things can occur, what must be the situation in other countries?

Paris, the 23rd of the Moon of Rhamazan 1718

LETTER 119

Usbek to the mullah Mehemet Ali, guardian of the three tombs at Qum

Of what use to us are the fasts of the imams, and the hair-shirts of the mullahs? Twice has the hand of God struck down the children of the Law; the sun has been obscured, its rays falling only upon their defeats; their armies rally, but are dispersed like dust.

The Ottoman Empire is shaken by the two worst defeats it has ever known; a Christian mufti can hardly continue to pursue the hostilities; the Grand Vizir of Germany* is the scourge of God, sent to punish the disciples of Omar; he proclaims on all sides the anger of God, who is incensed by their rebellion and their treachery.

Holy spirit of the imams, you weep night and day over the children of the Prophet, whom the detestable Omar has led astray; you are deeply moved by the sight of their tribulations; you desire their conversion and not their downfall; you would wish to see them gathered together under the flag of Ali, through the pitying intercession of the saints, and not scattered over the mountains and the deserts because of their fear of the infidel.

Paris, the 1st of the Moon of Chalval 1718

[SUPPLEMENTARY LETTER 6]

LETTER 120

Rica to ***

With all religions, it's a delicate matter to portray the pleasures in store for those who have lived virtuously. It's easy to frighten sinners with a long list of the punishments awaiting them; but in the case of good people, one does not know what to promise them; it appears that the very essence of pleasure is to be of short duration, and that the imagination has trouble conceiving of any other kind.

I've seen descriptions of paradise such as to dissuade any sensible man from wishing to go there; some depict the happy spirits as eternally playing the flute; others condemn them to the torture of walking all the time; and then there are others who, by showing them up there dreaming of the mistresses they had down here on earth, demonstrate that they do not believe one hundred million years long enough to cure their taste for such amorous concerns.

In this connection, I recall a story I heard from a man who had been in the country of the Mogul: it shows that Indian priests are just as sterile as all the others, when it comes to ideas about the pleasures of paradise.

A woman who had just lost her husband paid a ceremonial visit to the governor of the city, to ask his permission to burn herself; but since this cruel custom has been abolished, as far as possible, in countries subject to Muslim rule, he categorically refused her request.

When she saw that her prayers were futile, she flew into a great rage. 'Just look,' she kept saying, 'just look at how we are thwarted; a poor woman isn't even allowed to burn herself, when she wants to! Have you ever seen the like? My mother, my aunt, my sisters all burned themselves well and good, yet when I go and ask permission from this accursed governor, he gets angry and starts to shout like a madman.'

A young priest happened to be there. 'You infidel,' the governor said to him, 'is it you who has filled this woman's mind with this madness?' 'No,' he replied; 'I have never spoken to her; but if she believes me she will carry out her sacrifice; she will perform an act pleasing to the god Brahma, and consequently will be well rewarded, for in the next world she will be reunited with her husband and with him will begin a new marriage.' 'What!' exclaimed the woman in surprise, 'are you saying that I'll be reunited with my husband? Oh, I'm not going to burn myself; he was jealous, morose, and moreover so old, that unless the god Brahma has changed something about him, he most certainly has no need of me; burn myself, for *him*? Not so much as a fingertip, even if it saved him from the depths of hell. Two elderly priests who quite charmed me, and who were aware of what my life with him was like, were careful not to tell me everything;

but if that's the only gift that Brahma has in store for me, I renounce that blessing. Sir, I shall become a Muslim; and as for you,' she said, turning to the priest, 'you may, if you wish, go and tell my husband that I am very well.'

Paris, the 2nd of the Moon of Chalval 1718

LETTER 121
*Rica to Usbek, in A****

I expect you here tomorrow; however, I'm sending you your letters from Ispahan; mine inform me that the ambassador of the Grand Mogul has been ordered to leave the kingdom. They add that the king's uncle, the prince, who is responsible for his education, has been arrested,* imprisoned in a château under close guard, and stripped of all his honours; I am moved by the fate of this prince, and feel sorry for him.

I confess, Usbek, that I've never seen anyone weep without pitying them; I am filled with benevolence for the unfortunate, as if they alone were men; even the nobles, towards whom, while they are still powerful, my heart is like stone, the moment they fall I find I love them.

And indeed, what is the value to them, while they enjoy power, of useless affection? It is too similar to equality; they much prefer respect, which requires no return; but as soon as they fall from glory they have nothing but our lamentations to remind them of their loss.

For me there is something very candid, and even very great, in the words of a prince* who, about to yield to his enemies, told his weeping courtiers as they gathered round him: 'Your tears make me feel that I am still your king.'

Paris, the 3rd of the Moon of Chalval 1718

LETTER 122
Rica to Ibben, in Smyrna

You have often heard about the celebrated king of Sweden;* he was besieging a fortress in a kingdom called Norway when, while he was inspecting the trench, accompanied only by an engineer, he was shot in the head and killed. His prime minister was promptly arrested, the assemblies were convoked, and the minister was condemned to die on the scaffold.

He was accused of a heinous crime, namely, of having slandered the nation and destroyed the king's trust in his own people; an offence which, in my view, deserves the death penalty a thousand times over.

For after all, if it is an evil act to blacken the humblest of the king's subjects in the royal mind, what is it when the entire nation is blackened, and deprived of the goodwill of the individual appointed by Providence to ensure its happiness?

I would like men to be able to talk to kings the way angels talk to our holy Prophet.

As you know, at the sacred banquets where the Lord of Lords descends from the most sublime throne in the world to converse with his slaves, I have disciplined myself to keep tight control of my restive tongue; I have never been known to let slip a single word that could cause pain to the least of his subjects; when I have had to abandon sobriety, I have never ceased to be a decent and honourable man, and in this trial of our loyalty I have risked my life, and never my virtue.

I do not know how it happens that almost no prince is ever so bad a man that his minister is not an even worse one; if the prince commits an evil deed, it has almost always been suggested to him; so that the ambition of princes is never as dangerous as the baseness of soul of their councillors; but can you understand how a man who has only recently become a minister, and perhaps tomorrow will no longer be a minister, can become, overnight, the enemy of himself, his family, his homeland, and of the endless line of descendants of the man he is about to crush?

A prince has passions; the minister plays upon these passions; they determine how he directs his ministry; to manipulate them is his only goal, nor does he seek any other; the courtiers gratify the prince with their praise, the minister deludes him more dangerously with his counsel, with the schemes he suggests, and the maxims he propounds.

Paris, the 25th of the Moon of Saphar 1719

LETTER 123
Rica to Usbek, in ***

The other day I was crossing the Pont-Neuf with one of my friends
when he saw an acquaintance who, he told me, was a geometer.
Everything about the man confirmed this fact, for he was lost in
thought; my friend had to tug at his sleeve and shake him persistently before our geometer could bring himself down to his level, so
totally was his mind preoccupied with a curve, over which he had
been racking his brains for more than a week; the two men exchanged
a great many polite nothings and some literary gossip; this conversation took them to the door of a coffee house, which we all entered.

I noticed that everyone there greeted our geometer warmly, and
that the waiters treated him with much more deference than they did
the two musketeers who were sitting over in a corner; for his part he
seemed to find the place agreeable, for his face brightened a little, and
he began laughing, as if he lacked even the faintest tinge of geometry.

Meanwhile, his orderly mind was weighing everything that was
said during the conversation; he was like a man who walks round a
garden with his sword, lopping off the head of any flower that is taller
than the others; a martyr to his own precision, he was offended by a
flash of wit in the same way that delicate eyesight is offended by too
bright a light; for him nothing was unimportant, provided it was
true; his conversation, consequently, was peculiar. That very day he
had returned from the country with a man who had seen a superb
château surrounded by magnificent gardens; he himself had only
seen a building sixty feet in length and thirty feet in width, and an
oblong shrubbery of ten acres; he wished that the rules of perspective could have been observed, so that the shrubbery's avenues
would all have appeared to be of the same width, and he could have
provided an infallible method for achieving such a result. He seemed
very pleased with a sundial of a highly unusual design that he had
descried in the shrubbery, and he grew quite heated in talking to a
learned gentleman seated beside me, who unfortunately asked
him whether the sundial marked the hours in the Babylonian style.
A newsmonger mentioned the bombardment of the Château de
Fontarabie,* whereupon our geometer promptly gave us the

properties of the line the bombs had described in the air; delighted with knowing these details, he had no interest in hearing what had been the result of the bombardment. One man was complaining about being ruined the previous winter by a flood: 'What you are saying pleases me greatly,' remarked the geometer, 'I see that I did not err in the observation I made, that at least two inches more of rain fell on the ground than fell last year.'

After a moment he left the coffee house, and we followed him; as he was walking quite fast, and not bothering to look where he was going, he bumped straight into another man; the collision was quite violent; from this encounter they bounced back, each on his own side, in reciprocal proportion to their speed and mass; when they had recovered somewhat from their dazed condition, the other man, clapping his hand to his forehead, said to the geometer: 'I'm delighted that you ran into me, because I've a great piece of news for you; I've just presented my Horace* to the public.' 'How can that be?' asked the geometer: 'the public's been reading him for two thousand years.' 'You don't understand me,' replied the other, 'it's a translation of that ancient author that I've just published; translating has been my occupation for the past twenty years.'

'What, monsieur, you haven't thought any thoughts of your own for twenty years?' exclaimed the geometer. 'You speak for other people, and they think for you?' 'Monsieur,' said the scholar, 'don't you believe that I've rendered the public a valuable service, by giving them easy access to good authors?' 'I don't mean that exactly; I have as much respect as the next man for writers of genius, whom you misrepresent; but you will never match them; for although you never stop translating, nobody will ever translate you.

'Translations are like those copper coins which indeed have the same face value as gold pieces, and are even more widely used by the common people, but they are always light in weight, and base coin.

'You say that you want to give new life to those illustrious dead, and I agree that you do indeed give them a body, but life you do not give them; a spirit to animate them is always lacking.

'Instead, why not devote yourself to seeking all those beautiful truths which simple calculations enable us to discover every day?' After this modest word of advice, they went their separate ways, each of them very much displeased, I believe, with the other.

Paris, the last day of the Moon of Rebiab 2 1719

LETTER 124
Rica to ***

In this letter I shall tell you about a certain people called 'newsmongers', who meet in a magnificent garden* where their idleness always finds occupation. They are completely useless to the state, and for fifty years the effect of their utterances has in no way differed from what an equally long silence would have produced; however, they believe they are of consequence, because they spend their time on magnificent projects and discuss weighty matters.

Their conversations stem from a frivolous, ridiculous curiosity; there is no secret council so arcane that they do not claim to penetrate it; they cannot leave a single stone unturned; they know the number of wives our august sultan possesses and how many babies he makes every year; and although they spend nothing on spies, they know what measures he takes to humiliate the emperor of the Turks and the emperor of the Moguls.

Hardly have they exhausted the present than they charge into the future, racing ahead of Providence and anticipating her by predicting every human act; they take a general under their wing and, after praising him for a thousand follies that he never committed, prepare for him a further thousand that he will also not commit.

They make armies fly like flocks of birds and defensive walls fall like cardboard; they have bridges over all the rivers, and secret routes across all the mountains; immense armouries in scorching deserts; all they lack is common sense.

A man with whom I lodge received this letter from a newsmonger, and as I thought it unusual I kept it; here it is:

'Monsieur:
'I am rarely mistaken in my conjectures about current events; on January first of 1711 I predicted that the emperor Joseph would die* in the course of that year; it is true that as he was in excellent health, I was afraid of being ridiculed if I expressed myself in very unambiguous terms, and I therefore chose to use somewhat enigmatic language; however, people who think clearly understood me perfectly. On the 17th of April of that year he died of smallpox.

As soon as war was declared* between the emperor and the Turks, I went round collecting my colleagues from every corner of the Tuileries, gathered them together near the pond, and predicted that Belgrade would be besieged and taken. I have been fortunate enough to see my prediction accomplished; it is true that towards the middle of the siege I wagered 100 pistoles that the city would fall on the 18th of August, and this did not happen until the following day: can you call something so brilliant losing?

'When I saw that the Spanish fleet was landing in Sardinia, I deemed that it would conquer that island; I said as much, and the event proved me right. Full of this success, I added that this victorious fleet would then disembark at Finale, to conquer the Milanese; as I encountered some disagreement with my idea, pride made me insistent, and I wagered 50 pistoles, and lost them too; for that devil incarnate Alberoni,* despite the promises of the treaty, sent his fleet to Sicily and simultaneously deceived two great strategists, the duke of Savoy and me. All this, monsieur, has confused me to such a degree that I've resolved to go on predicting but never to wager again. In the past betting was quite unknown in the Tuileries; and the late M. le C. d. L.* would rarely permit it; but since a group of pretentious young bloods have attached themselves to us, we no longer know where we are. We barely open our mouths to impart some news than one of these young men proposes a wager against it.

'The other day, just as I was unfolding my manuscript and settling my eyeglasses upon my nose, one of those braggarts, taking advantage of the instant of silence between the first word and the next, said to me: "I wager 100 pistoles that that is not so." Pretending not to hear this piece of foolishness, I continued in a louder voice: "M. le Maréchal de ***, having learnt..." "That's not true," he told me, "your news is always idiotic, none of it makes any sense." I beg you, monsieur, do me the favour of lending me 30 pistoles, for I must confess to you that these wagers have been highly inconvenient to me; I am enclosing copies of two letters I have written to the minister. I am, etc.'

LETTERS FROM A NEWSMONGER TO THE MINISTER

'Monseigneur,

'I am the most zealous subject the king has ever had; it was I that induced one of my friends to carry out my idea of writing a book demonstrating that Louis the Great was greater than all the princes who had deserved the title of Great. I have been pursuing another project for a considerable time now, this project will bring even greater honour upon our nation, if your Magnificence will grant me a "privilège":* it is my intention to prove that, ever since the monarchy began, the French have never been defeated, and that until now, what historians have said about our misfortunes has been utterly fraudulent; I am obliged to set them right on frequent occasions; I dare flatter myself that I am most brilliant as a critic. I am, monseigneur, etc.'

'Monseigneur,
'Now that we have lost M. le C. d. L., we beg you to graciously permit us to elect a president; our meetings are becoming disorderly, and matters of state are not discussed as thoroughly as was formerly the case; our young men show absolutely no consideration for their elders, and have no discipline among themselves; it is truly a council of Rehoboam,* where the young dictate to the old. In vain do we point out that we enjoyed peaceful possession of the Tuileries twenty years before they were born; I do believe that they will finally drive us out of there, and that, forced to abandon the Tuileries, where we have so often evoked the shades of our French heroes, we will be obliged to hold our meetings in the Jardin du roi, or in some more out-of-the-way spot. I am...'

Paris, the 7th of the Moon of Gemmadi 2 1719

LETTER 125

Rhedi to Rica, in Paris

When I first arrived in Europe one of the subjects that most exercised my curiosity was the history and origin of republics. As you know, most Asians have not the faintest concept of this type of government,* and their imagination has not even enabled them to grasp that any form other than despotism can exist upon the earth.

The first governments in the world were monarchies; it was only by chance, and by the passage of time, that republics were born.

After Greece was engulfed by a flood it was repopulated by new inhabitants; almost all these immigrants came from Egypt or from the nearest Asian countries, which were governed by kings, and consequently the people from there were governed in the same way. But the tyranny of those princes becoming too burdensome, the people shook off their yoke, and there then arose, out of the debris of many monarchies, those republics that brought such glory to Greece, the only civilized country among so many barbarians.

Love of liberty and abhorrence of kings kept Greece independent for centuries, and spread republican government far and wide. The cities of Greece found allies in Asia Minor; they sent people there to form colonies that were as free as themselves, and which provided protection against the incursions of the kings of Persia. That is not all: Greece populated Italy, Italy populated Spain, and possibly Gaul. We know that the great Hesperis,* so celebrated by classical writers, was initially Greece, which its neighbours saw as a haven of felicity; however, the Greeks themselves, not finding this happy land on their own soil, sought it in Italy; those in Italy sought it in Spain, while those in Spain turned to Baetica, or Portugal: so that all these regions bore this name, for classical writers. Those Greek colonists brought with them a spirit of freedom nurtured in that pleasant land. Consequently, in those distant times monarchies were rare in Italy, Spain, and Gaul. As we shall soon see, the peoples of the north, and of Germany, were no less free, and if we find traces of monarchy there it is because they had chosen as king a head of the army or of a republic.

This was all taking place in Europe, for Asia and Africa have always been oppressed by despotism; the only exceptions are the cities in Asia Minor I mentioned earlier, and the republic of Carthage in Africa.

The world was divided between two powerful republics: that of Rome, and that of Carthage; nothing is so well known as the beginning of the Roman republic, and nothing so lost in obscurity as the origin of the Carthaginian one. Nothing whatever is known about the succession of African princes after Dido, or how they lost their power. The prodigious expansion of the Roman republic would have been of great benefit to the world, if it had not been for that unjust inequality between the Roman citizens and the vanquished peoples, if the governors of the provinces had been granted less authority, if the hallowed laws passed to prevent their tyranny had been observed, and if the governors had not used the very moneys that they had wrongfully amassed to subvert those laws.

It seems as if liberty is made for the spirit of the peoples of Europe, and servitude for that of the peoples of Asia. In vain did the Romans offer the Cappadocians this precious treasure: the cowardly nation refused it, and welcomed servitude with the same alacrity that other peoples show in welcoming freedom.

Caesar crushed the Roman republic and subjected it to arbitrary power.

For many long years Europe suffered under a brutal military government, and Roman clemency changed into cruel oppression.

Meanwhile, countless unknown peoples emerged from the north, and spread like raging rivers across the Roman provinces; finding it just as easy to make conquests as to practise their piracy, they divided up those lands and turned them into kingdoms. These were free peoples, and so strictly did they limit the authority of their kings that the latter were in fact no more than leaders or generals. These kingdoms, therefore, although created by force, never felt the yoke of the conqueror. When Asian peoples like the Turks and the Tartars made conquests, they, being themselves subject to the will of one man, thought only of giving him new subjects, and of establishing his inexorable authority by military force; but when northern people, who in their own country were free, took possession of a Roman province they did not give their leaders great power. Some of these peoples, such as the Vandals in Africa and the Goths in Spain, would even depose their king the moment he no longer suited them; and in other cases the authority of the monarch would be limited in a thousand different ways: his power would be shared among a large number of lords, whose agreement was required before a war could be undertaken; war booty was divided between leaders and soldiers; no taxes to benefit the king were permitted, and all laws were passed in national assemblies. Such were the fundamental principles of all those states which were created from the ruins of the Roman Empire.

Venice, the 20th of the Moon of Rhegeb 1719

LETTER 126

Rica to ***

About five or six months ago, in a coffee house, I noticed a rather well-dressed gentleman to whom people were listening attentively; he was saying how much he enjoyed living in Paris, and lamenting the fact that his finances obliged him to live in the country. 'I have an income of fifteen thousand livres tied up in my land; I'd consider myself better off if I had a quarter of that in cash, and in readily negotiable bills. It's useless to press my farmers, and burden them with legal costs, all I do is make their insolvency worse; I've never been able to lay my hands on a thousand francs all at once; if I owed someone ten thousand francs, my lands would be seized and I'd be in the poorhouse.'

I left without having paid much attention to this speech; but yesterday, happening to be in the area again, I entered the same establishment and saw there a solemn-looking man, with a long, pale face, who sat sunk in gloomy meditation amid a group of five or six chatterers; suddenly he began to speak: 'Yes, gentlemen,' he said, raising his voice, 'I'm ruined;* I've no longer enough to live on: at home, at the moment, I have two hundred thousand *livres* in banknotes, and a hundred thousand silver coins; I'm in a terrible fix, I thought I was rich, and here I am in the poorhouse; if only I owned a small estate where I could retire, I'd be sure of having something to live on, but I don't possess even the tiniest patch of land.'

I chanced to turn my head in another direction, and saw a different man; this one was grimacing like someone who had lost his wits. 'In future whom can we trust?' he exclaimed. 'There's a man I thought was such a good friend of mine that I lent him money, and he's paid me back! What a dreadful betrayal! No matter what he does now, I'll always think of him as dishonoured.'

Not far away sat a very badly dressed man who, raising his eyes to the heavens, was saying: 'May God bless the plans of our ministers, may I live to see the shares at two thousand, and all the footmen in Paris richer than their masters.' I was sufficiently inquisitive to ask his name. 'He's extremely poor,' I was told; 'moreover his occupation's a poor one, he's a genealogist; he's hoping that his expertise will turn a profit if these new fortunes continue, and that all these upstarts will require his services to rewrite their names, polish up their ancestors, and decorate their carriages; he imagines he's going to create as many gentlefolk as he chooses, and he's quivering with pleasure at seeing his clientele multiply.'

Lastly, I noticed a white-faced, dried-up old man walk in, whom I recognized as a journalist before he had taken his seat; he wasn't one of those who exude a triumphant confidence in the face of all reversals, and invariably predict victories and military tributes; he was, on the contrary, one of those apprehensive people who invariably have only bad news to impart. 'Things are going very badly over towards Spain,' he announced; 'we have no cavalry on the border, and it's to be feared that Prince Pio,* who heads a large body of men, will force all of Languedoc to pay a levy.' Sitting across from me was a rather unkempt philosopher, who seemed to feel sorry for the journalist, and kept shrugging his shoulders as the other kept raising his voice more and more; I went up to him and he whispered to me: 'As you see, that idiot's been regaling us for an hour with his alarm over Languedoc; well, yesterday evening I noticed a spot on the sun which, should it grow larger, might precipitate all of nature into a state of torpor, and I haven't said a single word.'

Paris, the 17th of the Moon of Rhamazan 1719

LETTER 127

Rica to ***

The other day, I went to visit a large library in a convent of dervishes;* these dervishes are, in a sense, curators of the collection, but they must allow the public access to it at certain hours.

Upon entering, I saw a grave-looking man walking about; a vast quantity of volumes surrounded him on every side. Approaching, I begged him to tell me about some particular books, which looked to be better bound than others. 'Monsieur,' he replied, 'here I'm in a foreign country; I know no one; many people ask me similar questions, but you can easily see that I'm not going to read all these books just to satisfy them; however, I have my librarian who will tell you what you want to know, for he's busy night and day deciphering everything you see about you; he's a man who is completely useless, and a great burden to us, because he does no work for the convent; but I hear the refectory bell summoning us; those who, like myself, are heads of a community, must be the first to discharge all its duties.' With these words the monk pushed me out of the library, closed the door, and vanished from my sight like a bird on the wing.

Paris, the 21st of the Moon of Rhamazan 1719

LETTER 128

Rica to the same

The following day I returned to that library, where I met a man who was very different from the one I'd seen the first time; his manner was straightforward, his expression unworldly, and his greeting most affable. As soon as I had explained my interest, he made a point of satisfying my curiosity, and even, since I was a foreigner, of instructing me.

'Father,' I asked him, 'what are those huge volumes that fill all that side of the library?' 'Those are commentaries on the scriptures,' he replied. 'There are a great many of them,' I remarked; 'in the past the scriptures must have been very obscure and now they must be quite clear; do any doubts still remain? Can there remain any points still in doubt?' 'Can any still remain, Lord in heaven, can any still remain!' he replied. 'There are nearly as many points in doubt as there are lines.' 'There are? So what did all those authors do?' I asked. 'Those authors', he retorted, 'did not seek in the scriptures what we ought to believe, but what they themselves believe; they did not approach the scriptures as a work containing dogmas that they ought to accept, but as a work that could provide authority for their own ideas; that is why they have corrupted every meaning and twisted every phrase; it's a place which men of every sect swoop down upon and plunder, it's a battlefield where confrontation between enemy nations leads to countless conflicts, and where there are assaults and skirmishes of a thousand kinds.

'Just beside them you have books on asceticism and piety, and after them the much more useful books on ethics; then works on theology, which are doubly unintelligible, first in the matter they treat, and again in their manner of treatment. Next comes the work of the mystics, that is, of devout writers with susceptible hearts.' 'Just a moment, Father,' I cried, 'don't go so fast; tell me about these mystics.' 'Monsieur,' he said, 'religious zeal excites a susceptible heart, and makes it send material particles* to the brain; these particles are then also stimulated, and beget states of ecstasy and trance. This condition is the delirium of piety; it often intensifies, or rather degenerates, into quietism; as you know, "quietist" is another name for a man who is mad, pious, and a freethinker.

'Here we find the casuists, who shine the bright light of day upon the secrets of the night, and create in their imaginations every monster that the demon of love can engender, assembling and comparing them, and making them the eternal focus of their thoughts; they are lucky if their heart remains untouched, and does not itself become the accomplice of so many aberrations, all so naively described and so clearly depicted.

'You can see, monsieur, that I think unconstrainedly, and tell you all my thoughts; I am by nature artless, and feel all the freer because you are a foreigner, and are eager to learn about things, and to learn about them as they really are; if I wished, I'd be speaking of all this with nothing but admiration; I'd be constantly telling you: "this is sublime, this is worthy of respect, there's something marvellous here;" one of two things would follow: either I would deceive you, or I would lose your good opinion of me.'

We said no more; a matter that arose requiring the dervish's attention interrupted our conversation until the following day.

Paris, the 23rd of the Moon of Rhamazan 1719

LETTER 129

Rica to the same

I returned at the appointed hour, and my man led me to the exact spot where we had parted. 'Here,' he told me, 'are the grammarians, the glossarists, and the exegetes.' 'Father,' I said, 'all those people can dispense with common sense, can't they?' 'Yes, they can,' he replied; 'and it doesn't even show; their works are none the worse for that, which is very convenient for them.' 'True,' I said, 'and I know plenty of philosophers who would do well to apply themselves to studies of that kind.'

'Now,' he went on, 'we come to the orators, who possess the gift of persuasion without recourse to rational argument; and then the geometers, who force a man to be persuaded in spite of himself, and convince him by tyrannical means.

'Here are the works on metaphysics, which deal with subjects of such great import, and where we constantly encounter infinity; books on physics, which find nothing more marvellous in the workings of this vast universe than exists in the simplest machine used by our craftsmen.

'Books on medicine: those monuments to the frailty of nature and to the power of science which, when they discuss even the most trivial maladies, so vividly portray the immediacy of death that we tremble with fear, but which fill us with complete confidence when they describe the properties of remedies, as if we had become immortal.

'Next to them are shelved the books on anatomy, which are far less concerned with describing the parts of the human body than they are with the outlandish names given to those parts: names which neither cure the patient of his disease nor the physician of his ignorance.

'Here you have chemistry, which by turn inhabits the poorhouse and the madhouse, finding itself equally at home in both.

'Next, books of science, or rather books of occult ignorance; for such are books containing some sort of devilry: most people call them abominable, but I see them as pitiful. The same is also true of works on astrological prediction.' 'What did you say, Father? Works on astrological prediction?' I retorted angrily. 'They are what we value most in Persia; they regulate all our actions in life, and determine all our ventures; strictly speaking, astrologers direct our lives; they do more, they are involved in the state government.' 'If that be so,' he told me, 'you live under a much harsher yoke than that of reason, one which surely deserves to be called the strangest of all tyrannies; I greatly pity a family, and even more a nation, that allows itself to be so powerfully dominated by the planets.' 'We use astrology,' I replied, 'the way you use algebra;* every nation has its own branch of knowledge, according to which it formulates its policies; all the astrologers taken together have never made such an idiotic miscalculation as was made here by just a single one of your algebraists. Do you believe that the chance conjunction of the stars cannot be fully as reliable a guide as the fine arguments of your system maker? If we kept score of the opinions on this matter in France and in Persia, the result would be a resounding triumph for astrology, and you'd see the mathematicians thoroughly humiliated: what crushing corollary might they not see drawn against them?'

Our argument was interrupted, and we had to part.

Paris, the 26th of the Moon of Rhamazan 1719

LETTER 130

Rica to the same

For our next interview my learned friend took me into a separate
room. 'We have books on modern history here,' he said; 'beginning
with works on the church and the popes; I read these for edification,
but they often have the opposite effect on me.

'Over there are the historians who describe the decadence of the
redoubtable Roman Empire, formed from the debris of so many
monarchies, and upon whose demise so many new monarchies
sprang up. A numberless horde of barbarians, as alien as the countries they inhabited, suddenly spread across the land like flood-
water, ravaging and dismembering the empire, and founding all
those kingdoms that you see in the Europe of today. Those people
were not, strictly speaking, barbarians, since they were free, but that
is what they became when, submitting for the most part to absolute
power, they lost that sweet freedom which accords so well with
reason, with humanity, and with nature.

'Here you see the historians of Germany, now but a shadow of her
first empire, but, I believe, the only power in the world which has
not been weakened by partition; the only one, I also believe, to grow
stronger in proportion to her losses; slow to profit from her
triumphs, she has become unconquerable by virtue of her defeats.

'Here are the historians of France; first we witness the development of the power of the crown; we see it expire twice, only to be
reborn twice, and then languish for several centuries; then, imperceptibly gathering strength from every side, attain its final period:
like those rivers that lose their waters as they course along, or that
disappear underground then reappear, swollen by the streams that
have emptied into them, and rapidly sweep away everything lying in
their path.

'In these next works we see the Spanish nation emerge from a
mountainous region; the Muhammadan princes subjugated as
imperceptibly as they had rapidly prevailed; a great many kingdoms
united in a vast monarchy which became almost unique until, overwhelmed by its spurious opulence, it lost its strength and even its
reputation, preserving only its pride in its original power.

'These are the historians of England, who portray liberty repeat-edly surviving the flames of discord and sedition; every monarch precariously occupying an invulnerable throne; an impatient nation, wise even in her anger, that, queen of the seas (something unheard of until then), combines commerce with empire.

'Close by are histories of that other queen of the seas, the Republic of Holland, so respected in Europe and so formidable in Asia, where her merchants find that so many kings bow down before them.

'The historians of Italy show you a nation that once ruled the world, and today is the slave of every other nation; her princes are divided and weak, without any attribute of sovereignty save futile policies.

'Here we find the histories of republics: that of Switzerland, symbol of freedom; of Venice, whose sole resource is her economy; and of Genoa, glorious only in her fortifications.

'And here are the histories of the northern countries, among them Poland, which makes such poor use of her liberty and the right she enjoys of electing her kings, that she seems to be trying to console the peoples of neighbouring states, which have lost both of these privileges.'

We then parted until the following day.

Paris, the 2nd of the Moon of Chalval 1719

LETTER 131

Rica to the same

The next day he showed me into a different room. 'These are the poets,' he told me, 'that is to say, those writers whose occupation it is to put shackles on common sense, and to smother reason* under embellishments, just as, in the past, women were buried in their finery and ornaments; you're familiar with poets, they aren't uncom-mon in the Orient, where the fiercer rays of the sun seem to inflame the imagination itself.

'Here we have epic poetry. And what are epic poems? To tell you the truth, I've no idea,' he declared; 'the experts say that only two epic poems* have ever been written, and that all others which claim to be epics are no such thing; there again, I don't know; furthermore, they say that it's not possible for new ones to be composed, which is even more surprising.

'These are the dramatic poets, who, in my opinion, are poets in the highest sense of the word, and masters of the passions; there are two kinds: comic poets, who move us very gently, and tragic poets, who disquiet us and arouse our emotions most powerfully.

'Now the lyric poets, whom I despise as much as I prize dramatic poets; they turn their art into melodious fantasies.

'Next come the writers of idylls and eclogues, who please even courtiers with the idea they give them of a kind of peace that the court lacks, and which the poets depict through the life of shepherds.

'Of all the writers we've seen these are the most dangerous: writers who hone the point of their epigrams, those tiny, sharp arrows that inflict deep wounds which no remedies can heal.

'Now we come to novels; their authors, who are poets of a sort, offend against both the language of the mind and the language of the heart; they spend their days seeking nature, and invariably missing it; they create heroes that are as out of place in the natural world as winged dragons would be, or hippocentaurs.'

'I've seen some of your novels,' I told him, 'and if you were to see ours, you would be even more shocked; they are just as unnatural, and furthermore, they are severely hampered by our customs; ten years of passion are required before a lover can see even the face of his mistress; nevertheless, authors are obliged to make their readers endure these boring preliminaries; it is impossible to vary the incidents, and consequently writers turn to a device worse than the evil it's supposed to cure: I mean the use of the marvellous; I'm sure you wouldn't approve of having a magician produce an army from beneath the ground, or of a solitary hero annihilating a force of a hundred thousand men. However, such are our novels; their uninspiring, repetitive adventures weary us, and their preposterous marvels disgust us.'

Paris, the 6th of the Moon of Chalval 1719

LETTER 132

Rica to Ibben, in Smyrna

Here, ministers succeed and annihilate one another like the seasons; in the space of three years I've seen the financial system change four times. Today, in Persia and in Turkey, the method of levying taxes is no different from what it was under the founders of those monarchies; quite the opposite obtains in France. It's true that we don't try to be as clever about it as do westerners; we believe that there is no more difference between administering the revenues of the prince and administering those of a private individual, than exists between counting 100,000 tomans and 100. But here a great deal more finesse and mystery is involved. It is necessary that great geniuses work night and day, and constantly and painfully bring forth fresh projects; that they listen to an infinite number of people who work for them without being asked, and that they withdraw from the world and hide themselves away in a secluded back room which the great cannot penetrate and the humble regard as sacred; that their minds be constantly filled with important secrets, miraculous schemes, and new systems; and that, sunk in cogitation, they be deprived not only of the use of speech, but even, sometimes, of politeness.

As soon as the late king had breathed his last, plans were afoot to form a new administration. People sensed that things were not right, but they could not see how to improve them. The limitless authority enjoyed by the previous ministers had not been popular, and the decision was taken to divide it up; for this purpose six or seven councils were created, and the resulting ministry may well be the most rational of all those that have governed France; it was of short duration, like the good that came of it.

France, at the death of the late king, was a body afflicted by a thousand ills; N***,* knife in hand, excised the useless flesh and applied remedies to the wounds. But there yet remained a deep-seated infection to cure. A foreigner came upon the scene who attempted this cure; after using a great many harsh remedies, he believed he had restored the patient to plump good health, but all he had done was to make him bloated.

Everyone who was rich six months ago now lives in poverty, and everyone who used to go hungry now overflows with riches. Never have those two extremes touched one another so closely. The foreigner has turned the state inside out the way an old-clothes dealer turns a coat; he has put on top what used to be underneath, turning what used to be underneath the wrong way up. How many unforeseen fortunes, incredible even to those who have made them! God himself does not snatch men faster out of the abyss.

How many footmen are being waited on by their friends, and perhaps, tomorrow, by their masters!

The consequences of all this are frequently bizarre. Footmen who made their fortune in the last reign are today boasting of their birth; they treat those who have just abandoned their livery in a certain street with all the scorn they themselves experienced six months ago; they shout as loudly as they can: 'the upper classes are ruined; our country is in dreadful disorder! What confusion in the ranks! We're always seeing nobodies making their fortunes!' I promise you: the latter will most certainly take their revenge upon those who follow after them, and thirty years from now *those* 'gentlemen' will be loudly giving voice to their complaints.

Paris, the 1st of the Moon of Zilcadé 1720

LETTER 133

Rica to the same

Here is a wonderful example of marital love, not only in a woman, but in a queen. The queen of Sweden* desired above all else to associate the prince, her husband, with the crown; in order to resolve all difficulties, she sent a declaration to the Estates General, announcing that she would abdicate the Regency if her husband were elected.

It is some sixty years since another queen, Christina, abdicated the throne in order to devote herself entirely to philosophy. I do not know which of these two examples should fill us with greater admiration.

Although on the whole I believe that each of us should stand fast in the position assigned us by nature, and although I cannot praise the weakness of those who, considering their post unworthy of their high rank, leave it, in a sense, by desertion, I am nevertheless impressed by the nobility of soul of these two princesses, and by seeing the mind of the one, and the heart of the other, superior to their destiny. Christina dreamt of knowing, at a time when others dreamt only of possessing, and the other princess desires possession of the crown only so that she can relinquish all her good fortune into the hands of her august husband.

Paris, the 27th of the Moon of Maharram 1719

LETTER 134

Rica to Usbek, at ***

The Paris Parlement has been relegated* to a small town called Pontoise. The Cabinet has dispatched, for registration or approval by the Parlement, a declaration that disgraces it, and this has been done in a manner that disgraces the Cabinet.

Other parlements of France are being threatened with similar treatment.

These bodies are invariably hated; they never approach the throne unless it is to impart painful truths; and, while a crowd of courtiers are repeatedly assuring the king that his people are content under his rule, they appear and give the lie to flattery, bearing the sighs and tears entrusted to them to the foot of the throne.

Truth, my dear Usbek, is a heavy burden when it must be conveyed to the knowledge of princes; the latter should consider carefully that those bearing this burden are obliged to do so, and that they would never bring themselves to take steps so unfortunate and distressing to themselves, were they not forced to do so by their duty, their respect, and even by their love.

Paris, the 21st of the Moon of Gemmadi 1 1720

LETTER 135

Rica to Usbek, in ***

I'll come to see you at the weekend: how pleasantly the time will pass when we're together!

A little while ago I was presented to a lady of the court, who wished to take a look at my foreign face. I thought her beautiful, worthy of the eyes of our monarch, and of a high position in the sacred place where his heart dwells.

She asked me a thousand questions about the customs of Persian men and the way of life of Persian women; it seemed to me that the life of the seraglio was not to her liking, and that she found distasteful the thought of one man shared between ten or twelve women.

She could not see the happiness of the one without envy, or the situation of the others without pity. As she loves reading, especially poetry and novels, she wanted me to speak to her about our literature; what I told her increased her curiosity, and she begged me to have translations made for her, of some parts of the works I had brought with me. I did so, and a few days later sent her a Persian story; you might perhaps enjoy reading it in this new guise.

In the days of the sheik Ali-Khan,* there lived in Persia a woman named Zulema; she knew the entire holy Qur'an by heart, and no dervish existed who understood the traditions of the holy prophets better than she; the scholars of Arabia had never made any pronouncements so arcane that she did not fully comprehend their meaning; and to this vast learning she united so playful a turn of mind, that it was almost impossible to guess whether she intended to entertain or to instruct those to whom she spoke.

One day, while she was sitting with her companions in a room in the seraglio, one of these asked her for her thoughts on the next life, and whether she believed in that ancient tradition of our learned doctors, which states that Paradise is only for men.

'That's the general belief,' she told them; 'there is nothing that has not been done to degrade our sex; there is even a people you can find spread throughout Persia which claims, on the authority of its sacred writings, that we have no soul.

'These pernicious opinions have no basis other than the pride of men, who wish to extend their superiority beyond their life, and do not reflect that in the bright light of day all creatures will seem as naught to God, without any advantages or rights to set one above another, except for those that virtue may have given them.

'God will not limit himself in his rewards; and just as those men who have lived virtuously, and have not abused the power they have over us here on earth, will inhabit a Paradise so full of heavenly, exquisite beauties, that if a mortal man had seen them he would instantly kill himself in his impatience to enjoy them; so too will virtuous women inhabit a place of pure delight, where they will be intoxicated by flowing streams of sensual pleasures, with sublime men who will submit to them; the women will each have her own seraglio* where these men will be confined, with eunuchs to guard them even more faithful than are our own.

'I have read a work in Arabic,' she added, 'about a man called Ibrahim who was intolerably jealous; he had twelve exceedingly beautiful wives whom he treated very harshly; he no longer trusted his eunuchs, or the walls of his seraglio; he kept his wives locked in their rooms almost all the time, so that they could neither see nor speak to one another, for he was even jealous of an innocent friendship; all his actions reflected his innate brutality, for he never spoke a kind word or made the smallest sign that did not in some fashion add to the rigours of their servitude.

'One day, when he had assembled all his wives in a room in his seraglio, one, bolder than the others, reproached him for his cruel disposition. "When someone is so determined to find ways to make himself feared," she told him, "he will invariably first find ways to make himself hated; we are so unhappy that we cannot help longing for a change; in my position another would hope for your death, but I desire only my own; having no hope of being separated from you by any other means, I shall nevertheless be very happy to be free of you." These words, which should have moved him, filled him with a terrible rage; he drew his dagger, and plunged it into her breast. "My dear companions," she said, her voice sinking, "if Heaven takes pity on my virtue, you will be avenged;" and with these words she departed this ill-fated life to enter into the abode of bliss, where women who have lived virtuously find a happiness that is eternally renewed.

'First she saw a sunlit meadow, where the green of the grass was set off by flowers of the brightest hues, with a stream whose waters, purer than crystal, seemed to meander on for ever; then she found herself in charming woodlands, where the silence was broken only by the sweet song of the birds; next she came to splendid gardens, decorated by nature with her simplicity and all her magnificence; finally she reached a superb palace that had been prepared for her, and was filled with sublime men intended for her pleasure.

'Two of these men immediately started to undress her; others conducted her to the bath, perfuming her with the most delicious essences; then she was given garments that were infinitely more sumptuous than her own; after which she was led into a spacious room where she found a fire of aromatic wood burning, and a table spread with the most exquisite dishes. Everything seemed designed to fill her senses with rapture; she listened to music so caressing as to seem divine, while her eyes delighted in the dancing of those godlike men, whose sole business was to please her. But the purpose of so many pleasures was purely to lead her gradually to greater pleasures. She was taken to her bedroom, and after being undressed once more she was carried to a superb bed where two entrancingly handsome men received her in their arms. It was then that she knew true ecstasy, and that her rapture exceeded even her desires. "I am so utterly lost in bliss," she told them, "that I would think I was dying, if I was not certain of my immortality. This is too much; leave me; I am faint with the frenzy of pleasure. Yes, now you're calming me a little, I can breathe now, I feel better. Why have the torches been removed? Why may I not gaze upon your celestial beauty? Why cannot I see... But why see? Ah, you're taking me back to my former raptures. Oh God, how kindly these shadows are! What, am I then immortal, and immortal with you? Am I... No, have mercy, I beg you; I can clearly see that *you* will never ask for it."

'After repeated requests she was obeyed, but only when she spoke with real earnestness; she lay languidly resting, then fell asleep in their arms. A few minutes of sleep cured her fatigue; she felt two kisses that quickly aroused her, and made her open her eyes. "I'm uneasy," she said; "I'm afraid that you no longer love me;" this was a doubt which she could not long endure, but she received from her companions all the clarification she could desire. "I am now sure," she exclaimed, "forgive me, please forgive me, I am sure of your love; you do not speak to me, but you have a better way of proving it than by anything you might say to me. Yes, yes, I admit it, no one has ever loved so well. What! You're fighting for the honour of convincing me? Ah, if you fight, if you unite ambition to the pleasure of defeating me, I am lost; you will both be victorious, and I alone vanquished; but I shall ensure that victory costs you dearly."

'All this was interrupted only by the approach of daylight; her loyal and amiable servants entered her room and made the two young lovers rise; two elderly men returned them to the place where they were kept for her entertainment. Then she rose from her bed, and first appeared to her adoring court in all the simple charms of informality; later, she came wearing the most sumptuous ornaments. That night had made her more beautiful; it had given life to her complexion, and eloquence to her charms. The entire day was filled with dancing, concerts, feasts, games, and excursions; and it was observed that from time to time Anaïs would slip away and fly off to meet her two young heroes; after joining them for a few precious moments she would return to the gathering she had left, her expression always more serene. Eventually, towards evening, she disappeared completely; she went and shut herself into the seraglio, where she wished, she said, to make the acquaintance of her immortal captives, who were destined to live with her for ever. To this end she went all through the quarters, visiting the most remote and the most delightful chambers of the seraglio, where she counted fifty slaves, all miraculously beautiful; the whole night long she wandered from room to room, in each being paid homage that always varied, and was always the same.

'That is how the immortal Anaïs spent her life, now in splendid public festivities, now in solitary pleasures; admired by a brilliant gathering, or worshipped by an infatuated lover; often, she would leave her enchanted palace to visit a rustic grotto; as she walked, flowers seemed to spring up beneath her feet and diverting amusements press about her.

'She had spent more than a week in this joyful place, in a continual state of rapture, without even once pausing for reflection; she had enjoyed her happiness without knowing it, and without having passed a single one of those quiet moments when the soul takes stock of itself, as it were, and listens to its own voice, in the silence of the passions.

'The blessed know such intense pleasures that they can rarely enjoy this freedom of spirit; that is why, unwaveringly absorbed by the present moment, they lose all memory of the past, and no longer feel any interest in things which in their other life they knew or loved.

'But Anaïs, whose mind was truly philosophical, had spent almost her entire life in meditation, and her thoughts had evolved to a much higher level than would normally be expected of a woman left to her own devices. The rigid isolation that her husband had imposed upon her had given her this single advantage; it was this strength of mind which made her disdain the fear that overpowered her companions, and disdain death, which would mark the end of her sufferings and the beginning of her felicity.

'Thus, little by little, she moved beyond the delirium of pleasure and shut herself away, alone, in a room in the palace. She let her thoughts dwell most pleasantly on her past existence and on her present happiness; she could not stop herself pitying her companions in their misfortunes; people are deeply affected by suffering in which they themselves have shared. Anaïs was not content with simply being compassionate; full of tenderness for those unfortunate women, she felt impelled to help them.

'She commanded one of the young men who attended her to assume the appearance of her husband, to go to the seraglio, assert his rights as its master, evict the husband, and remain there in his place until she recalled him.

'She was instantly obeyed; he plunged through the heavens and arrived at the door of the seraglio, whose master was out. He knocks; the doors open before him; the eunuchs prostrate themselves at his feet; he flies to the rooms where Ibrahim's wives are imprisoned; he had already, in passing invisibly by the jealous husband, removed the keys from his pocket. He enters and first surprises the wives by his gentle, amiable manner, and soon afterwards surprises them even more with his eager attentions and the rapidity of his advances; they all had reason to feel astonished, and would have supposed him a dream had he been less real.

'While these new scenes are being played out in the seraglio, Ibrahim knocks, declares who he is, rages and shouts; after much difficulty he enters and throws the eunuchs into terrible confusion; he strides rapidly in but recoils, thunderstruck, when he sees the false Ibrahim, his exact double, enjoying all the freedoms of the master. He shouts for help; he wants the eunuchs to help him kill this imposter, but he is not obeyed; his sole recourse—hardly a powerful one—is to turn to his wives for support. In the space of one hour the false Ibrahim has won over all his judges; the jealous husband is rejected and shamefully cast out of the seraglio; he would have been killed a thousand times over had not his rival ordered that his life be spared. Finally the false Ibrahim is left master of the field of battle, and, proving himself ever more worthy of this choice, distinguished himself by miraculous feats never witnessed hitherto. "You're not at all like Ibrahim," said his wives. "Say rather that that imposter is not at all like me," replied the triumphant Ibrahim; "what must I do to be your husband, if what I'm doing now is not enough?"

'"Oh, we haven't the least desire to doubt that you're our husband," said his wives. "If you are not Ibrahim, it is enough for us that you so well deserve to be him; in the course of a single day you've proved yourself to be more Ibrahim than he himself did in the course of ten years." "So you promise", he went on, "that you'll declare yourselves for me, against that imposter?" "Don't doubt it for a moment," they replied with one voice, "we swear eternal loyalty to you; we've been abused too long, the traitor had no notion of our virtue, he only knew about his own weakness; now we can see clearly that men are not like him; they must surely be like you; ah, if only you knew how you've made us detest him!" "Oh, I shall frequently give you fresh cause to detest him," replied the false Ibrahim; "you do not yet know the full extent of the wrong he did you." "We judge his injustice by the dimensions of our revenge," they replied. "Yes, you're right," said the godlike lover; "I made the reparation fit the crime; I'm delighted that you are satisfied by my style of punishment." "But," objected the women, "if this imposter returns, what shall we do?" "I think it would be hard for him to deceive you," he replied, "the place I occupy is not one that can be held by subterfuge, and besides, I shall send him so far away, that you'll never again hear word of him; meanwhile I will be responsible for making you happy; I won't be jealous, I'll know how to be sure of you without restricting you; I have a sufficiently high opinion of myself to believe you will remain faithful to me; if not with me, then with whom would you be virtuous?" This conversation continued for some time between him and the wives, who, more impressed by the differences than by the similarities between the two Ibrahims, never even considered enquiring closely into all these many marvels. Eventually, the desperate husband returned once more to trouble them; he found his household full of joy, and his wives even more incredulous than before. This situation was unbearable to a jealous man, and he departed in a fury; a moment later the false Ibrahim followed him, snatched him up, and carried him through the skies to a place four hundred leagues away, where he left him.

'Dear God! What misery reigned among those wives during the absence of their dearest Ibrahim! Their eunuchs had already reverted to their natural severity; the entire household was in tears; at times the women supposed that everything that had happened to them had been nothing but a dream; they would stare at one another and recall the most trivial details of those strange adventures. Finally Ibrahim returned, more amiable than ever; they gathered that his journey had not been arduous; the new master's behaviour contrasted so greatly with his predecessor's that it surprised all the neighbours. He dismissed all the eunuchs; he opened his house to everybody; he did not even want his wives to veil their faces; it was indeed strange to see them on feast-days, mingling with the male guests and enjoying the same freedom as they did. Ibrahim believed, with good reason, that the customs of the country were not made for citizens like himself. Meanwhile, he did not refuse himself any expense, he disbursed with great liberality the fortune of the jealous Ibrahim, who, returning after three years from the distant country to which he had been transported, found only his wives, and thirty-six children.'

Paris, the 26th of the Moon of Gemmadi 1 1720

LETTER 136

*Rica to Usbek, in ****

Here is a letter I received yesterday from a learned scholar; I believe you will find it curious:

'Monsieur,
'About six months ago I came into an inheritance from a very rich uncle, who left me 500,000 or 600,000 livres, and a superbly furnished house. It is a pleasure to own wealth when one knows how to make good use of it. I have no ambition, nor any taste for pleasures; I spend almost all my time shut away in a small study, where I lead the life of a scholar; in that study you will find a meticulous collector of our venerable classical antiquity.

'When my uncle breathed his last I would have dearly loved to have him buried with the ceremonials observed by the ancient Greeks and Romans; but at that time I owned neither lachrymatories, nor urns, nor antique lamps.

'Since then, however, I have provided myself amply with those rare and precious objects; a few days ago I sold my silver to buy an earthenware lamp, which had been used by a Stoic philosopher. I've disposed of all the mirrors with which my uncle had covered the walls of his rooms, in order to acquire a tiny, slightly cracked looking-glass which once belonged to Virgil; I find it delightful to see my own face reflected there, instead of that of the Swan of Mantua.* But that's not all: I spent 100 gold coins on five or six copper pieces which were current 2,000 years ago. To the best of my knowledge, I do not now possess, in my house, a single item of furniture that was not made before the decadent period of the Empire. I have a small collection of extremely precious, and extremely expensive, manuscripts; although I'm ruining my sight deciphering them, I much prefer reading them to reading printed copies, which are not as correct, and which anyone can own. I hardly ever go out; however, that does not prevent me from being passionately interested in finding all the old roads that date from the Romans. There is one such road near my property, which was built by a proconsul of Gaul about 1,200 years ago. Whenever I travel to my country house I never fail to take it, although it's very inconvenient, and lengthens the distance by more than a league. But what infuriates me is that wooden posts have been set up along it at regular intervals, to mark the distances from neighbouring towns; I am filled with despair when I see those wretched signposts instead of the military pillars that stood there in the past; I shall most definitely ensure that my heirs have them restored; I shall require them to pay for this in the terms of my will. If, monsieur, you happen to own a Persian manuscript, I would consider it a great favour if you let me have it; I would pay whatever you asked, and I would give you, in addition, a few works of my own which would demonstrate to you that I am not a useless citizen of the Republic of Letters; you will note, among other things, a treatise in which I prove that the crown which was used, in the past, in triumphal ceremonial was made of oak, not laurel; you will be impressed by another in which I prove, by means of learned conjectures drawn from the most venerated Greek authors, that Cambyses was wounded in the left leg, not the right; and another where I prove that, for the Romans, a narrow forehead was a beautiful and desirable feature. I shall also send you a volume *in Quarto*, a commentary on a line in Book Six of Virgil's *Aeneid*; you won't receive all this for a few days; for the present I am sending you this fragment from an ancient Greek mythologist, which until today has remained unknown; I discovered it covered in dust in a library. I leave you now for an important task I have undertaken, namely the restoration of a fine passage in Pliny the Elder, which the fifth-century copyists had strangely distorted.

'I remain, etc.

FRAGMENTS FROM AN ANCIENT GREEK MYTHOLOGIST*

'On an island near the Orkneys a baby was born whose father was Aeolus, god of the winds, and whose mother was a nymph of Caledonia. It is said of him that he learnt all by himself to count on his fingers, and that he could so well distinguish between different metals, that when his mother tried to give him a ring made of brass instead of one made of gold, he knew he was being deceived and flung it down onto the ground.

'As soon as he was grown, his father taught him the secret of imprisoning the winds in a goatskin bottle, which he would then sell to all travellers; but as this commodity was not greatly valued in his own country, he left, and set off to travel the world in the company of the blind god of chance.

'On his travels, he heard that in Baetica all the land shone with gold, so he hurried there. He was not at all welcomed by Saturn,* the then ruler, but when the god had departed this earth he decided to present himself at all the public gathering-places and repeatedly proclaim, in a hoarse voice: "People of Baetica, you think you are rich, because you possess gold and silver; your error makes me pity you; trust me, abandon the country of base metals and come into the empire of the imagination, and I promise you such riches as will astonish you." Whereupon he opened a large number of the goatskins he had brought, and distributed his wares among all those who desired them.

'The following day he returned to the same places and shouted: "People of Baetica, do you want to be rich? Tell yourselves that I am very rich, and that you are very rich also: imagine every morning that your fortune has doubled during the night; then get up, and if you have creditors, go and pay them with what you have imagined, and tell them to imagine in their turn."

'After a few days had passed he reappeared, and spoke thus: "People of Baetica, I can clearly see that your imaginations are not as lively as they were at first; let yourselves be guided by mine; every morning I shall set up, where you can see it, a board which will be the source of your wealth; there will only be four words on it, but those words will be highly significant, for they will determine the dowry of your wives, the portion your children will inherit, and the number of your servants; and as for you," he said to those listeners nearest to him, "as for you, my dear children— I can call you by that name, for I have given you a second birth—my board will determine the magnificence of your carriages, the opulence of your banquets, and the quantity, and allowances, of your mistresses."

'Some days later he arrived at the meeting-place quite out of breath and in a great rage: "People of Baetica," he cried, "I had advised you to use your imaginations, and I can see you are not doing that; well now I command you to do so." He then abruptly left them, but reconsidered, and retraced his steps. "I have discovered that some among you have been so despicable as to hold on to your gold and silver; the silver, well that's not so bad, but as for the gold... as for the gold... Oh, that really infuriates me... I swear by my sacred goatskins, that if these people do not hand over their gold to me, I shall punish them severely;" then he added, in most persuasive tones: "Do you believe that it's because *I* want to keep those wretched metals that I'm asking you for them? A proof of my good faith is that when you brought me your gold and silver a few days ago, I promptly returned half to you."

'The next day, people watched him from far away, as, his voice soft and wheedling, he attempted to worm his way into favour: "People of Baetica, I have heard that you keep a part of your treasure in foreign countries; I beg you, have this sent to me, you will please me greatly, and I shall be eternally grateful to you."

'The son of Aeolus was addressing people who had no real desire to laugh; they could not, however, stop themselves doing so, which made him turn away, much embarrassed; but then, with renewed courage, he tried another little entreaty. "I know that you own some precious stones; in the name of Jupiter, rid yourselves of them; nothing will impoverish you like things of that kind; rid yourselves of them, I tell you; if you cannot manage to do so on your own, I can connect you with some excellent agents; what great wealth will be yours, if you follow my advice! Yes, I promise you the very purest part of what is in my goatskins."

'Finally, he climbed up onto a stand and spoke with greater confidence: "People of Baetica, I have compared the happy state you now enjoy with the state in which I found you on my arrival here; I see before me the wealthiest people on this earth; but to put the finishing touch to your fortunes, permit me to divest you of half your possessions." With these words, the son of Aeolus vanished on gossamer wings, leaving his audience overcome with indescribable consternation; because of this he came again the following day, and said: "I perceived yesterday that my remarks displeased you greatly. Well, let us assume that I said nothing to you; it's true, half is too much; we must simply find different expedients to attain the goal I have set myself; let us gather together all our resources in one place; we can easily do this, as they do not take up much space;" and thereupon, three-quarters of the wealth promptly disappeared.'

Paris, the 9th of the Moon of Chahban 1720

LETTER 137

Rica to Nathaniel Levi, a Jewish doctor in Leghorn

You ask what I think of the worth of amulets and the potency of talismans. Why do you consult me? You are a Jew and I am a Muslim, which is to say, we are both very credulous.

I always carry on my person more than two thousand passages from the holy Qur'an; I tie to my arm a small packet containing the names of more than two hundred dervishes; the names of Ali, of Fatima, and of all the pure of soul, are concealed in more than twenty places in my clothing.

I do not, however, disapprove of those who reject this power we attribute to certain words; it is much harder for us to counter their reasoning than it is for them to explain our experiences.

I wear all the sacred strips of cloth from long-established habit, following a universal practice; I believe that if they possess no more virtue than do the rings and other ornaments with which people adorn themselves, they possess no less; but *you* place all your trust in some mysterious letters, and without that safeguard you would be in a permanent state of terror.

Men are indeed unhappy creatures: they vacillate endlessly between false hopes and ridiculous fears, and instead of putting their trust in reason, they fashion monsters that frighten them or phantoms that deceive them.

What effect do you suppose the arrangement of certain letters can produce? What effect do you suppose their disarrangement can confound? How do they relate to the wind, so that they can calm storms;

to artillery powder, so that they can abort cannon-fire; to what physicians term 'malignant humour', and to the pathological causes of disease, so that they are able to restore health?

The extraordinary thing is that those who ransack their reason to find connections between certain events and the occult powers, have to make just as great an effort to prevent themselves seeing the true cause of those events.

You will tell me that a particular marvel of magic caused a victory in battle; and I will tell you that you are deliberately blinding yourself if you cannot see that the disposition of the terrain, the number or the courage of the soldiers, and the experience of their captains are sufficient to bring about the result whose cause you are trying to ignore.

For the moment I will grant you that marvels do occur; grant me, in my turn, the possibility that they do not, for this is not impossible. This concession you are making to me will not prevent the two armies from joining battle; do you claim that in such a case neither army would be able to achieve victory?

Do you believe that their fate will remain uncertain until some invisible power arrives to decide it? That every blow will be wasted, all forethought will be futile, and all courage will be unavailing?

Do you think that death, which these occasions render so immediate in so many ways, will not be capable of producing, in men's spirits, that panic and terror that you find so hard to explain? Are you suggesting that in an army of one hundred thousand it is possible that there might not be a single cowardly man? And do you believe that this man's faint-heartedness will not communicate itself to another? And that, when the second deserter leaves *his* companion, that soldier will not also soon abandon a fourth? That is sufficient to make an entire army suddenly despair of achieving victory; the larger the army, the more easily will despair seize hold of it.

Everybody knows, and everybody feels, that man, in common with every creature that strives to survive, is passionately attached to life. This is accepted as a generally established fact, and yet people wonder why, on a particular occasion, man should fear losing his life.

Although the holy books of every nation are full of examples of these supernatural or inexplicable panics, such examples seem to me utterly futile, because in order to be certain that a result which could come from a thousand different natural causes is supernatural, it is necessary first to have examined whether any of these causes was involved, and that is not possible.

I will say no more, Nathanael; I do not feel that this subject deserves to be given such serious consideration.

Paris, the 20th of the Moon of Chabban 1720

PS. As I was concluding, I heard the cries of a street vendor proclaiming the sale of a letter from a physician in the country to a physician in Paris (for here every trifle is printed, published and sold). I thought it appropriate to send you it, because it has a bearing on our subject; there is much in it that I don't understand, but you, being a doctor, will surely comprehend the language of your colleagues.

LETTER FROM A COUNTRY PHYSICIAN* TO A PHYSICIAN IN PARIS

'There was in our town a sick man, who had been unable to sleep for thirty-five days; his physician prescribed opium, but he could not bring himself to take it; holding the glass in his hand, he felt more reluctant than ever to drink the potion; finally he said to his physician; "Monsieur, I beg for mercy just until tomorrow; I know a man who is not a physician, but who has in his home a vast number of remedies against insomnia; permit me to send for him, and if I cannot sleep tonight I promise to return to you."

'Having dismissed the physician, the patient ordered the curtains closed, and said to a young lackey: "Go to the house of Monsieur Anis,* and tell him to come and see me." Monsieur Anis arrives: "My dear Monsieur Anis, I'm dying; I can't sleep; in your shop, have you by any chance the *C. of the G.*,* or perhaps some work of piety composed by a R.F. of the J.* that you have not succeeded in selling? For sometimes the remedies that remain on your shelves longest are the best."

'"Monsieur," said the bookseller, "I have at home *The Holy Court* by Father Caussin,* in six volumes; it's at your service, I shall send you it: I hope that it will do what you desire; if you would like the works of the Spanish Jesuit the Revd Father Rodriguez,* don't hesitate to ask, but believe me, let's stick to Father Caussin; I hope that with God's help, one sentence of Father Caussin will work as well for you as an entire page of the *C. of the G.*" Monsieur Anis left, and hurried to his shop to fetch the remedy. *The Holy Court* arrives; they shake the dust off it; the sufferer's son, a young schoolboy, begins to read; he is the first to be affected, by the second page he can no longer articulate clearly, and all those present are already beginning to flag; a moment later they are all snoring except for the patient, who after being long put to the test, finally falls asleep.

'In the morning the physician arrives: "Well, did he take my opium?" They say nothing in reply; instead, the wife, the daughter, and the small boy delightedly show him Father Caussin. He asks what this is, and they say: "Long live Father Caussin; we must send him to be bound; who would ever have thought it? Who would ever have believed it? It's a miracle; here, monsieur, here's Father Caussin; this is the book that put my father to sleep;" whereupon they told him about what had happened.

'The physician was an astute man, steeped in the mysteries of the Cabala and in the power of words and spirits; this cure impressed him deeply; after much careful consideration he resolved to completely change his own methods. "This is most strange," he reflected. "I have this one case; I must pursue the experiment further. Why should a spirit not transmit to his writings the same qualities that he himself possesses? Do we not observe this every day? It's at least worth trying; I'm tired of apothecaries; their syrups, their juleps, and all their Galenic drugs bankrupt the patients and ruin their health; I'll change my approach and try the power of the meanings of treatises." Based on this idea, he set up a new kind of pharmacy, as you will see from the description I shall give you of the principal remedies he employed.

Purgative infusion

'Take three pages of Aristotle's *Logic* in Greek; two pages of a treatise of Scholastic Theology (the most mordant—perhaps that of the penetrating Scot); four of Paracelsus; one of Avicenna; six of Averroes; three of Porphyry and as many of Plotinus and Iamblicus; infuse all these for twenty-four hours and take four times a day.

Much stronger purgative

'Take ten A**. by C***. on the subject of the B**. and the C**. of the I.**,* distil them in a steamer, macerate a drop of the resulting sharp, bitter humour in a glass of ordinary water, and drink the whole with confidence.

Vomitive

'Take six sermons, a dozen funeral orations (any will serve, except those of M. de N.,* which must be scrupulously avoided); a collection of new operas, fifty novels, thirty new memoirs: put all together into a flask, leave to dissolve two days, then distil at high heat. If this does not suffice:

Another, still more powerful

'Take a sheet of marbled paper which has been used to cover a collection of the plays of J. F.:* infuse it for three minutes, heat a spoonful of this infusion, and swallow.

Very simple remedy for curing asthma

'Read all the works of the former Jesuit, the Reverend Father Maimbourg,* taking care to stop only at the end of every sentence; you will find your ability to breathe gradually returns, without your having to repeat the cure.

To prevent mange, itch, ringworm, equine farcy

'Take three of Aristotle's *Categories*, two degrees of metaphysics, one philosophical "distinguo", six lines of Chapelain's* verse, one sentence from the letters of Monsieur l'Abbé de St Cyran:* inscribe all these on a piece of paper which should be folded, tied with a ribbon, and worn round the neck.

*Miraculum chymicum de violenta fermentatione cum fumo, igne, & flamma**

'*Misce Quesnellianam infusionem, cum infusione Lallemaniana: fiat fermentatio cum magna vi, impetu, & tonitru, acidis pugnantibus, & invicem penetrantibus alcalinos sales: fiet Evaporatio ardentium spirituum: pone liquorem fermentatum in Alembico: nihil inde extrabes, & nihil invenies, nisi caput mortuum.*

Lenitivum

'*Recipe Molinae Anodini chartas duas; Escobaris relaxativi paginas sex; Vasquii emollientis folium unum: infunde in aquae communis lib. iiij ad consumptionem dimidiae partis colentur & exprimantur; & in expressione dissolve Bauni detersivi, & Tamburini abluentis folia iii.*

'*Fiat Clister.*

In chlorosim, quam vulgus pallidos colores,
aut febrim amatoriam, appelat

'*Recipe Aretini figuras quatuor; R. Thomae Sanchii de Matrimonio folia*
ii. infundantur in aqua communis libras quinque.

'*Fiat ptisana aperiens.*

'These are the medicines that our physician began to use, with what
success you may imagine. He did not, he said, out of concern for his
patients' health, want to use remedies that were rare or hard to find:
as, for instance, a dedicatory epistle that had not made anyone yawn;
a too-short preface; a pastoral letter from a bishop; a work by a
Jansenist that was despised by another Jansenist, or admired by a
Jesuit. He said that remedies of this type only served to support char-
latanism, for which he felt an insurmountable dislike.'

[SUPPLEMENTARY LETTER 7]

[SUPPLEMENTARY LETTER 8]

LETTER 138

Usbek to Rhedi, in Venice*

It has long been said that good faith is the soul of a great minister.

A private individual can take shelter behind the obscurity he lives
in; he dishonours himself in the eyes of only a few, and remains
secure before the others; but a minister who sullies his integrity has
as many witnesses and as many judges as there are people he governs.

Dare I say this? The greatest evil done by a dishonest minister is
not in harming his monarch, or in bankrupting the people; it is something else, which I consider a thousand times more dangerous: it is
the bad example he sets.

As you know, I have spent much time travelling in the Indies;
there I have seen a naturally generous nation instantly perverted,
from the humblest to the greatest among them, by the bad example
of a minister; an entire people, whose generosity, probity, candour,
and good faith have always been thought innate characteristics,

suddenly become the least of all nations; I have seen the evil spread, sparing not even the most saintly among them; the most virtuous men committing unworthy acts, and at every opportunity life offered violating the most basic principles of justice, on the vain pretext that their own just rights had been violated.

They appealed to abominable laws to justify the most despicable acts, and gave the name of necessity to injustice and perfidy.

I have seen the good faith of contracts denied, the most hallowed of covenants abolished, the whole of family law turned upside down. I have seen avaricious debtors, proud of their shameless poverty, unworthy instruments of the law's wrath and the harshness of the times, pretend to make a payment instead of actually doing so, and plunge a knife into the bosom of their benefactor.

I have seen others, even more ignoble, buy, for practically nothing, or rather collect oak leaves from the ground in order to substitute them for the money widows and orphans need to survive.

I have seen a sudden, insatiable craving for riches be born in every heart. I have seen a detestable conspiracy to acquire wealth suddenly, instantaneously, come into being: wealth acquired not from honest labour or noble industry, but from the ruin of the prince, the state, and fellow-citizens.

I have seen, in these unhappy times, a gentleman retire for the night only when he could say: 'Today I've bankrupted one family; tomorrow I'll ruin another.'

'I'm going,' said another man, 'with a man dressed in black, who carries a writing-desk and sports a sharpened quill behind his ear, to bring despair to the heart of everyone to whom I am indebted.'

A third remarked: 'I'm settling my affairs now; it's true that three days ago, when I went to make a certain payment, I left an entire family weeping, that I squandered the dowry of two decent young girls and deprived a little boy of his education; this will make the father die of anguish; the mother's pining away from grief; but I only did what the law permits.'

What greater crime can there be than that committed by a minister, when he corrupts the morals of an entire nation, depraves the noblest souls, tarnishes the glory of titles, blackens virtue itself, and involves those of the noblest birth in the universal contempt?

What will posterity say when it finds it must blush for the shame of its forebears? What will the coming generation say when they compare the bravery of their ancestors with the venality of those who fathered them? I have no doubt that the nobility will expunge from their coat of arms an unworthy degree of elevation which dishonours them, nor that they will abandon the present generation to the horrifying void into which it has cast itself.

Paris, the 11th of the Moon of Rhamazan 1720

LETTER 139

The head eunuch to Usbek, in Paris

Things have come to such a pass,* that they cannot continue as they are; your wives seem to have imagined that your departure granted them complete impunity; horrible things are happening here; I myself tremble at the grim account I am about to give you.

Zelis, on her way to the mosque a few days ago, allowed her veil to fall, and appeared before all the people with her face almost uncovered.

I found Zachi in bed with one of her slaves, which is strictly forbidden by the laws of the seraglio.

It was only by the merest chance that I happened upon a letter, which I am sending to you; I have been quite unable to discover to whom it was addressed.

Yesterday evening a youth was seen in the seraglio garden; he escaped over the walls.

To this must be added all that is hidden from me; for undoubtedly you have been betrayed. I await your orders, and until the happy moment when I receive them I shall be in terrible suspense, but if you do not give me leave to handle your wives as I think fit I cannot answer for any of them, and every day I shall have news as wretched as this to send you.

The seraglio in Ispahan, the 1st of the Moon of Rhegeb 1717

LETTER 140

Usbek to the head eunuch, at the seraglio in Ispahan

With this letter I grant you unlimited power over the entire seraglio; command there with all the authority that I myself would wield;

may fear, may terror be your companions; hasten from room to room bearing punishment and retribution; may they all pass their days in dread, may they all weep bitterly in your presence; question the entire seraglio, beginning with the slaves; do not spare my love, let them all be answerable to your formidable justice; uncover the most hidden secrets, purify that infamous place and restore to it banished virtue; from this moment the most trivial offences shall be upon your head; I suspect Zelis of being the one to whom the letter you discovered was addressed; watch her with the eyes of a lynx.

From *.*.*., the 11th of the Moon of Zilhagé 1718

LETTER 141

Narsit to Usbek, in Paris*

The head eunuch has just died, Magnificent Lord; as I am the oldest of your slaves, I have taken his place until such time as you inform us of your choice of a replacement.

Two days after his death I was brought a letter from you addressed to him; I was most careful not to open it; I have wrapped it up respectfully, and put it away until you inform me of your sacred wishes.

Yesterday a slave roused me in the middle of the night to tell me he had found a young man in the seraglio; I arose and enquired into the matter, but I found that it was an illusion.

I kiss your feet, Noble Lord, and beg you to have faith in my devotion, my experience, and my venerable years.

The seraglio at Ispahan, the 5th of the Moon of Gemmadi 1 1718

LETTER 142

Usbek to Narsit, at the seraglio in Ispahan

Wretched man, you have in your possession letters that contain urgent, inexorable orders: the smallest delay could bring me to despair, and yet you, on a futile pretext, do nothing!

Unspeakable things are happening; perhaps half of my slaves deserve to die; I am sending you the letter concerning this that the head eunuch wrote to me before he died. If you had opened the packet addressed to him you would have found it contained ruthless orders; so read those orders: you die if you fail to carry them out!

From *.*.*., the 25th of the Moon of Chalval 1718

LETTER 143
Solim to Usbek, in Paris

If I remained silent any longer, I would be as guilty as are all the criminals you keep in your seraglio.

I was in the confidence of the head eunuch, the most loyal of your slaves. When he realized he was about to die, he sent for me, and spoke to me in these words: 'I am dying, but the only pain I feel upon quitting this life is that my expiring eyes should have witnessed the criminal conduct of my master's wives. May Heaven protect him from all the misfortunes I foresee; and after my death, may my menacing ghost appear as a warning to these perfidious women to do their duty, and to threaten them once more! Here are the keys to this formidable place; take them to the oldest of the black slaves; but if, after my death, he fails in vigilance, remember to warn your master.' As he said this, he died in my arms.

I know not whether, some time before his death, he wrote to you about the conduct of your wives: there is a letter in the seraglio which, had it been opened, would have spread terror everywhere.* The letter you wrote later was intercepted three leagues away from here; I do not know what is happening, but everything is turning out wretchedly.

Meanwhile, your wives no longer conduct themselves with any prudence; since the death of the head eunuch it is as though anything is permitted; Roxane alone remains dutiful and behaves with decorum. I see the conduct of the others grow daily more lax. I no longer observe, on the faces of your wives, that resolute, severe virtue that I used to see; a new joyfulness, which is everywhere evident, is to my eyes infallible proof of some new satisfaction; I notice, in the smallest things, a bold freedom hitherto unknown; even among your slaves there is a certain indolence in fulfilling their duties, and in observing the rules, that surprises me; they no longer display that zealous ardour to serve you that once inspired the entire seraglio.

Your wives spent a week in the country, in one of your least-frequented houses. It is said that the slave who takes care of it was suborned, and that the day before their arrival he had two men hidden in a stone recess in the wall of the principal bedchamber, whence they emerged at night, after we had gone to bed. The old eunuch who is in charge of us at present is an imbecile, who can be made to believe whatever one chooses.

I am filled with avenging fury against all this treachery; and if it were Heaven's will that, for the good of your service, you judged me capable of governing, I promise you that if your wives were not virtuous, they would at least be faithful.

The seraglio in Ispahan, the 6th of the Moon of Rebiab 1 1719

LETTER 144

Narsit to Usbek, in Paris

Roxane and Zelis desired to go to the country; I did not think it right to refuse them. Fortunate Usbek, you have faithful wives, and vigilant slaves; I rule over these quarters, which virtue seems to have chosen as its abode; rest assured that nothing occurs here that your eyes could not witness.

A misfortune has occurred which I deeply regret. Some Armenian merchants, newly arrived in Ispahan, had brought me a letter from you; I sent a slave to fetch it; on his return here he was robbed, so that your letter was lost. Therefore write to me promptly, for I imagine that with all these changes you must have important instructions for me.

Fatmé's seraglio, the 6th of the Moon of Rebiab 1 1719

LETTER 145

Usbek to Solim, at Fatmé's seraglio in Ispahan

I put my sword into your hand. I entrust to you what I now hold dearest in the whole world: my revenge. Take up your new role, but bring to it neither magnanimity nor pity; I am writing to my wives to obey you without question; overcome with shame at their many offences, they will fall before your gaze. To you I must owe my happiness and my tranquillity; give me back my seraglio as I left it, but first you must purify it; destroy those that are guilty, and fill with terror those who were planning to become so. What can you not expect from your master, to reward such notable services? It will depend entirely on your own powers to rise above your present condition, and obtain all the recompense that you have ever desired.

Paris, the 4th of the Moon of Chahban 1719

LETTER 146

Usbek to his wives at the seraglio in Ispahan

May this letter fall upon you like a thunderbolt that strikes amid lightning and tempestuous rain! Solim is now your head eunuch, not to guard, but to punish you. Let the entire seraglio humble itself before him; he is to be the judge of your past conduct; as for the future, he will ensure that you live under so rigid a yoke that you will mourn your lost freedom, even if you do not mourn your lost virtue.

Paris, the 4th of the Moon of Chahban 1719

LETTER 147

Usbek to Nessir, in Ispahan

Happy is the man who, recognizing the true worth of a quiet and tranquil existence, lets his heart remain at rest in the bosom of his family, and knows no land other than the one which gave him birth!

I breathe the air of an alien country; wholly aware of all that torments me, and wholly deaf to all that interests me; prey to an oppressive melancholy, I am sinking into hideous depression; I feel I am destroying myself, and that I only find myself again whenever a dark jealousy flares up within me, begetting fear, suspicions, loathing, and regrets.

You know me, Nessir; you have always seen into my heart as if it were your own; you would pity me, were you to see my deplorable state; sometimes I have to wait for six whole months to receive news of the seraglio; I count each moment as it passes, and my impatience always makes them longer; when finally the awaited moment approaches, a sudden change takes place in my heart; my hand trembles at the thought of opening a fatal letter; that anxiety which filled me with despair seems to me the happiest state I could experience, and I am fearful of being forced out of it by news that would be crueller to me than a thousand deaths.

But whatever the reason that made me leave my homeland, and although I owe my life to my departure, I cannot, Nessir, remain in this dreadful exile any longer. For would I not die anyway, of sorrow? I have urged Rica countless times to leave this foreign land, but he objects to all my decisions; he keeps me here on a thousand pretexts; it seems he has forgotten his homeland, or rather, it seems he has forgotten me, so indifferent is he to my unhappiness.

Wretched that I am! I long to see my homeland again, perhaps to become more wretched yet! And what shall I do there? I shall be returning to hand over my head to my enemies. That is not all: I shall enter the seraglio, where I must demand an account of the calamitous years of my absence; if I discover culprits there, what will become of me? If the very thought of it overwhelms me at this distance, what will happen when my presence makes it reality? What will happen when I must see and must hear what I dare not imagine without shuddering? What will happen if it is necessary that the retribution I myself choose shall be an everlasting symbol of my shame, and my despair?

I shall shut myself away behind walls that will be more terrible for me than for the women who are guarded within them; I shall bring with me all my suspicion; their ardour will not erase any of it from my mind; in my bed, in their arms, I shall dwell only on my misgivings; at a time so little suited to reflection, my jealousy will find food for thought. Worthless rejects of the human race, base slaves whose hearts have been forever closed to feelings of love, you would no longer lament your condition if you knew the misery of mine.

Paris, the 4th of the Moon of Chahban 1719

LETTER 148

Roxane to Usbek, in Paris

Horror, darkness, and terror hold sway in the seraglio, which is shrouded in ghastly mourning; at every moment a tiger gives vent in it to all his rage; he has tortured two white eunuchs, who confessed nothing but their innocence; he sold some of our slaves, and forced us to exchange among ourselves those that remained. At dark of night, in their chambers, Zachi and Zelis were subjected to shameful treatment; the sacrilegious creature did not shrink from laying his foul hands upon them. He keeps us locked up separately in our rooms; although we are alone, he makes us wear the veil; we are no longer permitted to speak to one another; it would be a crime to write to one another; our sole remaining freedom is in tears.

A troop of new eunuchs has been brought into the seraglio, where they harass us night and day; our sleep is constantly interrupted by their feigned or genuine suspicions. My consolation is that all this will not last long, and that these torments will end with my life; it will not be a long one, cruel Usbek, and I shall not allow you the time to put a stop to these outrageous affronts.

The seraglio in Ispahan, the 2nd of the Moon of Maharram 1720

[SUPPLEMENTARY LETTER 9]

[SUPPLEMENTARY LETTER 10]

LETTER 149

Solim to Usbek, in Paris

I weep for myself, Magnificent Lord, and I weep for you; never before has a faithful servant felt despair as terrible as what I am now experiencing; I shall lay before you both my own misfortunes and yours, and can only write of them with a trembling hand.

I swear, by all the heavenly prophets, that since you entrusted your wives to me I have watched over them night and day, and that never for one moment have I allowed my anxious vigilance to lapse; I began my stewardship with punishments; but when I stopped the punishments, I never relaxed my natural severity.

But what am I saying? Why boast of a loyalty that has been of no use to you: forget all my past services; look upon me as a traitor; punish me for every crime that I have been powerless to prevent.

Roxane, the proud Roxane—heavens! Who, henceforth, is to be trusted? You suspected Zachi, and had complete confidence in Roxane; but her fierce virtue was a cruel deception, the veil that concealed her perfidy; I surprised her in the arms of a young man who, the instant he saw he was discovered, attacked me; he stabbed me twice with his dagger; alerted by the noise, the eunuchs quickly surrounded him. He defended himself for a long time, wounding several of them; he tried to get back inside Roxane's room, to die, he said, in her presence; but finally, outnumbered, he was subdued, and expired at our feet.

I know not, Sublime Lord, whether I shall await your implacable commands; you have entrusted your vengeance to my hands, I ought not to let it languish in idleness.

The seraglio in Ispahan, the 8th of the Moon of Rebiab 1 1720

[SUPPLEMENTARY LETTER 11]

LETTER 150

Roxane to Usbek, in Paris

Yes, I have deceived you; I have bribed your eunuchs, I have played upon your jealousy, and I have managed to make of your dreadful seraglio an abode of delights and pleasures.

I am about to die: soon the poison will be coursing through my veins, for why would I remain here, when the only man who gave me a reason for living is dead? I am dying, but my shade will be well escorted on its flight; I have dispatched ahead of me those sacrilegious guards who spilt the most precious blood in the world.

How could you suppose me so credulous as to believe that the sole purpose for my existence was to adore your caprices? That while you refused yourself nothing, you had the right to frustrate every desire of mine? No: I may have lived in servitude, but I have always been free: I have rewritten your laws to conform to those of nature, and my spirit has always remained independent.

You should still be thanking me for the sacrifice I made you, in my degrading pretence of being your faithful wife, and in cravenly keeping secret in my heart what I should have proclaimed before the whole world; in short, that I profaned virtue, in allowing my submission to your caprices to be described by that word.

You were amazed at not seeing in me the ecstasies of love: if you had truly known me, you would have seen in me all the violence of loathing.

But you have long enjoyed the conviction that a heart like mine had surrendered to you; we were both happy: you believed me deceived, and I was deceiving you.

My language will no doubt seem new to you: after dealing you such an agonizing blow, might I also perhaps force you to admire my courage? But it is over; the poison consumes me, my strength abandons me, the pen falls from my hand; I feel that even my hatred is fading away… I am dying.

The seraglio in Ispahan, the 8th of the Moon of Rebiab 1 1720

SUPPLEMENTARY LETTERS

LETTER 15

The head eunuch to Jaron, a black eunuch at Erzeron

[SUPPLEMENTARY LETTER 1]

I pray that Heaven will bring you back here, and keep you safe from all dangers.

Although I have hardly known the bond that people call friendship, and have always been wholly wrapped up in myself, nevertheless you made me feel that I still had a heart; while I was as unfeeling as stone towards all the slaves living under my rule, I took pleasure, during your childhood, in watching you grow.

The day came when my master turned his eyes upon you. Nature had not yet awakened in you when the knife separated you from nature. I will not tell you if I pitied you, or if I rejoiced at seeing you raised up to my level. I soothed your tears and your cries. I believed you were being granted a second birth, leaving a servitude in which you must always obey, to enter a servitude in which you must command. I watched over your training. My severity, which is an essential part of any training, meant that for years you did not know that you were dear to me. However, you were indeed dear to me, and I would tell you that I loved you as a father loves his son, could the names of father and son be applied to our destiny.

You will be travelling through countries inhabited by Christians, who have never been believers. It will be impossible for you to avoid many defiling encounters. How could the Prophet watch over you among so many millions of his enemies? It is my hope that my master, upon his return, will make a pilgrimage to Mecca: you would then all purify yourselves in the land of the angels.

The seraglio in Ispahan, the 10th of the Moon of Gemmadi 1711

LETTER 22

Jaron to the head eunuch

[SUPPLEMENTARY LETTER 2]

The farther Usbek travels from the seraglio, the more does he turn his head in the direction of his sacred wives; he sighs, he weeps; his anguish grows more bitter, his suspicions more deep. He plans to increase the number of their guards. He is going to send me back, with all the black slaves who form his escort. He no longer fears for himself; he fears for what is a thousand times dearer to him than himself.

I shall therefore be living under your rule, and sharing in your duties. Great God! How much is required to make one man happy!

Nature seemed to have created women as dependants, but then to have withdrawn them from that state; discord between the sexes was born, because the rights of men and women were reciprocal. Now we have entered into a period of a different balance: we have put hatred between women and us, and love between men and women.

My countenance will become severe. My eyes will gaze darkly upon the world. My lips will know no joyful smiles. My expression will be calm, my spirit uneasy. I need not wait for the wrinkles of old age, for my face to reveal its sorrows.

I would have enjoyed following my master in the West, but I and my wishes belong to him. He wants me to guard his wives and I shall guard them faithfully. I know how to conduct myself with that sex, who, even when vanity is forbidden them, are haughty, and who are less easily humiliated than destroyed. I prostrate myself before you.

Smyrna, the 12th of the Moon of Zilcadé 1711

LETTER 77

Ibben to Usbek, in Paris

[SUPPLEMENTARY LETTER 3]

It seems to me, my dear Usbek, that for a true Muslim misfortunes are not so much punishments as warnings. They are so very precious, those times when we feel impelled to expiate our offences. It is the periods of prosperity that we should abridge. Of what use are all those impatient longings, except to show that we seek happiness independently of him who bestows all happiness, because he is happiness itself?

If a being is made up of two parts, body and soul, and the need to preserve their union is seen more as evidence of submission to the creator's will, then this can be made a law of religion; if the need to preserve this union is seen more as a guarantor of men's good behaviour, then this can be made a civil law.

Smyrna, the last day of the Moon of Saphar 1715

LETTER 91

Usbek to Rustan, in Ispahan

[SUPPLEMENTARY LETTER 4]

A personage has appeared here masquerading as an ambassador of Persia;* he is making a shameful mockery of the two mightiest monarchs on this earth. He brings, as gifts for the French king, offerings that our king would not deign to present to a ruler of Irimette or Georgia; his despicable avarice has sullied the majesty of two empires.

He has made himself ridiculous in the eyes of a people that claim to be the most courteous in Europe, and he has caused westerners to say that the subjects of the King of Kings are nothing but barbarians.

He has been received with honours which his own demeanour seems to have been designed to preclude; and, as if the French court cherished Persian greatness more than he himself did, they presented him with all due dignity to a people that despised him.

Say nothing of this in Ispahan; spare the life of an unfortunate man. I do not want our ministers to punish him for their own imprudence and the unworthy choice they have made.

Paris, the last day of the Moon of Gemmadi 2 1715

LETTER III

Usbek to ***

[SUPPLEMENTARY LETTER 5]

The reign of the late king lasted for so long that its end made people forget its beginning. It's the fashion today to be interested solely in things that happened during the king's minority, and no one is reading anything but the memoirs of that period.

Here is a speech* given by one of the generals of the city of Paris during a war council; I confess that I don't understand much of it:

'Messieurs: Although our troops have suffered losses and been repulsed, I believe that we can easily remedy this setback. I have six verses of a song all ready to circulate, which I'm certain will restore everything to normal. I've selected some very penetrating voices which, issuing from the depths of certain very mighty chests, will stir the common people in a marvellous way. They are sung to a melody which, until now, has had a very special effect.

'If that does not suffice, we will produce a print depicting Mazarin* hanging from the gibbet.

'Fortunately for us, he does not speak French well; he butchers it so dreadfully that his affairs must inevitably degenerate. We shall most emphatically draw his ridiculous pronunciation to the attention of the people. We pointed out, a few days ago, a grammatical error so glaring that it inspired lampoons performed at all the crossroads.

'I hope that before the week is out, the people will turn the name Mazarin into an all-inclusive term for beasts of burden and carthorses.

'Since our defeat, our songs about original sin have so enraged him that, to avoid seeing his supporters reduced by half, he has been forced to dismiss all his pages.

'So be of good heart, take courage once again; you can be sure that we'll drive him back over the mountains with our whistle blasts.'

Paris, the 4th of the Moon of Chahban 1718

LETTER 124

Usbek to Rhedi, in Venice

[SUPPLEMENTARY LETTER 6]

What can be the motive for those enormous gifts that monarchs shower upon their courtiers? Are they trying to win them over? They have already done this to the extent that they are able. And besides, if they secure some of their subjects by buying them, it surely follows, by the same token, that they lose innumerable others by impoverishing them.

When I consider the position of princes, invariably surrounded by avid, insatiable men, I cannot do other than pity them, and I pity them all the more when they lack the strength to resist demands that always impose burdens upon those who demand nothing.

I never hear about their liberalities, and the favours and pensions they grant, without a thousand thoughts filling my head; ideas come crowding into my mind, and it seems as if I hear a voice proclaiming the following statute:

'The indefatigable zeal displayed by some of our subjects in requesting pensions having unceasingly exercised our royal munificence, we have finally yielded to the multitude of demands we have received, which have, until now, constituted the principal concern of the crown. Our subjects have pointed out that not once, since the day we acceded to the throne, have they failed to attend our levée; that invariably, as we pass by, we have seen them waiting motionless as statues, and that by climbing onto the tallest shoulders available, they have attained heights such that they have been able to gaze upon our Serenity. We have even received several requests from members of the fair sex, begging us to remember that their maintenance is notoriously demanding; some among them, well past their prime, have implored us, nodding their heads, to note that they were the ornament of the courts of our royal predecessors; and that, if generals of armies made the state formidable with their military prowess, they made the court fully as celebrated with their intrigues. Accordingly, desirous of treating these suppliants with generosity, and of acceding to all their requests, we have issued the following orders:

'That every labourer having five children shall each day withhold a fifth part of the bread he gives them. We enjoin fathers of families to reduce each child's portion as exactly as possible.

'We expressly forbid all who engage in cultivating their inherited lands, or who have let them as farms, to undertake any repair thereupon of any kind whatsoever.

'We command that all persons engaged in base or mechanical work, who have never attended the levée of our majesty, shall henceforth only buy coats for themselves, their wives, and their children once in every four years; we further forbid them, most strictly, those little celebrations that they were accustomed to enjoy with their families on the principal festivals of the year.

'And, in as much as we have been apprised that most of the good citizens of our towns are wholly preoccupied in ensuring the establishment of their daughters, whose sole claim to favour in our realm is a dreary and tiresome modesty; we command that they shall delay marrying them until they attain the age established by law, when these daughters can force their fathers to find husbands for them. We forbid our magistrates to make provision for the education of their children.'

Paris, the first of the Moon of Chalval 1718

LETTER 144

Rica to Usbek

[SUPPLEMENTARY LETTER 7]

The other day, in a country house I was visiting, I encountered two scholars who are very celebrated here. Their character struck me as remarkable. The conversation of the first—which was greatly appreciated—could be summed up as follows: 'What I have said is true, because I have said it.' The conversation of the other centred on something different: 'What I have not said is not true, because I have not said it.'

I quite liked the first; if someone is obstinate, it doesn't bother me in the least, but if someone is irrational, that does indeed bother me. The first is defending his own opinions, which is his right; the other is attacking the opinions of others, and therefore attacking the rights of everyone.

Ah, my dear Usbek! How dangerous is vanity to those with a larger share of it than is needed to preserve the essence of their being! Such people seek admiration by being deliberately unpleasant. They mean to be superior to others, and they are not even their equal.

Modest men, come, let me embrace you. You give life its sweetness and charm. You think that you have nothing, but I tell you that you have everything. You believe that you humble no one, but you humble every one. And when I compare you in my mind to the autocratic men I see on all sides, I hurl them off their podiums, and set them at your feet.

Paris, the 22nd of the Moon of Chahban 1720

LETTER 145

Usbek to ***

[SUPPLEMENTARY LETTER 8]

A clever man is commonly aloof in company. He seeks out few people; he is bored by a great many whom he chooses to call poor company; it is impossible for some not to sense his dislike. Those men become his enemies.

Confident of pleasing when he so desires, he very often neglects to do so.

He is inclined to be critical, because he sees more than others see, and feels these things more acutely.

Almost invariably he loses his fortune, because his mind shows him more ways to go about this.

His enterprises fail, because he takes great risks. His vision, which is always extensive, offers him objects that are too far distant. Not only that: at the start of a project he is less impressed by the difficulties inherent in the plan, than by the remedies that he can supply, and for which he draws on his own abilities.

He neglects the tiny details, upon which, however, depends the success of almost all great undertakings.

The second-rate man, by contrast, works hard to turn everything to advantage; he knows very well he cannot afford any loss through negligence.

Universal approval is more commonly accorded to the second-rate man. People are pleased to give their approval to him, and very gratified to withhold it from his rival. While envy pounces upon the latter, forgiving him nothing, it supplies all that the former lacks, for vanity is on his side.

But, if an intelligent man suffers from so many disadvantages, what can we say about the hard lot of the truly learned?

I never think of this without remembering a letter a learned man wrote to a friend. Here it is:

'Monsieur,

'I am a man that spends every night gazing, through thirty-foot lenses, at the vast bodies that circle above our heads; and, when I want to relax, I take my little microscopes and study a mite or a tick.

'I am not rich, and live in only one room; I dare not even light a fire in it, because I keep my thermometer there, and the extra warmth would make the thermometer rise. Last winter I thought I would die of cold; and although my thermometer, which went down to its lowest degree, warned me that my hands were about to freeze, I did nothing about it. And I have the consolation of being precisely informed of the tiniest fluctuations in the temperature over the entire course of last year.

'I have very little contact with people, and among those I do see there are none that I know. But there is a man in Stockholm, another in Leipzig, and another in London whom I have never seen, and no doubt shall never see, with whom I maintain such a regular correspondence that I never fail to write to each of them with every mail.

'However, although I know nobody in my area, I have such a bad reputation here that eventually I shall be forced to leave. Five years ago I was coarsely insulted by one of my neighbours, for having dissected a dog that she claimed belonged to her. A butcher's wife, who happened to be present, joined in. And while the former was heaping insults upon me, the latter began throwing stones at me and at Doctor ***, who was with me and received a terrible blow upon his frontal and occipital bones, a blow that badly jolted his seat of ratiocination.

'Ever since that day, as soon as some dog is lost at the end of the street it is instantly decided that it has fallen into my hands. A good woman who had lost a little dog that she loved, as she said, more than her children, came to my room the other day and fainted; not finding her dog, she had me summoned before the magistrate. I believe I'll never be free of the importunate malice of these women, who, with their yapping voices, are constantly stupefying me with the funeral orations of all the automata that have died in the last ten years.

'I am, etc.'

All learned men were, in the past, accused of magic. This does not surprise me. Everyone told himself: 'I've developed my natural talents as far as they will go; however, a certain scholar has gone further than me; the devil must have a hand in it.'

Nowadays accusations of that type are not well thought of, so a different approach has been tried, and a scholar can hardly avoid being reproached with irreligion or heresy. In vain does the populace absolve him; the wound has been opened and will never close properly. It will always be, for him, a vulnerable place. An adversary will approach him thirty years later, and modestly say: 'God forbid that I should claim that what you are accused of is true; but, you were obliged to defend yourself.' That is how even his justification is turned against him.

If he writes a history, and he is blessed with some nobility of mind and purity of heart, he will be persecuted in a thousand ways. He will be accused before the magistrate over an event that occurred a thousand years ago. And some will claim that, while his pen may not actually be for sale, he writes what he is told to write.

He is, however, luckier than those despicable men who abandon their faith for an insignificant pension; who, if one considers all their many lies one by one, sell them for next to nothing; who turn upside down the constitution of an empire, diminish the rights of one power and increase those of another; give to princes and take away from the people, restore outdated privileges, flatter those passions that are fashionable in their day and those vices favoured by the throne, deceiving posterity all the more shamefully, the less it will possess the means to demolish their testimony.

But it is not trial enough, for an author, to have experienced all these affronts, nor is it enough that he should have suffered constant anxiety over the success of his work. Finally, this work which has cost him so dearly sees the light of day. It draws contention upon him from every quarter. And how could it be otherwise? He had an opinion; he supported that opinion in his work; he did not know that at a distance from him of 200 leagues a man had written the exact opposite. Nevertheless, war is declared.

And yet, if he could at least hope for a little respect! No. At best, he is respected by those who have dedicated themselves to the same kind of work as he has. A philosopher feels supreme scorn for him whose head is filled with facts; he, in his turn, is thought a visionary by the man with a good memory.

As for those who profess an arrogant ignorance, they would like the entire human race to be buried in the oblivion which they themselves will soon enjoy.

A man who lacks a certain talent will compensate himself by despising it; he eliminates the obstacle which blocks his path to excellence, and, as a consequence, sees himself as the equal of the rival whose work he fears.

Finally, we should add to an uncertain reputation the deprivation of pleasure and the loss of good health.

Paris, the 26th of the Moon of Chahban 1720

LETTER 157

Zachi to Usbek, in Paris

[SUPPLEMENTARY LETTER 9]

God in Heaven! A brute has insulted me even with the style of punishment he visited on me! He dared to inflict on me that punishment which first shocks a woman's modesty, then humiliates her to the uttermost degree, then reduces her, as it were, to childhood.

My spirit, at first overwhelmed by shame, regained its power of feeling and I was filled with indignation, while my screams raised echoes from the ceiling of my chambers. People heard me begging for mercy from the vilest of beings, and attempting to inspire pity in him, as he grew ever more implacable.

Ever since that day, his insolent, servile spirit has shown disrespect for me. His presence, his looks, his words, every misfortune press down unbearably upon me. When I am alone at least I know the consolation of shedding tears, but when I catch sight of him I am filled with rage; I find it is of no avail, and I fall into despair.

The beast dares to tell me that you are the author of all this cruelty. He is trying to deprive me of my love, and desecrate the very emotions of my heart. When he utters the name of him whom I love, I no longer feel I can complain; my sole remaining recourse is to die.

I have endured your absence, and by the strength of my love for you I have been able to preserve it. The nights, the days, the moments have all been yours. I gloried proudly in that very passion, and your love for me made me respected here. But now... No, I can no longer bear the humiliation to which I have been reduced. If I am innocent, come back to love me; come back if I am guilty, so that I may die at your feet.

The seraglio at Ispahan, the 2nd of the Moon of Maharram 1720

LETTER 158

Zelis to Usbek, in Paris

[SUPPLEMENTARY LETTER 10]

At a thousand leagues away from me, you judge me guilty; at a thousand leagues away from me, you punish me.

If a cruel eunuch lays his base hands upon me, he is acting upon your orders; it is the tyrant who commits the outrage, and not he that is the instrument of tyranny.

You can, as you desire, redouble your harsh treatment. My heart is at peace, since it can no longer love you. Your soul is being degraded, and you are growing cruel. Know that you are wretched. Farewell.

The seraglio at Ispahan, the 2nd of the Moon of Maharram 1720

LETTER 160

Solim to Usbek, in Paris

[SUPPLEMENTARY LETTER 11]

I have made my decision; your misfortunes are about to vanish; I mean to punish.

Already I feel a secret joy; your soul and mine will know peace, for we shall wipe out crime, and watch innocence grow pale.

And you, who seem born only to deny all your senses and to resent your very desires, eternal victims of modesty and decorum, why cannot I have you brought in great numbers to this unhappy seraglio, so that I may witness your terror at all the blood I am about to spill here!

The seraglio at Ispahan, the 8th of the Moon of Rebiab 1 1720

SOME REFLECTIONS ON THE
PERSIAN LETTERS

Nothing has given readers of the *Persian Letters* greater pleasure than finding, without expecting to, a kind of novel in it. They see the beginning, the development, and the end; the various characters are set in a chain that links them. The longer they remain in Europe, the less do the customs of that part of the world seem to them wonderful and strange; and they are less, or more, struck by this strangeness and this wonder, according to how their characters differ. On the other hand, the disorder in the eastern seraglio grows in proportion to the duration of Usbek's absence, that is to say, as the women's anger increases, their love diminishes.

Furthermore, novels of this type are usually successful because the writers are describing their own feelings at the actual moment, which means that emotions are conveyed more powerfully than any third-party account of them could do. And that is one of the reasons for the success of some charming works which have appeared since the *Persian Letters*.

Lastly, in an ordinary novel digressions cannot be permitted unless they themselves form a new novel. One could not include debate in it, because, since none of the characters was put there to engage in reasoning, this would not conform to the nature of the work. But in the letter form, where the participants are not chosen and the subjects treated do not depend on any design or predetermined plan, the author allows himself the advantage of adding philosophy, politics, and ethics to the novel, and of linking it all together by a secret and, in a sense, unrecognized chain.

The *Persian Letters* were such an immediate and extraordinary success that the booksellers did all they could to obtain sequels. They pestered everyone they encountered, saying: 'Monsieur, write me some Persian Letters.'

But what I have just described is sufficient to demonstrate that they are not appropriate material for the addition of any sequel, even less for any combination with letters penned by a different hand, however ingenious these might be.

There are some passages that many people have thought too daring. But they should, I beg, consider the nature of this work. The Persians, who had such an important role to play in the novel, found themselves suddenly transplanted into Europe, that is, into another universe. They necessarily had to be portrayed, for a certain time, as full of ignorance and prejudice. What was important was to show the genesis and progress of their ideas. Their first thoughts were bound to be bizarre; so the solution was to make them bizarre in a way that is compatible with intelligence. It was necessary to describe the Persians' emotional reaction to each thing that seemed to them extraordinary. Far from intending to involve in this any principle of our religion, their creator did not even suspect himself of imprudence. These passages are invariably associated with a feeling of surprise and amazement, and never with any idea of scrutiny, even less with that of criticism. In speaking of our religion, the Persians must not appear better informed than when they speak of our customs and practices. And, if sometimes they find our dogmas singular, this singularity always bears the stamp of their total ignorance of how those dogmas and our other truths are related.

The author offers this justification out of love for these great truths, quite apart from the respect he feels for his fellow-men, whom he certainly had no wish to wound in their most vulnerable spot. The reader is therefore urged never, for one moment, to stop seeing the passages in question as the fruit of surprise experienced by people who ought to be surprised, or else as paradoxes written by men who lack even the knowledge necessary to think them through. The reader is urged to note that the entire charm of the work resides in the constantly recurring contrast between actual reality and the singular, naïve, or strange manner in which reality is perceived. Certainly, the nature and purpose of the *Persian Letters* are so obvious, that the work can never delude any readers except those who wish to delude themselves.

APPENDIX
EXTRACTS FROM MONTESQUIEU'S SOURCES

The extracts in this Appendix are designed to supplement Montesquieu's references to eastern practices with documentary descriptions, and to amplify the intellectual context. The passages are drawn from three of Montesquieu's most important sources: Jean Chardin, *Voyages de Monsieur le chevalier Chardin, en Perse, et autres lieux de l'Orient* (Amsterdam, 1711); Jean Paul Marana, *L'Espion dans les cours des princes chrétiens* (Cologne, 1717); Jean-Baptiste Tavernier, *Les Six Voyages de Jean-Baptiste Tavernier, chevalier baron d'Aubonne, qu'il a fait en Turquie, en Perse, et aux Indes, pendant l'espace de quarante ans* (Paris, 1679).

Christianity

The Protestant religion, as it is called, which is accused of having caused so many troubles in the kingdom, is presently in retreat owing to the capture of La Rochelle,* which was, as you know, the main stronghold of this party. It seems that this king would like to emulate our powerful and frightening emperors, and that following your example is not inclined to tolerate two rival religions in his states. (Chardin)

Europe is a fertile field for rebellion, tumult, disorder, and extraordinary wars. There is no other place in Christendom so stained by treachery, perfidy, and carnage, and scarcely a corner that is not steeped in human blood [. . .]. Religion has no more control over the passions than the fables of the ancient poets. (Marana)

Bishops enjoy great veneration here. They are not invested with absolute authority since they depend on the Roman prelate and on the king. However, the extent of their jurisdiction is great: the kingdom of France is full of churches, and these churches are visited by millions of people. Bishops wear a gold cross around their neck. They have an active public role and are obliged to know everything about their law. They must be doctors and may not marry. They must be sober, charitable, prudent, irreproachable, and do no harm to anyone else. They must never get intoxicated nor shed human blood. They are dressed in a long robe of black or purple silk that extends to the ground. They rarely go about on foot, and have themselves carried in carriage to avoid getting tired in a city that seems to be the largest in the world. (Marana)

In the West you have a multitude of people who not only scorn and despise their own law as well as ours, but who openly mock all the religions of the world. They go by the name of atheists and libertines; that is, declared enemies of God's creation [. . .]. These foolish libertines are not only found at the court of France, but in general across all of Europe. Their illness is an epidemic, an infection that has spread among clergymen as well as among the lay people, aristocrats, and peasants [. . .]. For once religion has become an object of contempt, it then becomes a political trick and ruse devised by clergymen in order to keep fools respectful and dependent. Even those who have a better opinion of themselves and would like to be seen as sensible people use the opportunity to attack the tenets of religions and to argue against the existence of God. Instead of calmly submitting to the dogmas that they appear to respect or consider as obvious falsehoods, they shake off the yoke not only of natural religion, as though they were a fierce and untamed bird, but also that of common morality. And since they have too much sense to be duped by religious trickery, they lack no confidence in exposing all the pious frauds of the church, such as oracles, about which they have no doubts. They aim mainly to be sceptics in everything and wish only to satisfy their passions. In their view there is no use of time worse than contemplating the afterlife. (Marana)

Science and Philosophy

Women of high birth have recently undertaken the study of philosophy, just like men. They judge that their education would be deficient if they cannot refute Aristotle and his disciples [. . .]. A new star has recently appeared on the French horizon, and his influence has incited the noblest of women to feel devotion for the study of philosophy. This is the famous Monsieur Descartes, whose brilliance surpasses many of the ancient Peripatetic philosophers* and eclipses the Stagirite* and all the ancient luminaries of Greece and Italy. It is this incomparable man who has attracted such a large number of the fair sex to his school: the women consider that being a follower of Descartes and defending his principles is an honour even greater than their noble and illustrious pedigree.

I know that our serious and wise Muslims would condemn the indulgence that the French show their women, and would accuse them of being weak because they grant women rights that are comparable to those of the intelligent sex. But despite our severity in the Orient, I cannot completely disapprove of the westerners. If we regard women as our enemies, it seems cowardly and base to prevent them from having the same means that we use. But if they deserve to be called our friends, then it is inhumane and tyrannical to deprive them of the privilege of a rigorous education; for both sides would find their friendship more charming and more agreeable. It has rarely been noticed that nature has been generous in endowing this sex with its most excellent gifts. In general, their senses are as acute as our senses, their reason very strong, and their judgement as mature and solid. If to these natural perfections they added the advantages of acquired learning, would not their natural beauty, for as long as it lasted together with their charms and politeness, augment rather than obscure the brilliance of their mind? In trying to perfect their natural merits, we must never fear losing the dominion that we have over them, since it is the case that where learning, sensibility, and knowledge are greater there is also more modesty and regularity of conduct. I therefore see no reason why we should fear women and not grant them an education as good as our own. (Marana)

Venerable Sage, allow me as your pupil to have a brief conversation with you, since you are a source of wisdom, and beyond the perfect knowledge that you possess of Divine Law there is nothing written about mankind that you do not know.

There is a man of great spirit and exalted intelligence who in certain quarters staunchly maintains the idea that the earth is in movement while the sun is not. He is not the first author of this dogma, which has several defenders among men of learning. But he has done a great deal to perfect the theory. The reasons that he adduces in support of his opinion are almost as convincing as mathematical demonstrations; and nothing in them appears to contradict the authority of Moses and Judaic scripture. Christians are averse to a philosophy that does not conform to what they call the Bible, even though on a daily basis their practical conduct belies the contents of this book. There is no doubt that the Divinity is free of envy, and that he who knows all will never punish men for wishing to perfect their knowledge. The study of nature is full of innocent pleasures; and he who gave men the desire to be learned would not prevent them from attaining the means to achieving this. For that matter, I do not see why this new philosophy contains greater contradictions than the simple text of their Bible, which I have read in different languages. Even the Jews who were the recipients of the original Hebrew allow a Cabbalistic interpretation that is different from the literal version. Similarly, the Arab prince and the philosopher Avicenna* explain the poetry of our holy Qur'an, where paradise is discussed, with much more refinement than the text would seem to support. When we read these mysterious books we must be like subtle chemists and purify the terms of everything coarse, sublimate, as it were, everything that is low and earthly and accept only the spirit and soul of the language.

That the sun be the centre of the world, and that the earth and planets move around this star, is a thesis that squares perfectly with human reason and seems to accord naturally with the faculties of our intelligence. This system puts all the routes of this great and marvellous machine in exact and proportionate circulation. From this one can conjecture about the true revolutions of the planets. Ptolemy's model of the world seems Roman when he says that the sun, moon, and stars are all hours on an immense path that we do not know how to explain according to the rules of motion. Tycho Brahe* revised this by surrounding the globe with external epicycles, etc. The first wanted the stars to be fixed in perpetual and incomprehensible disorder; the second placed the planets in a type of perplexity. Neither one of these two systems is a patch on that of the excellent astronomer Copernicus, who resolved all the difficulties in placing, as he did, the sun at the centre of the world in a manner that fits very well with the reality. Arguments made from the senses are inconclusive, and if one does reach a conclusion it is equally opposed to both solar and lunar movement, since it is more extraordinary that the sun should move so many hundreds of thousands of miles hour after hour, and that the motion never looks longer than the length of a horse.

[. . .] There are scientists who say that the moon and the other planets are as habitable as our world is. Speaking personally, I would like it if this were the case, and think that this is a belief that would have the approval of society. When I sometimes cast my eyes on high I cannot help feeling chagrined at the thought of the vast expanse of the sky that is uninhabited, while there is scarcely a corner of our spoiled earth without dwellers. It is possible to demonstrate that the moon is a solid body of the same material as the earth that we inhabit, and that all the light of the moon is reflected from the sun. Why, therefore, is it heretical to suppose that the moon and the earth were created for the same purpose? I hope that the holy empire of Islam will never experience guilt for a murder like that of the Christian bishop who was burned by decree of the Roman church because he supported the existence of the Antipodes; which is now a truthful fact acknowledged by all nations, thanks to progress made in navigation and trade. Galileo would have met with the same fate in Rome ten years ago for saying that the earth was not fixed and that the sun is the centre of the world, and nothing could have saved him had he not retracted the view. Such severe treatment does an injustice to learning, and hinders the progress that one could make in the arts and sciences. (Marana)

This astronomer is famed throughout the West and passes for the best philosopher ever to write on the natural world. His name is René Descartes. I had frequent conversations with him and took utter pleasure in the abstract and subtle ideas he has about the world. He analyses the fabric of all the elements with such skill that it is as though he was with the creator when he extracted them from the inchoate mass. He is able to see the proper shape of the tiniest particle of matter that the eyes of others fail to perceive. He speaks easily of atoms that are round, square, and triangular, as if he measured them. If so admirable a genius were not stigmatized with gross impiety, because he mocked the holy Qur'an, the book of glory and guide to Paradise, I would believe him to be inspired by Heaven. (Marana)

Western philosophers, and above all the followers of Monsieur Descartes, maintain that the souls of all creatures, excepting man, are material and mortal; and that a beast is no different to a machine like a watch or a clock;* and that the intelligence animating it is material; and that it acts mechanically and in proportion to the external impressions that it forms.

[. . .] I shall not believe that they are in Paradise until I have the good fortune of seeing them there, but nonetheless I do not share the view of the modern philosophers who suppose their souls to be purely material. I agree that men and animals move only in accordance with the rules of mechanics; but I believe that this machine is regulated by an overriding principle that weakens the impression of external objects on animals by comparison with the impressions made on men.

It seems to me that all animals share a faculty that is very similar to reason even if one cannot give it that name. Empedocles, Pythagoras, Plotinus, Porphyry,* and several other wise men of antiquity took this view. It is true that this faculty is far more obvious in some animals than in others.

I cannot but admire the harmonious architecture of the bees, their industry and their political economy, which is superior to even the best form of government found in mankind. I have no less pleasure in considering the spider, which builds with admirable artistry a little palace made of silk and spins its canvas to capture unwise flies. There is something pleasant and amusing in watching the behaviour of ants, their wise prudence, and to see how they work during the entire summer to amass the stores of food that they need during the winter. There is not a bird, not a four-legged beast, not a fish, that does not refute this hypothesis by Descartes [. . .]. Is it possible that all these actions come only from matter? On that basis it would be appropriate to say that even human nature is only matter modified in one way or another; and that all the noise man makes in the world is nothing more than the effect of a body that is better constructed and of a machine that is more refined and better constructed.

I remain in agreement that we surpass many another living creature in all the activities of our souls, in our use of reason. However, we must admit that we have our own flaws, just like them. The greatest among them,

I believe, is not granting reason to creatures that often have more sense than we have. Man behaves this way from a principle of naivety and envy that I am obliged to condemn even though I know you are not guilty of it. (Marana)

There is in Paris a man who, while not born blind, lost his sight in an accident. It seems that nature wished to compensate this man for the loss of his eyes by giving him an exquisite sense of touch. We might say that he has eyes at the end of his fingers, for he distinguishes by touch things that could not be differentiated by sight. I am persuaded that this man is not deceitful, and that he is genuinely blind and does not dissemble so as to blind those who are not. I have seen him with his face covered by a blindfold. In front of him a table was set up on which various samples of oriental silk cloth in different colours were arrayed. He touched each of them carefully and told us the colour of each of them. I, who do not usually rush to judgement, suspected that the fabric of the blindfold around his eyes might have allowed him to perceive the different colours, or that perhaps one of the other spectators might have tipped him off with prearranged signals. I made everyone leave the room, apart from a single wise dervish who was a close friend. We wrapped the man's head in a coat made of thick velvet that reached down to his midriff. He was completely encased and only his arms were free. I then picked up pieces of silk that were so small they could be hidden in the palm of my hand. I raised them to the level of his chin in such a manner that he could not have seen them even if he had not been blind. He touched them and didn't make the slightest error in discerning the different colours. We changed the order of the pieces of silk and gave him the same sample four or five times in a row. But no sooner did he touch them than he responded with some irritation that it was the same colour.

I swear to you, dear friend, that such an unusual experience filled me with great pleasure and admiration. It led me to conclude that nature is not mean with her gifts. When nature creates someone whose senses are defective, she replaces this fault with great delicacy of another sense. We asked the blind man how he managed to discriminate between the colours without the aid of his eyes. He was unable to describe to us the specific quality of the different sensation, and replied that in general the difference he felt between black and red silk was just like the difference he could feel between Persian silk and fine linen from Europe when he still had his eyesight—a difference to the touch that is, as you know, like that between paper and parchment [. . .]. You who daily have insight into the faculties of the human body can judge better than anyone if the extreme sensitivity of this man lies in the fineness of his skin, in the subtlety of his intelligence, or in the extraordinary virtue of a powerful and delicate soul; or if all these things work together. (Marana)

Now that printed books have vastly increased in number they are common and cheap. Histories and learned works that earlier were only available in Latin and Greek, or in other oriental languages, are now in translation and speak the language of every nation. This has made it possible for even the most humble people to read, if they have the time. They can even become as learned as their superiors, and the slave is able to argue points of science with his master. It is for this reason that Christians accuse those who are truly pious of ignorance and barbarism, since we do not allow printing anywhere in the entire extent of the Muslim empire. They draw attention to the fortunate results of this art, but do not consider its irritating consequences. They show no awareness that the freedom to print has filled the world with errors and lies. Moreover, they are ignorant of how Muslims are raised and do not know that from childhood everyone as a rule is taught Arabic and Persian. How otherwise could celebrated writings in these two languages exist? There is nothing essential to wisdom that has not already been included in the writings of the wise men of the East. As for these nugatory little books that the Europeans acquire, they are superstitious and a nuisance. Authors waste their time and readers waste their money. Let us also note, in addition, the baleful effects that the unfortunate permission to print has produced in Christianity. How many acts of sacrilege, how many massacres, rebellions, and acts of impiety has one seen in this permissive century in most western countries? How much hatred among the Christians, how many rebellions among subjects, what diverse opinion about religion, what scorn for divine, human, and natural laws? (Marana)

Politics

The ancient kings of France granted to this court the power to approve and verify the laws and declarations that they issued. This was a barrier that these wise men comfortably placed between their subjects and their sovereign authority. From this it would appear that a part of the government of France was in the hands of the aristocrats; since in the view of the wise men the state could not last long without such a mixed government. In this century princes have submitted to tribunals, appointed by themselves, the decisions that they would wish to take; and they do this in order to exculpate themselves before God, to whom they are obliged to make their account just like all other mortals; and in order to gain the confidence of their subjects they appoint from the ranks of the aristocrats the magistrates who resolve any differences that arise between them. However, they retain the right to invoke their absolute power [. . .]. As the king today rules with absolute power, and has complete control of his coffers, which are well filled, he has brave and experienced officers, brave and energetic soldiers, large armies and a good navy. In this manner he lets this powerful body know that, while it was established in order to aid and advise the king, it must not think that its laws apply to the sovereign. For this purpose he made an appearance at the courts bearing all the regalia normally reserved for ceremonial occasions, accompanied by a mob of lords who paid tribute to the power of the monarch. He gave these men to understand that he wished them to pass without reservation the edicts and declarations that he had sent them, and he pretended that they had passed them immediately. He then forbade them to meddle in future affairs of state; and in order to give them an even greater shock, he declared that henceforth he would distribute favours and offices and reward the deserving. (Marana)

A cloud of sadness covers France; the Sun of France has set; Louis, the powerful king for whom Europe would have been too small had he lived longer, is now confined within the limits of his tomb. Yesterday, on the fourteenth day of the fifth moon, he died at St-Germain: he left a queen as regent and Cardinal Mazarin* as prime minister. He was a prince of great virtue, and his virtue, his successful conquests, and his victories attracted the envy of his neighbours. (Marana)

At present, then, the government of the Persians is a monarchy—despotic and absolute, since it is entirely in the hands of a single man who is the sovereign chief both in spiritual as well as in worldly affairs; the complete master of the life and goods of his subjects. There is certainly no other sovereign in the world who is as absolute as the king of Persia; for one completely and faithfully heeds his orders without examining his reasons or the circumstances, even when one sees as plainly as day that there is rarely any sense of justice in his injunctions and that they often lack even common sense [. . .]. Nothing can hinder the extravagant nature of his capriciousness—not honesty, not merit, not devotion, not past service. It takes nothing more than a change in his fancies, suggested by a single word from his mouth, to overthrow in a second people who are well established and most deserving of their status; to deprive them of their possessions and their life; and all of this can occur without any type of trial and without an obligation to verify the crime of which they are accused. (Chardin)

Orientals and the Orient

Persia is the greatest empire in the world, if you consider it according to the geographical description given by the Persians who represent it to the full extent of its ancient boundaries, which are four great seas; the Black Sea, the Red Sea, the Caspian Sea, and the Gulf of Persia; with six rivers almost as famous as those seas, viz., the Euphrates, the Araxes, the Tigris, the Phase, the Oxis, and the Indus. One can hardly be more precise in pointing out the limits of this vast kingdom, which is not like the states of petty sovereigns, whose frontiers are marked out with a brook or a rivulet, or some little landmark. Persia on every side has the space of four or five days journey from its confines, which is uninhabited, although the soil is the best in the world in many places, as on the eastern and western sides [. . .]. The Persians, in naming their country, make use of the one word, which they indifferently pronounce Iroun, and Iran; an ancient term invented by the Tartars, from whom the modern Persians proceed. (Chardin)

The blood of the Persians is naturally thick; it may be seen by the Guebres, who are the remainder of the ancient Persians; they are homely, ill shaped, dull, and have a rough skin, and dark complexion. The same thing is observed also in the provinces next to India, where the inhabitants are little better shaped than the Guebres [. . .]. But in other parts of the kingdom the Persian blood is grown clearer, by the mixture of the Georgian and Circassian blood, which is certainly the people of the world which nature favours most in respect of their shape and complexion and their boldness and courage; they are likewise sprightly, courtly, and affectionate [. . .]. As to the men, as a rule they are tall, straight, ruddy, vigorous, have a good air and a pleasant countenance. The temperateness of their climate, and the temperance they are brought up in, do not a little contribute to their physical beauty [. . .]. As for intelligence, it is as beautiful in the Persians as their bodies; their fancy is lively, quick, and fruitful; their memory easy and copious; they have a ready disposition to sciences and to the liberal and mechanical arts, and to war also; they love glory, or rather vanity, which is only glory's shadow; they are of a flexible and obliging temper, of a quick and clever wit; they are courtly, civil, polite, and well bred; they have naturally a proclivity for voluptuousness, luxury, extravagance, and excess; for which reason, they are ignorant both of frugality and trade [. . .]. They are true philosophers on what is good and bad in the world, and on the hope and dread of the future; they are little guilty of covetousness, and are only desirous of getting so that they may spend; they love to enjoy the present and deny themselves nothing that they are able to procure, taking no thought for tomorrow, and relying wholly on providence and their own fate; they firmly believe it to be sure and unalterable, and carry themselves honestly in that respect; so when any misfortune happens to them they are not cast down, as most men are, they only say quietly, *Mek toub est*, i.e., *That is written*, or, *it is ordained*, that that should happen. (Chardin)

This mad taste for tobacco is an ill habit that has bewitched almost all the world. Our people in the West smoke it, take it as snuff, and chew it, as everyone knows; and some people, particularly the Portuguese, have noses always full of snuff. The eastern people only smoke it, but with the same insatiable greediness, and most of them, especially the Persians, always have a pipe in their mouth. (Chardin)

The most commendable trait in the manners of the Persians is their kindness to strangers; the reception and protection they afford them, and their universal hospitality, and toleration, in regard to religion. The exception to this are the clergy of the country, who, as in all other places, hate furiously all those who hold different opinions. (Chardin)

The Persians are the most civilized people of the East, and the greatest flatterers in the world. The polite men among them are on a level with the politest men of Europe. Their air, their countenance, is very well composed, lovely, grave, majestic, and as affable and tender as possible. (Chardin)

These people are of the opinion, as I have observed, that one cannot better attain to virtue, nor have a fuller taste of pleasure, than by resting and dwelling at home and that it is not good to travel except for the purpose of acquiring wealth. Similarly, they believe that every stranger is a spy if he is not a merchant, or a craftsman [. . .]. It is from this spirit of theirs, no doubt, that the Persians are so grossly ignorant of the present state of other nations of the world, and that they do not much understand geography [. . .]. The majority have only a confused idea of Europe, which they look upon to be some little island in the North Sea, where there is nothing to be found that is either good or handsome; this explains why, they say, the Europeans travel all over the world in search of fine things, and of those which are necessary, since they are destitute of them. (Chardin)

The men wear no breeches, only a pair of lined drawers, which hang down to their ankles, but which have no feet; they are not open and must be undone when they have occasion to make water. You must take notice that the men put themselves all in the same posture as the women when they answer the call of nature, and in that posture they untie their drawers and pull them down, though but a little way [. . .]. On solemn occasions wealthy women, and sometimes the men, border the neck of the shirt or shift with pearl embroidery about a finger's breadth. The men don a cotton waistcoat, which they fasten before, upon their stomachs, and which falls down to their *hames*, and over it a robe, which they call *cabai*, as wide as a woman's petticoat, but very straight on top, passing twice over the stomach. It is fastened under their arms, the first round under the left arm, and the other, which is uppermost, under the right arm [. . .]. Depending on the season, they will put a short or tight-fitting sleeveless coat, which they call *courdy*, over the robe; or a long one with sleeves, which they call *cadabi*. These close-fitting coats are cut like robes, that is to say, they are wide at the bottom and narrow at top, like bells; they are made of cloth, or gold brocade, or a thick satin, and they daub them all over with gold or silver lace, or galloon, or they embroider them; they are furred, some with sable skins, and others with the skins of the sheep of Tartary, and Bactriana, the wool of which is finer than that of the horses [. . .]. The footwear is of different sorts or fashions in Persia; but they are all without ears, and not a bit open on the sides; they are nailed down under the heel, and they trim the sole of the shoe with little nails, at the place where the bottom of the foot rests, to make it last the longer [. . .]. The shoes worn by wealthy people are made like women's slippers, that they may throw them off the easier when they enter their houses, where the floors are covered with carpets. These shoes are of green shagreen, or some other colours; the sole, which is always a single one, is as thin as a pasteboard, but it is the best leather in the world. None but that type of shoe have heels, the rest are flat [. . .]. The Persian turban, which they call *dulbend*, that is to say, a band that winds round, and which is the finest part of their dress, is a piece so heavy that it is a wonder they can wear it; some are so heavy as to weigh twelve or fifteen pounds; the lightest of them weigh half as much [. . .]. These turbans are made of coarse white linen, which they use to shape it, and they cover it with a fine luxurious silk fabric, or with silk and gold. The materials of the turban have the ends richly woven with floss fringes about six or seven inches wide, which they tie in a knot, in the middle of the turban, like a plume of feathers [. . .]. The Persians, for the most part, let the beard grow on the chin and all over the face, but short and which only covers the skin, but the clergy and pious wear it longer. (Chardin)

Women

I am living rather well here [in Paris]. The country is pleasant and wealthy. People are of good society and appear frank and polite. I have yet to make the acquaintance of women and must find a way of effecting introductions. They are a sex that is unforgiving should they consider themselves scorned. Women are good at discovering what one would like to know and divulging those things that one would like to make public [. . .]. One does not find here the same peace and quiet that we have in Constantinople. The throng of carriages, horses, and carts is so great that the imagination boggles. You might find it strange that smart people who suffer from no ailment of the limbs have themselves transported in a machine with four wheels. But I am most surprised to find that the very same people are resolved to put up with the incommodious noise and to spend so much money from sheer vanity. The more modest French do not approve of this luxury, and say that in the time of Henri III there were no more than three carriages in Paris, of which two belonged to the king. But today the number is so large that they cannot be counted. (Marana)

The chastity and fidelity from which you benefit cannot be overestimated. It is a virtue that makes women worthy of the highest praise. Her caring and diligence; the respect and duties that she shows you, are qualities that must charm you. Should you mistreat her, you are surely too magnanimous to feel anger even a moment later. Should you follow the usual route and issue her, according to the law, a letter of divorce, you will repent in less than forty-eight hours. (Marana)

Their head is very well clothed, and over it they have a veil that falls down to their shoulders, and covers their neck and bosom before. When they go out, they put over all a great white veil, which covers them from head to foot, not suffering any thing to appear in several countries but the balls of their eyes. The women wear four veils in all; two of which they wear at home, and two more when they go abroad. The first of these veils is made like a kerchief, falling down behind the body, by way of ornament; the second passes under the chin, and covers the bosom; the third is the white veil, which covers all the body; and the fourth is a sort of handkerchief, which goes over the face, and is fastened to the temples. This handkerchief, or veil, has a sort of network, like old point, or lace, for them to see through [. . .]. The custom of these veils for the women is the most ancient of which their histories speak. But it is difficult to know whether it was pride, vainglory, or modesty which induced them to wear them first; or whether it was the jealousy of their husbands. (Chardin)

Eunuchs

There are a great number of eunuchs throughout the kingdom of Persia, and it is possible to describe the manner in which they govern and of what they are masters, they who have the confidence of their Lord, the custody of his possessions, and the management of his affairs. In particular, women fall under their surveillance and under their tutelage. They are in charge of access to the harem, which is the dwelling-place of the women—or, better said, their prison—and they accompany them everywhere, even when they bathe and pay visits. Nonetheless, the eunuchs do not have the right to enter the chambers of the women when they are on their own. Among the great families the eunuchs are also the teachers and tutors of the children [. . .]. It is costly to buy and maintain eunuchs. Those aged between eight and sixteen sell for between one thousand and two thousand francs, provided they are of good intelligence and education. It is not desirable to purchase them when older than this age since they are castrated young, that is, between the ages of seven and ten years, when they sell quickly and scarcely ever change their master, since once they enter into service they are put to work, sometimes under severe punishment if required, which shapes their character as desired by those whom they serve. They recognize that, on the one hand, their happiness depends on their master since they are slaves and he is the arbiter of their fate; and, on the other hand, that they are only able to aspire to his benevolence and trust through good service. For these reasons they attempt to serve with all their power; and they usually succeed so well that they manage and run everything [. . .]. The number of eunuchs in the homes of the greatest lords is usually from six to eight. In the homes of lesser nobility the smaller number is between three and four, and in the homes of people who are merely rich there are just a couple [. . .]. It is the jealousy that men bear their women in the East that has produced the cruel and unnatural impulse to create eunuchs. But while they were initially destined to guard women, they have been found suitable for other offices and for greater affairs. Given the state in which they have been placed, eunuchs are less prone to the passions of love and ambition, which are the great sources of disorder in public life; they ought to get less carried away than other men, and since they are not burdened by children, wives, or even relations, since they always come from the lowest people and hardly even know which country they are from, they therefore have only to be concerned with the state of their body and will be more devoted to their duties than other men [. . .]. Some people maintain, as I've said, that there are eunuchs who experience the passion of love and who seek relations with women [. . .]. What I can say for certain is that as a rule in the Orient women have a mortal hatred of eunuchs as the Argus looking over their actions. (Chardin)

Seraglio

The Persians call the apartments of the wives a harem or sacred space. The Turks give them the name of the seraglio, which means a palace, a large residence. This word 'harem', which is Hebrew, occurs in a hundred places in the Books of Moses, where it means 'illicit', 'prohibited', 'taboo', 'abominable', 'execration', 'excommunication'. In Persian one uses it with respect to that part of the residence inhabited by women in order to indicate that all men are prohibited from entering with the exception of the master; and that this is a sacred space [. . .]. Women are guarded more strictly in Persia than anywhere else on the face of the earth. The seraglios of the Turks and of the Grand Seigneur look like public places in comparison. I attribute the reason for this to the opulence natural to the Persian climate; and to the religion of the country, which permits one to find satisfaction in numerous women provided that they do not belong to anyone else. The reason for this lies in the climate, which is generally hot and dry to the point where one feels acutely the turbulence of love, and for that reason a passion for women is extremely violent. As a result jealousy is even stronger than in the surrounding countries, where love is clearly felt less strongly [. . .]. The Persians explain their jealousy differently. They recount that on his deathbed their Lawgiver told them in his final utterance to guard their religion and their women. Gripped by their furious zealousness, his followers have since cited these words as the commandment that authorizes them to lock their women away in seraglios or harems where the walls are not only raised but sometimes doubled and tripled. And since the manners of a nation derive in part from the dogmas of their faith, in Persia it is said that it is a matter of the glory of God and their well-being that one may do no more than cast one's eyes towards the apartments where women are enclosed.

[. . .] Oriental women have always been regarded as lesbians. I have heard it confirmed so often and by so many people that this is the case and that they have many ways of mutually satisfying one another, that I take this to be highly likely. Attempts are made to thwart them, since one assumes that this diminishes their desire and renders them less susceptible to the love of men. The women who have been in the seraglio report surprising things about the passions with which the women there make love, about the jealousy that is involved, and about the furious jealousy that the favourites have for one another, and about their hatreds, their treachery, their malicious tricks [. . .]. The Persians say that women are good for nothing apart from pleasure and childbirth, and they make no allowances for their skill, for their intelligence and for their commitment to all sorts of activities. Similarly, they have no involvement in communal activities, nor is their involvement in housekeeping any greater than in anything else. They spend their life in a state of sloth, laziness, and lassitude, all day reclining on their beds so as to be scratched and patted down by their little slaves, which is one of the great pleasures of the Asiatics, or in smoking tobacco, which is so mild that one can take it in the morning and evening alike without feeling the effects. (Chardin)

EXPLANATORY NOTES

In composing my own Explanatory Notes, I have learned a great deal from the scholarly work of editors whose versions are listed in the Select Bibliography. Every student of Montesquieu, and Enlightenment thought, will owe a debt to the scholarly apparatus of the Voltaire Foundation edition, which is of such compendiousness on Montesquieu's sources as to serve virtually as an index of his colossal erudition and map of his thought-world. Readers interested in learning more about Montesquieu's ideas about religion and, more specifically, the contribution of Pierre Bayle to the views expressed in the *Persian Letters*, are now advised to consult the extensive comments in this great critical guide.

Preface

3 *But that . . . anonymous*: Montesquieu's use of the device of the fictional persona of the translator would become fashionable in later oriental fictions.

Asian style: other works of the period, such as Marana's *The Turkish Spy* and J. F. Bernard's *Moral, Satirical and Comic Reflections on the manners of our Century*, also frame their tale as the work of a fictional translator who speaks of the oriental style as a 'beautiful fire of imagination', the excesses of which must be tempered to suit French classical taste. Letter 15 provides a pastiche of this elaborate oriental style.

Letter 1

4 *Qum*: city holy to Shiite Muslims, where the burial-places of Fatima and kings Sefi I (1642) and Abbas II (1632–66) are shrines.

twelve prophets: Montesquieu appears to have confused Fatima, the daughter of Muhammad, from whom twelve successors descended, with a different Fatima whose tomb was located in the Great Mosque at Qum.

Erzeron: Armenian capital.

5 *Tabriz*: according to Tavernier, the journey from Tabriz to Ispahan lasted twenty-four days by caravan.

Saphar: this is the month of April. The travellers left Ispahan on 19 March (Maharram) 1711 and arrive in Paris at the beginning of May (Rebiab 1) 1712. Their final letter from Paris is dated 11 November (Rhamazan) 1720 and coincides with the crash of John Law's System (see note to Letter 126). For more information on the calendar, see the 'Note on the Chronology of the *Persian Letters*', p. xlvii.

Letter 2

5 *chief black eunuch . . . seraglio*: the chief eunuch was in charge of the seraglio or harem. So-called white eunuchs assisted the black eunuchs and were banned from entering the living spaces in the seraglio. White eunuchs had their testicles removed, while black eunuchs underwent more radical castration. See also the sections on 'Eunuchs' and 'Seraglio' in the Appendix.

laws of chaste and seemly behaviour: the letter introduces the world of the seraglio as a realm governed entirely for the sake of the pleasure of the master. But while the women exist to serve their master, their subordination to the discipline of chastity, order, and quiet is in keeping with religious strictures and is seen as a matter of laws or rules rather than personal whim. The Persians use the word law to designate religious rules until Letter 36, where Rica raises the notion of 'natural law' in connection with the status of women. Usbek's harem is of a modest size, housing five wives (Fatmé, Roxane, Zachi, Zelis and Zephis); four black eunuchs (the chief eunuch, Jaron, Ismael, and Solim), and three white eunuchs (Cosrou, Nadir, and their chief). Montesquieu brings almost all of them to life as characters by giving them their own letters. There has been considerable debate about whether the seraglio is also meant to represent by analogy the situation of France under an oppressive monarchy. For further comments on despotism, see Letter 101.

Always remember the abyss: a paraphrase of line 524 from Racine's *Bajazet* (1672), 'Rentre dans le néant dont je t'ai fait sortir'.

Letter 3

6 *boxes*: sedan-chair.

Letter 5

8 *whatever reasons . . . you may give me*: Usbek supplies different addressees with different motivations for his trip. Letter 1 cites an 'appetite for learning', but Letters 5 and 8 suggest he is menaced after falling into disfavour at court.

Letter 6

Erivan: Armenian city on the border of Turkey and Persia.

Ottomans: named for Osman or Othman I, the founder of the Turkish Empire. Montesquieu captures both the political tensions between the Persians and Turks and the religious divisions, the latter being Sunni Muslims while the Persians are Shiites. In Letter 19 Usbek confirms the sense that not all Orientals are alike by painting a negative portrait of Turkey, which stands as an emblem of the corruption and despotism with which the Oriental is sometimes associated in the eighteenth century.

Letter 10

15 *mullahs*: the 'doctors of law' who read and interpreted the Qur'an during Friday prayers.

Letter 11

Troglodytes: among Montesquieu's sources for the utopian age of the Troglodytes are Pomponius Mela (*De orbis situ*), who says that they whistle rather than speak, and the description of Bétique from Fenelon's *Télémaque* (1699), a narrative that was read throughout the Enlightenment for its instruction on good kingship and virtue, and the Earl of Shaftesbury's writings on the relation of self-interest and selfishness to the welfare of larger entities like society and the state. On the influence of Hobbes on Montesquieu, see Ursula Haskins Gonthier, 'Montesquieu and England: Enlightened Exchanges in the Public Sphere (1689–1755)', DPhil thesis, Oxford University (2006), 32.

Letter 15

23 *Zufagar*: Muslim tradition holds that the Archangel Gabriel gave the sword to Ali, the son-in-law of Muhammad, who, after his martyrdom, was revered as one of the founders of Shiite Islam.

O thirteenth Imam: according to Shiite belief there were twelve imams or leaders in the succession from Muhammad and his son-in-law Ali. Usbek means to flatter his addressee. Throughout the work, Islam is rarely considered for its own sake and exists, rather, in counterpoint to Christianity (see e.g. Usbek's observations in Letter 44, on casuistry in Letter 55, and on hypocrisy in Letter 73). While the Persians' criticism of Islamic practice would seem implicitly to advantage Christianity, this is nothing more than a ruse on Montesquieu's part, since the travellers' bemusement clearly has the Judaeo-Christian tradition, and religious belief more generally, as its target.

Letter 16

all meats: dietary restrictions on impure food for Jews are articulated in Leviticus 11. Similarly, the Qur'an legislates against eating animals 'slain in their own blood' and against pork. As observant Muslims, Montesquieu's letter-writers are continually on the lookout for fresh water in which to bathe and fulfil their religious obligations, e.g. Letters 29 and 44. Montesquieu is generally fascinated by the notion of rules and rituals that govern both western and eastern institutions that at least superficially seem to run according to personal choice.

Letter 17

25 *Abdias Iben Salon*: Montesquieu follows closely his source Hermannus Dalmata, *Machumetis Saracenorum principis doctrina* (1550), which includes a dialogue between Muhammad and the Jewish doctor.

Letter 18

26 *Tokat*: in the seventeenth century Tokat, the ancient Hadrianopolis,
remained a great trading depot and crossroads between Constantinople,
Persia, and Smyrna.

after thirty-five days of travel: the letter is dated to 2 November. The duration of itineraries mentioned in the letters correspond closely to information given in accounts by Chardin and Tavernier (see Introduction,
p. xix), and thereby convey a sense of verisimilitude. The travellers are
likely to have departed Erzeron just after the middle of September. From
Smyrna they will travel by sea to the Tuscan port of Livorno. The journey normally took forty days.

materializing out of a rock: presumably the Knights of Malta.

Letter 21

29 *by elderly women*: the *dueña* was a familiar character in Spanish fiction.
The 'jalousie', which made it possible to gaze outwards without being
seen, was a borrowing from Arab architecture.

only one veil: Italian women wore a covering when entering a church.

Letter 22

30 *Paris is as large as Ispahan*: true to the tradition of satirists of urban life,
from Juvenal to the seventeenth-century poet Nicolas Boileau (especially
Satire VI), Rica, the younger and the more ironic of the travellers, gives
a mixed picture of the city, which is monumental and chaotic.

They run, they fly: the observation about the quickness of the French
remains a standard observation among Enlightenment travellers, as does
attention to the crush of traffic on the streets of Paris.

31 *this king is a great magician*: a hint of Montesquieu's interest in the connection between ritual and hierarchies and the mystique of power. The
king, like the pope, pursues a political programme based on the illusion of
omnipotence, infallibility, and wealth.

if . . . in his treasury: the currency was devalued on 23 December 1715, and
its value continued to fluctuate sharply until 1726.

called Constitution: the Bull *Unigenitus*, urged on Pope Clement XI by
Louis XIV, condemned the hundred propositions contained in Pasquier
Quesnel's Jansenist statement (*Nouveau Testament en français*). Jansenism
was a Christian sect that owed allegiance to the doctrines of the Dutch
theologian Otto Jansen (1585–1638), who set out fundamental beliefs in
his *Augustinus* (1640). Jansenism embraced a theological determinism
concerning man's ability to achieve divine grace; and it expressed a theological pessimism reflected in the moral rigour and harshness of the
movement. It was condemned as heretical by Pope Innocent X in 1653. It
had an important influence among followers of the Port-Royal logic and

gained sympathy in France among the Oratorians, who were responsible for the training of priests. The Papal Bull was promulgated in September 1713, after the date of this fictive letter (4 June 1712) and a deliberate anachronism by the author. The collaboration between king and church was particularly alarming since the French church had traditionally maintained its independence from Rome according to the Gallican tradition.

32 *fomenters of this revolt*: the Bull *Unigenitus* condemned the 73rd of Quesnel's propositions, which asserted the right of women to read holy scripture and learn the mysteries of religion.

war against his neighbours: after the death of Charles II, the last Spanish Habsburg king, in the War of the Spanish Succession (1701–14) England, the Low Countries, and the Holy Roman Empire fought to thwart French expansion.

invisible enemies: allusion to the Jesuits, who were implacable opponents of the Jansenists.

Letter 26

36 *late afternoon*: the Comédie-Française, where performances took place in the late afternoon. In Diderot's *Rameau's Nephew* (1760) the hero rushes off to the Opéra, which starts at 6 p.m.

the theatre: the entire description of the theatre, seen from Rica's *faux-naif* viewpoint, is a good example of Montesquieu's use of alienation technique. He misunderstands the relation of audience and stage and regards the spectators in the boxes as actors. Yet he astutely notices the tension between members of the audience, who sit according to social classes.

37 *the right*: allusion to the extrovert behaviour of Oronte in Molière's the *Misanthrope* (1666).

sacrifice I made him: aristocrats notoriously preyed on the artists for sexual favours.

Letter 27

39 *will burn*: namely, the Inquisition.

little wooden beads: rosary beads.

Galicia: site of pilgrimage to St James of Compostella.

sanbenitos: a garment worn by both penitents and impenitents of the Spanish Inquisition. Penitents wore sanbenitos that were yellow with red crosses. Impenitents—heretics burned at the stake during autos-da-fe—wore black sanbenitos decorated with devils and flames.

Letter 28

40 *I found portraits of me*: these images are likely to refer to portraits of other 'exotic' visitors, such as the Siamese ambassadors from 1686, Moroccans

from 1699, and the Persian ambassador of 1715 (described in Supplementary Letter 4 and painted by Antoine Coypel in his *Louis XIV Receives the Ambassador of Persia*, 1715).

Letter 30

41 *three hundred people*: the Hôpital des Quinze-vingt, located on the rue Saint-Honoré near the Palais-Royal, was founded by St Louis in 1254 as a hospice for the blind.

42 *'What,' I said, 'you're blind?*: philosophers of the period, including Locke and Berkeley, speculated on the capacity of the blind to perceive. Later in the Enlightenment Diderot and others will interest themselves in the Molyneux problem. For a contemporary parallel, see the letter by Marana in the Appendix, p. 234.

Letter 31

42 *divine Qur'an*: the Qur'an prohibits the consumption of fermented drinks.

43 *Seneca*: Roman philosopher of the first century AD, admired since the Renaissance as an exemplary figure of Stoic virtue whom various philosophical schools and Christian thinkers claimed as their own.

if the blood flows: Descartes describes the 'movement of the heart and arteries' in Part V of the *Discourse on the Method* (1637).

potions: coffee.

Letter 33

45 *Polygamy Triumphant*: Johann Leyser, *Polygamata triumphatrix, id est Discursus politicus de polygamia* (London, 1682).

Letter 34

46 *Coffee*: from the foundation of the Café Procope in Saint-Germain in 1688, cafés and coffee were a key institution of the Parisian public sphere, associated with freethinking and regarded as centres of intellectual activity. A classic literary treatment of café life as an intellectual centre of the time can be found in Diderot's *Rameau's Nephew*.

ancient Greek poet: the appearance of Mme Dacier's translation of the *Iliad* (1699) would rekindle in 1714 the famous Quarrel of the Ancients and Moderns that dated back to the mid-seventeenth century.

47 *dense, black confusion*: the area in the Latin Quarter near the Sorbonne and Monastery of Sainte-Geneviève, destroyed in the French Revolution, where ecclesiastical colleges were located.

an entire nation: allusion to Irish Catholics expelled after the deposition of James II in 1688.

Letter 35

The king . . . old: Louis XIV, born in 1638, was 75 at the time of Usbek's letter. By the end of his reign the finances of the state were highly precarious. The vast expenditure on the building of Versailles was only one commonly cited cause for the financial crisis that the Regent faced.

he has a minister who is only eighteen, and a mistress who is eighty: Mme de Maintenon was born in 1635. A number of aristocratic scions attained high posts at precocious ages in the late stages of the reign.

Letter 36

48 *Whether . . . women*: the question was treated by Poullain de La Barre, *On the Equality of the Two Sexes* (*De l'égalité des deux sexes*, 1673), an evident source for Montesquieu.

49 *very worldly*: the French word *galant* refers to mixture of intellectual and social qualities that was cultivated by men who frequented the salons. Conjectures about the philosopher identify either François Poullain de La Barre or Bernard le Bovier de Fontenelle, the French Academician and an important writer on metaphysics and natural philosophy.

Semiramis: fabled Babylonian queen.

Of the Romans . . . obeyed their wives: the source is Plutarch's *Life of the Elder Cato*.

Sarmatians: a people mentioned by Herodotus that settled in the region from the Baltic to the Caspian Sea and were eventually devastated by the Huns.

The Prophet decided the question: Qur'an 2: 228.

Letter 37

50 *Haggi Ibbi*: the sole appearance of this correspondent. In a note Montesquieu recorded that 'Haggi' is the name of someone who has made pilgrimage to Mecca (*hajj*).

Letter 42

54 *excellence of his chosen craft*: reference to Molière, *Le Bourgeois Gentilhomme* (1671), I. ii, where the dancing master, philosopher, music-master, and marksman each claim to be superior in his skill.

that conqueror: Alexander the Great, of whom it was said 'He undertook many campaigns, gained possession of many fortresses, and put the local kings to death. So he advanced to the ends of the earth' (1 Maccabees 1: 3).

Letter 43

55 *rue St Honoré . . . Faubourg St Germain*: during the Regency these streets were renowned for their elegant mansions. The large sum

mentioned conveys the importance the *petit-maître* attaches to conspicu-
ous expenditure as a sign of social status.

56 *Nicolas Flamel*: a fabled alchemist from the fourteenth century.

   Raymond Lull: Catalan mystic and missionary of the thirteenth century.

Letter 45

58 *courouc*: Montesquieu's source Chardin uses the term to describe the cry
made by eunuchs who clear the way when a woman leaves the harem.

Letter 46

60 *man of quality*: the meaning of *homme de qualité* is close to 'gentleman' at
this period.

   a tax farmer: tax-collectors paid a fee for the privilege of collecting revenue for the Crown and received a handsome 'cut' as payment. They were
the butt of ridicule by satirists like La Bruyère.

   a rubicund complexion: a quotation from Molière's *Tartuffe* (1664): 'Il a
l'oreille rouge et le teint bien fleuri' (I. iv).

62 *fancy hair*: the coiffure of *the petit-maître* was a pile of elaborate curls
raised high in the front.

63 *resemble the angels, and the incorporeal powers*: Matt. 22: 30.

Letter 47

64 *Capuchin friar*: the Capuchins, an autonomous branch of the Franciscan
order of monks, maintained a residence in Ispahan. Montesquieu had a
critical view of missionary work, as he was convinced that the religions of
each country grew out of an individual matrix of ethnographic and geo-
graphic factors.

Letter 49

65 *the tsar*: Peter the Great became tsar in 1689. He visited Paris in 1721. His
towering appearance attracted enormous crowds. Peter was an absolute
ruler or despot, unchecked by a parliament or constitution of any kind.
Montesquieu draws on the observations of Olearius, *Voyage to Muscovy,
Tartary and Persia* (*Voyage en Moscovie, Tartarie et Perse*, 1666), where he
came across the legend that Russian women had a positive taste for being
abused by their husbands—although Russian law did permit husbands to
discipline their wives quite severely.

67 *the present ruler*: as part of his westernizing reforms in 1698 Peter required
nobles to adapt their appearance to European custom. Courtiers were
henceforth to be clean-shaven; the oriental-style caftan of the boyar was
shed for European dress. Such reforms led Orthodox believers to think of
Peter as an antichrist.

new kingdoms: in the Northern Wars (1704–21) Peter succeeded in smashing the power of Sweden, the rival empire in the region. This enabled him to extend control over Baltic trade-routes and raise the international diplomatic status of Russia.

Letter 51

69 *the white eunuch*: whether or not eunuchs could feel desire was discussed by Charles Ancillon, *Treatise on Eunuchs* (*Traité des eunuques*, 1707), a source on their psychology and physiology.

Zelide: in Letter 4 Zelide belonged to Sephis. In Letter 19, the chief eunuch divulged his intention of confiscating her for himself.

Letter 52

71 *seat in the Academy*: the Académie Française, founded in 1635, was the pre-eminent learned society devoted to the cause of the French language. Montesquieu was elected a member in 1728.

Letter 53

the first few hours of marriage: the ironical viewpoint comes from Molière's *School for Wives* (*L'École des femmes*, 1662).

72 *the Turks were taking Baghdad from us*: the siege of Baghdad by the sultan Amurat IV on 15 August 1638 (which is described in Marana's *Turkish Spy*).

Letter 54

73 *Gambling . . . in Europe*: the taste for gambling and the figure of the gambler became literary themes in the period, as treated by La Bruyère in his *Characters* (*Les Caractères*, 1688) and in numerous plays. The acquisition (and loss) of wealth through chance epitomizes for the Persians a disrespect for the rational control of life consistent with the ethics of their religion. But the aristocratic pastime, on the other hand, captures the speculative spirit of the period of John Law.

Letter 55

74 *rakes*: Montesquieu uses the term *libertin*, which commonly referred to freethinkers who showed insufficient religious respect; there was a close association between religious scepticism and hedonistic behaviour.

75 *Great Sophy*: a title of the ruler of Persia.

Letter 57

77 *I visited a house*: in the seventeenth century the Salon was the place where the 'beau monde' gathered for good conversation and a display of refined

manners. From the early eighteenth century until 1789 much of the intellectual discussion of the Enlightenment took place in the Salons of famous hostesses, where intellectuals, writers, and political figures mingled.

77 *Colbert*: Jean-Baptiste Colbert (1619–83), great reforming minister of finance and architect of central government in the reign of Louis XIV.

Letter 58

78 *Jews in France*: from 1394, by law, Jews no longer had the right to reside in the kingdoms of France. Queen Isabella of Castille expelled the Jews from Spain in 1492. A royal decree of 1715 restored to Jews the right to be in France if they resided there: the ban on Protestants in 1685 eliminated concern that Jews might be won over to the Protestant cause and undermine Catholicism. Montesquieu would treat the status of the Jews and also defend tolerance in the *Spirit of the Laws*.

79 *Abu Bakr*: father-in-law of Muhammad (b. 573, d. 634). Elected caliph in 632 after the death of the Prophet.

Letter 59

80 *conqueror of China*: reference to the conquest of China in 1643 by the Tartar emperor Chun-Chi.

Theodosius: the massacre by Theodosius I of 3,000 inhabitants of Thessalonika occurred in AD 390.

Letter 65

88 *Zoroastrian*: Montesquieu uses the Persian word *Ghebr* (borrowed from the account of Tavernier), which signifies a Zoroastrian. It has been determined that his information about these cultic practices comes from Thomas Hyde, *Historia religionis veterum persarum* (1700).

Cambyses: king of Persia from 530 to 522 BC. According to Herodotus, he married his sister.

92 *Zoroaster*: founder of the Persian religion Zoroastrianism, a monotheistic faith, said to have lived in around 1300 BC.

Balq: fortress city in the Turkish plateau, bordering Azerbaijan and Iran.

94 *Tartars*: Montesquieu means nomadic peoples of Muslim faith from the north of Asia.

Letter 67

96 *how a painter*: Pliny the Elder recounts in his *Natural History* that Zeuxis (464–398 BC) produced a composite portrait of Helen by selecting features of five beautiful women from the town of Croton.

he is never limited: this seems compatible with Descartes' position in his *Meditations*, where he affirms the infinite perfections of God which cannot be fully comprehended by the human mind. For a detailed discussion of Montesquieu's philosophical sources, see the article by Paul Hoffman, 'Usbek Metaphysicien: recherches sur les significations de la 69ᵉ *Lettres persanes*', *RHLF* 92 (1992), 779–800.

Letter 69

99 *their ancient legislator*: possibly a reference to Deuteronomy 22: 13–15.

Letter 70

100 *Messrs Tavernier and Chardin*: Jean Chardin (1643–1713) published the first edition of his travels in 1688. Jean-Baptiste Tavernier (1605–89) published his *Six Voyages* in 1676–77; both men were Huguenots and merchant travellers.

Letter 71

French Academy: Montesquieu's election to the Académie Française was contested in 1727 owing to the heretical nature of Letter 22. In 1751 the abbé Gaultier published the pamphlet *The Persian Letters Convicted of Impiety*, in which he argued that the work should be censured, and warned readers of the profound irreligiousness and impiety behind its surface charm.

a Code of its decrees: meaning the *Dictionnaire de l'Académie Française*, 1st edn. 1694, revised 1718.

at birth by a bastard: a reference to the history of the French Academy's landmark project of the *Dictionnaire de l'Académie Française*, which was marked by conflict and long delays.

Letter 74

103 *the laws . . . kill themselves*: under French law of 1670 suicide was regarded as a civil crime as well as a religious offence. This letter provoked the wrath of the abbé Gaultier, who noted that ending one's life in no way put an end to one's troubles (as Montaigne had argued), but earned eternal woes. In the *Spirit of the Laws*, Montesquieu treats suicide as a cultural practice, conditioned by custom and factors like climate. For example, he observed that suicide goes unpunished in England because it results from the climate.

Letter 75

107 *The only one of their books*: Cervantes's *Don Quixote* famously parodies the romance tradition.

Letter 78

110 *types of government*: the passage anticipates fundamental aspects of Montesquieu's political theory as worked out in the *Spirit of the Laws* concerning the relation of geographical and physical factors and the constitution of a state.

111 *Osman . . . deposed*: Osman II was deposed on 20 May 1622 after ruling for four years.

Letter 79

the empire of the Mogul: founded by Baber in northern India in the early sixteenth century.

Muscovy: the Tartars overran Kiev in 1247 and subjected the lands of Russia to their administration and taxation as run by the Golden Horde; their grip was weakened after a Russian victory in 1389.

Letter 80

112 *cut off their tongues*: despite vows of silence, Carthusians did not practise such mutilation.

Letter 81

that justice is eternal: Montesquieu's thinking about Natural Law is indebted to Cicero's *De Legibus* and *De Officiis*. Other sources on the question of Justice include Malebranche, *Treatise on Morality* (*Traité de morale*, 1683) and the Earl of Shaftesbury's *Sensus Communis, an Essay on the Freedom of Wit and Humour* (1711).

Letter 82

Invalides: a sanatorium constructed by Louis XIV from 1670 to 1706 for the benefit of veteran soldiers, it is much admired as an architectural monument of the period. Enthusiasm for the building and the treatment of soldiers did little to mitigate the sense of ruin caused by the King's foreign policy.

Letter 83

115 *Shah Soliman*: Suleiman III reigned from 1666 to 1694.

By banishing the Armenians: mention of the expulsion of Armenians from Persia during the reign of Soliman reminds readers of the Revocation of the Edict of Nantes (1685), which led to the exodus of 200,000 Huguenots from France to England, the United Provinces, and other Protestant countries. Apart from disapproving of intolerance, Montesquieu, like others, felt that this weakened France economically.

Shah Abas: Persian ruler from 1587 to 1629; see Letter 89.

Letter 85

118 *sociable animal*: this idea is a quotation from Aristotle's *Politics*, which had recently appeared in Addison's *The Spectator*.

Letter 87

120 *glory*: a distinction was made in the period between glory (*la gloire*), associated with military success, and honour (*l'honneur*), deriving from social standing.

Letter 88

122 *duels solved every problem*: attempts by the government to curb duelling as a means of settling scores of honour were largely futile. In 1679 Louis XIV made it a crime punishable by death for both the protagonists and the seconds, but the practice survived well into the nineteenth century.

Letter 89

123 *The monarch . . . is dead*: Louis XIV died on 4 September 1715. The new king was Louis XV, but power belonged to his uncle, Philippe d'Orléans (1674–1723), who had the backing of the Parlements and ruled as Regent. In his will, Louis XIV had stipulated that a Regency Council be established, of which his nephew would be only the chairman. Through brilliant manoeuvring, Orléans dismissed the provisions and eliminated most limits on his power. In September 1715, wishing to give the appearance of being more consensual, he restored some of these privileges (a fact Montesquieu recorded in his notebooks). On the position of the Parlements, see Letter 134.

Letter 90

124 *santon*: term for a monk of the Islamic faith.

Paul, Anthony, and Pachomius: the life of St Paul the Hermit was told by St Jerome. After fleeing into the desert of the Thebaid in Egypt, he lived in a cave until he was 113. Anthony and Pachomius were fourth-century Egyptian ascetics who became models for the hermit-ideal of monasticism. Pachomius founded a community of ascetics in the Thebaid, while Anthony renounced wealth and retreated to the desert.

Letter 91

125 *public law*: the major system of public law in the eighteenth century was the Reichsrecht, the law governing the relations between the members of the Holy Roman Empire. The position here is consistent with Montesquieu's later position that laws should coincide with reason, and that law was not a static system but one that evolved in accordance with social conditions and was sensitive to human institutions.

Letter 92

127 *Egyptian monarch*: the Pharaoh Amasis in the sixth-century BC.

Letter 94

130 *The Creator . . . in motion*: the entire letter is suffused with ideas from Descartes. The reference here is to an idea in his *Principles of Philosophy*: according to Cartesian physics, God is the ultimate cause of the quantity of motion in the universe; the immutability of God underlies the conservation of energy, who neither adds nor subtracts energy from the world.

observed, without any exception: this position implicitly excludes the possibility of miracles, although both Descartes and his follower Malebranche reconcile the existence of immutable laws of nature with miracles.

first law . . . and the second: references to two presuppositions of Cartesian mechanics, namely, that the universe operates in accordance with immutable laws established by God, and that the human mind has the innate capacity to discover those laws.

rich in miracles: the remark is rich in irony, since by miracles Usbek means the discoveries of science rather than the claims of revealed religion.

Letter 95

132 *Chamber of Justice*: on 14 May 1716 the Regent created by edict a Chamber of Justice to investigate financial malfeasance by the tax farmers. The minister is likely to be the duc de Noailles, who was president of the Council of Finance from 1715 to 1718.

Letter 96

132 *French fashion*: the entire letter, which uses exaggeration and irony, raises again (see Letters 24 and 50) the theme of artificiality in society and the value of appearances.

133 *the coiffures*: La Bruyère's *Characters* devotes a chapter to the subject of hairstyles. The excesses of fashion in the Regency were also a commonplace of the period. Here Rica's irony pushes the detail to absurd exaggeration in suggesting that domestic architecture was modified to suit hairstyles, and that children can scarcely recognize their parents after a 'makeover'.

Letter 97

134 *Roman laws*: the sixth-century Code of Justinian and the *Corpus Juris Civilis*.

Letter 98

135 *the Papal Bull*: in the French text, *Constitution*; see the note on the Bull *Unigenitus* in Letter 22.

Letter 99

137 *created a guard*: it was said that Philip-Augustus (12th century) employed a Swiss guard.

Letter 100

138 *Henri IV*: through his personal charisma Henri IV was able to moderate strife between the Protestants and Catholics. His assassination in 1610 helped to create the myth of a great king who saved the monarchy and his people. It was during the Regency that Voltaire began composing his epic poem about Henri IV and the Religious Wars (*La Ligue*, later known as *La Henriade*, 1728).

Letter 101

139 *submission and obedience*: Montesquieu couches his own anti-absolutist bias in these comments on English republicanism. He was clearly struck by John Locke's view that an abused people had the right to revolt against an unjust king, as argued in his *Treatise on Civil Government* (1690).

one of their kings: Charles I, executed in January 1649.

140 *captured a prince*: the anecdote apparently relates to Prince Edward, son of Henry VI, speaking to King Edward IV after the Battle of Tewkesbury in 1471.

Letter 104

145 *the late king*: see Letter 35.

Letter 105

type of book: literary journals began to circulate in the early eighteenth century. Montesquieu's library at La Brède contains a few examples.

Letter 106

147 *The University of Paris*: according to legend, Charlemagne was the founder.

over the letter Q . . . like a K: this anecdote concerns the scholar Ramus (at the Collège de France in 1551) whose enemies at the Sorbonne picked a quarrel over his pronunciation of the letter Q. Montesquieu's source is Bayle's *Dictionnaire historique*.

Letter 108

149 *so sparsely populated . . . former ages*: the answer to Rhedi's question extends through to Letter 118. In 1685 the scholar Isaac Vossius, whose views were disseminated by Pierre Bayle, published calculations showing that the population of Europe was in decline. In his 1751 essay, 'Of the Populousness of Ancient Nations', David Hume disputed the figures, but while it is now known that the population of Europe was in fact growing, Montesquieu and other contemporaries were pessimistically convinced of the opposite.

150 *Irimette, Circassia, and Guriel*: all are mentioned by Chardin as civilized places. Guria and Imereti are in the Black Sea region near the area now known as Georgia. Circassia extended from the Azov Sea to north of the Black Sea.

Letter 109

15 *one in particular*: the Black Death of 1350.

shameful of all maladies: in the eighteenth century stories circulated that syphilis originated in the New World. Voltaire has fun with this idea in *Candide*.

152 *that such cataclysms*: reconciling the geological age of the earth with biblical dating would become a concern in Enlightenment thought. In 1681 Thomas Burnet had advanced a theory on the number of catastrophes that the earth had undergone, and Montesquieu advanced views of his own in a preliminary presentation to the Academy of Bordeaux of a project entitled *The History of the Ancient and Modern Earth (Histoire de la terre ancienne et moderne)*. Travellers' accounts from the period call attention to depopulated cities in Persia and in Turkey.

Letter 110

152 *'Look to your wives . . . are yours'*: Qur'an, 2: 187.

153 *'Your wives . . . you will find Heaven'*: Qur'an 2: 223.

Letter 111

154 *peculium*: slaves were not allowed to own property under Roman law, but they were entrusted with a sum called the *peculium*. While this was technically the property of the master, it was considered to be the property of the slave and could be used for purchasing his freedom.

Letter 113

157 *chastity is the supreme virtue*: the demographic danger posed to society by clerical celibacy is a theme of numerous religious thinkers in the seventeenth century. On one estimate France had 270,000 priests in 1667.

marriage laws: the emperor Augustus, concerned about morals and the decline of native Roman stock, promulgated sumptuary legislation penalizing couples who did not marry and offering financial reward to those who did.

158 *the earliest authorities*: the marriage of priests is sanctioned by St Paul (1 Timothy 3: 2). The highly positive attitude evinced in the letter towards Protestantism, after the Revocation of the Edict of Nantes, was considered inflammatory by the church.

Letter 114

159 *colonies in America*: the Portuguese engaged in slave-trading from Africa, starting in the mid-fifteenth century. The trade expanded greatly following the discovery of America.

Letter 115

160 *population*: Montesquieu remarks in his *Pensées* that the Chinese reproduce out of a religious sense, 'in order to provide their ancestors with people who can service their cult'.

T'ien: notion of heaven in Confucianism.

Letter 117

162 *Ever since the Jews were wiped out*: AD 135.

163 *expulsion of the Moors*: by Philip III in 1610.

recovered their health: a history of Madagascar published in 1658 contained an anecdote to this effect.

164 *exterminate them*: Montesquieu had read Bartolemeo de Las Casas's *Short Account of the Destruction of the Indies* (1542), the great critique of the brutal colonial techniques Spain employed in South America.

Letter 119

166 *the Grand Vizir of Germany*: reference to the campaigns of Charles VI against the Turks in 1716–17.

Letter 121

168 *has been arrested*: Cellamare, the ambassador of Philip V of Spain, was implicated in the conspiracy to topple the Regent and install Philip in his place. His co-conspirators included the duc de Maine, the natural son of Louis XIV, who was arrested on 29 December 1718. Their grievance concerned the Regent's decision to concentrate power in his own hands rather than ruling with a Council, as Louis XIV had wished. In August 1718 Orléans forced through a series of measures that severely limited the powers of the *parlementaire*, preventing them, among other things, from intervening in financial matters.

168 *in the words of a prince*: as recounted by Quintus Curtius Rufus, *De gestis Alexandri* (5.8). On his defeat by Alexander the Great in 333 BC, King Darius III of Persia is alleged to have told the surviving members of his retinue: 'Your loyalty and devotion make it possible for me to believe that I am still king.'

Letter 122

king of Sweden: Charles XII was murdered during the siege of Fredrikshald in November 1718, and his assassin, Baron Henry de Goertz, was executed early in 1719.

Letter 123

170 *Château de Fontarabie*: reference to the siege of the Spanish citadel laid in June 1719 by James Fitzjames, duke of Berwick.

171 *Horace*: André Dacier published his edition of the Roman poet Horace between 1681 and 1689.

Letter 124

172 *'newsmongers' . . . garden*: the *Dictionary* of the French Academy defines the *nouvelliste* as 'someone who knows the news and who likes to retail it'. Such news was exchanged at gatherings in the Tuileries and circulated to the public in handwritten sheets (*nouvelles à la main*).

the emperor Joseph would die: he died of smallpox in April 1711.

173 *war was declared*: war broke out in July 1716, and the Turks were routed.

Alberoni: minister to Philip V of Spain, who engineered the reconquest of Sardinia in 1717. Montesquieu met the cardinal during his travels in 1728–9.

M. le C. d. L.: the French soldier Count Joachim of Lionne, who died in March 1716.

174 *privilege*: royal permission to publish.

council of Rehoboam: reference to 1 Kings 12: 8 where King Rehoboam consults the elders who had served his father Solomon and rejects their advice but accepts the counsel given by younger men.

Letter 125

type of government: Montesquieu's early research into the history of ancient Rome laid the basis for his interest in comparative government, one of the recurrent topics in the remaining part of the *Persian Letters*. He was to explore it further in his *Considerations on the Causes of the Greatness of the Romans and their Decline* (1734). Of his sources on oriental despotism, Chardin was clear about the Persian ignorance of the republican form of government.

175 *great Hesperis*: mythical garden located in Greece.

Letter 126

177 *I'm ruined . . .*: these anecdotes capture the beginning of the collapse of John Law's System, as shares in his Mississippi enterprise became grossly inflated in June 1719 and then started to deflate. This letter, dated to 17 November 1719, anticipates the crisis that ensued from January 1720. For an accessible account, see Janet Gleason, *The Moneymaker* (London: Bantam Books, 1999), ch. 13.

178 *Prince Pio*: Pio de Savoye-y-Corte Real was governor of Catalania in 1715 and fought against the duke of Berwick on behalf of Spain in the War of the Spanish Succession (1701–14).

Letter 127

a convent of dervishes: most likely the Abbey of St Victor, a twelfth-century scholastic foundation, which from 1707 was open to the public on Mondays, Wednesdays, and Saturdays. It was suppressed during the French Revolution and no longer exists.

Letter 128

179 *material particles*: the French term *esprit* has several meanings and appears in medical vocabulary with this significance.

Letter 129

181 *We use astrology . . . you use algebra*: a further dig at the false science of Law's financial scheme.

Letter 131

183 *to smother reason*: Montesquieu is decidedly sympathetic to the Moderns in the Quarrel, and approves of their rational approach to literary criticism.

two epic poems: Homer's *Iliad* and *Odyssey*.

Letter 132

185 *N****: Adrien-Maurice, the third duke of Noailles, who fought in the War of the Spanish Succession and was head of the finance council from 1715 to 1718.

Letter 133

186 *queen of Sweden*: Ulrika Eleanora (1688–1741) proclaimed herself queen of Sweden after the death of her brother Charles XII in December 1718. She abdicated in favour of her husband Frederick I of Hesse-Cassel.

Letter 134

187 *The Paris Parlement has been relegated*: in May 1720 Law provoked public
fury by devaluing share prices and banknotes. The Parlement of Paris lost
faith in the System and refused to sanction certain royal edicts. The
Regent punished its resistance by banishing its members temporarily.

Letter 135

188 *sheik Ali-Khan*: he became Grand Vizir in 1668, during the reign of
Soliman III.

each have her own seraglio: compare Letter 22, where the exclusion of
women from Paradise is cited. Chardin qualifies this by observing that
women do enter, provided they reside separately from men.

Letter 136

195 *Swan of Mantua*: name given to the Roman poet Virgil, who was born in
Mantua.

196 *Fragments from an Ancient Greek Mythologist*: the history of the Scotsman
John Law is told here as an allegory in the style of Fénelon; Bétique, the
mythical setting of his *Télémaque*, represents France. The allegory is rife
with allusions to Law's attempts from late January 1720 to shore up the
value of paper assets by placing strict control on the circulation of tangible
assets like gold and silver coin and diamonds.

Saturn: Law's banking plans came to nothing during his first visit to
France in 1699–1700. He established himself more successfully in 1714,
just before the death of Saturn (who is clearly Louis XIV). His System
took effect from August 1719.

Letter 137

200 *Letter from a Country Physician*: here, as in Letters 127 to 131 on libraries,
Montesquieu contrasts humanist learning and even a medieval view of the
world with the progressive, post-Cartesian thought of his own day. With
Rabelaisian flair, the interpolated letter satirically spoofs scholastic learning as a type of unscientific alchemy. The figure of the quack doctor
derived from the *commedia dell' arte* and was familiar from Molière's plays.

Monsieur Anis: director of the Royal Print Office at the Louvre.

the C. of the G.: reference to Mme Dacier's work *Des causes de la corruption du goût* (1714) in which she defended the superiority of the ancients
over the Moderns.

R.F. of the J.: Révérend Jesuit Father.

Father Caussin: Nicolas Caussin (1583–1651), a religious writer.

Spanish Jesuit . . . Rodriguez: Alonso Rodriguez (1526–1616), also a
religious writer.

201 *ten A**. by C*** . . . I.***: scholarly commentators have glossed the abbreviations as satirical references to legal documents concerning the affairs of Law's Banque and the Compagnie des Indes.

202 *M. de N.*: the celebrated preacher, Esprit Fléchier, bishop of Nîmes.

J. F.: the Jeux de Floraux of Toulouse, a sixteenth-century group of troubadour poets.

Maimbourg: a Jesuit expelled from the Order by the pope in 1681 for his defence of Protestantism.

Chapelain's: Jean Chapelain (1595–1674), a poet mocked by Boileau.

St Cyran: the abbé de St Cyran (1581–1643), a founding leader of Jansenism in the 1640s.

Miraculum . . . flamma: the three final remedies are in Latin and are translated below. The Jansenist Pasquier Quesnel (1634–1719) was a target of the Bull *Unigenitus*. Lallemant is any one of a number of Jesuits with the name. The cod-Latin recipes use the names of a number of prominent (if now obscure) Spanish Jesuits and casuists, such as Molina, Escobar, and Tamburini, who were anti-Jansenist. The 'illustrations' refer to a notorious set of engravings by Giulio Romano showing various sexual positions, accompanying a sequence of erotic sonnets by Pietro Aretino (1492–1557), while Sanchez was the author of a 1637 volume on marriage containing explicit descriptions.

A miraculous chemical reaction from violent fermentation with smoke, fire, and flame

Mix an infusion of Quesnell with an infusion of Lallement. Fermentation will occur with great power, impetus, and thundering as the acids and alkaline salts react violently and combine; a vapour of burning essences will result. Place the fermented liquor in an alembic: you will extract nothing from it and find nothing in it except a death's head.

Laxative

Take two leaves from the anodyne Molinae; six pages from the laxative Escobar; one leaf from the emollient Vasquez; douse in four pints of ordinary water until half the water has been absorbed, whereupon they should be sieved and wrung out. In the liquid thus produced dissolve three leaves of the corrosive Bauny and the ablutive Tamburini. For use as an enema.

For Chlorosis, commonly called pallor, or love-fever

Take four illustrations from Aretino; two leaves from the Revd Thomas Sanchez *On Marriage*. Infuse in five pints of ordinary water. For use as a laxative mixture.

Letter 138

203 *Usbek to Rhedi*: the date of this letter (11 November 1720) makes it the last to be written, since the final letter from Roxane is dated 8 May 1720. However, given the distance it has to travel, her suicide note is likely to have been the last to reach Usbek.

Letter 139

205 *such a pass*: the last twelve letters of this edition form a single consecutive account of the mayhem in the seraglio as it unfolds in 1719 and 1720. Historical time and novelistic time diverge. For dramatic reasons, Montesquieu groups them together and thereby disrupts the actual chronology of the entire book. On the basis of its date of 1717, Letter 139 should be Letter 101 in the sequence. Montesquieu keeps these letters in reserve for the end, and interpolates them as a self-contained unit in order to give a unified structure to the events recounted in Letters 139 to 147, concluding with the final Letter 150 which follows chronologically Letter 138. From February 1718 Usbek has been aware of the growing insurrection in the seraglio, but his attention in Letters 108 to 119 is on more abstract matters until he receives Letter 141 from Narsit in December 1718, and is jolted into a late attempt to restore order.

Letter 141

206 *Narsit to Usbek*: Narsit's response to Usbek's order in the previous letter takes five months and six days to arrive. The dramatic irony, of course, is that the reader learns about the death of the chief eunuch long before Usbek, and knows that the rebellion is irreversible before Usbek receives confirmation. Montesquieu wishes to maintain the unity of the seraglio sequence and places Letters 147 and 148 consecutively, although Usbek's latest letter (Letter 138), which is to Rica, is dated 11 November 1720. As of Letter 147 (9 October 1719), Usbek continues to wait for news of the seraglio, which makes the arrival of Roxane's penultimate letter all the more devastating. By then he is likely to have received Letter 148 from Roxane, followed shortly by her final message.

Letter 143

207 *there is a letter . . . spread terror everywhere*: this is Usbek's message (Letter 140), which arrives after the head eunuch's death.

Supplementary Letter 4 [91]

216 *ambassador of Persia*: the embassy of Mehemet Riza Beg was formally received by Louis XIV at Versailles on 19 February 1715, but his awkward demeanour and modest gifts caused diplomatic embarrassment and a number of courtiers suspected that he was an impostor (the incident is recounted in the *Memoirs* of the comte de Saint-Simon). The splendour

of the reception accorded by the French king was captured in a painting by Antoine Coypel (see note on Letter 28).

Supplementary Letter 5 [111]

217 *a speech*: this invented speech mimics (and mocks) discourse dating to the aristocratic rebellion called the Fronde from early 1649, when the French court fled and army commanders took charge.

Mazarin: Cardinal Jules Mazarin (1602–61), Italian-born first minister of France from the death of Richelieu in 1642, devoted to an absolute monarchy (on behalf of the boy king Louis XIV) and to crushing the Fronde. During the five years of unrest numerous hostile pamphlets, known as 'Mazarinades', circulated. He was reviled popularly for his greed and reported homosexuality.

Appendix

229 *La Rochelle*: after fourteen months of siege, from August 1627 to October 1628, this Huguenot stronghold surrendered to French troops. The fall of the city represented the end of the Huguenot War.

230 *Peripatetic philosophers*: followers of Aristotle. The name was derived either from the *peripatos* in the Lyceum grounds, where Aristotle had taught, or from Aristotle's habit of lecturing while walking.

Stagirite: a title sometimes used of Aristotle, who was born in Stagirus.

231 *Avicenna*: Abu ʿAli Al-Husayn ibn Sina (980–1037), great medieval Islamic philosopher. Born in Bukhara in Central Asia, he produced significant writings on the nature of God, the nature of the human faculties, and the soul.

232 *Tycho Brahe*: Danish astronomer of the Renaissance. In his system, the immobility of the earth was maintained from the Ptolemaic system, but the other planets were seen to revolve around the sun, as in the Copernican system; this was an attempt to find a middle ground between the Ptolemaic and Copernican systems, but it failed to convert Galileo from the Copernican view.

233 *beast is . . . like a watch or a clock*: Descartes took a highly reductionist view of all non-human animals: since they were without consciousness, he believed that much of their behaviour, such as the sounds they make, could be explained purely mechanically.

Empedocles, Pythagoras, Plotinus, Porphyry: Empedocles (*c*.493–*c*.433 BC), major Greek philosopher of the pre-Socratic period, author of a poem *On Nature* which views reality as an arena of ceaseless change and process of harmonization and dissolution; *Pythagoras*, Greek pre-Socratic philosopher of the sixth century BC, who taught a doctrine of reincarnation and advocated an arithmetical interpretation of nature as grounded in different geometric structures; *Plotinus*, founder (AD 204–70) of

Neoplatonism, the main philosophical movement of the Graeco-Roman world in late antiquity. He developed a complex spiritual cosmology involving three entities, the One, the Intelligence, and the Soul. It is from the productive unity of these three Beings that all existence emanates. He expressed his theory about the realm of intelligible things in the *Enneads*, as collected by his student *Porphyry*, who, as well as editing the writings of Plotinus, was responsible for the resurgence of interest in Aristotle. He also attacked Christianity, which he thought appealed to the irrational. His commentaries on Aristotle's *Categories* had an important influence on medieval philosophy.

236 *Cardinal Mazarin*: see note to Supplementary Letter 5.

CONCORDANCE OF LETTER NUMBERS

The following table gives equivalent numbers for letters as changed between the first (1721) edition, which is the basis of the Voltaire Foundation text used for this translation, and the edition of 1758 prepared after Montesquieu's death (for details see the Note on the Text). Eleven Supplementary Letters were added by Montesquieu to his revised edition of 1754, where they were printed in a block at the end (as in the present translation). He also changed the position of one letter (no. 76), altering its fictional date and renumbering it as Letter 129. In the 1758 edition the Supplementary Letters were incorporated into the body of the text itself.

1721 edition	1758 edition	1721 edition	1758 edition
1	1	33	35
2	2	34	36
3	3	35	37
4	4	36	38
5	5	37	39
6	6	38	40
7	7	39	41
8	8	40	42
9	9	41	43
10	10	42	44
11	11	43	45
12	12	44	46
13	13	45	47
14	14	46	48
	15 [Suppl.1]	47	49
15	16	48	50
16	17	49	51
17	18	50	52
18	19	51	53
19	20	52	54
20	21	53	55
	22 [Suppl.2]	54	56
21	23	55	57
22	24	56	58
23	25	57	59
24	26	58	60
25	27	59	61
26	28	60	62
27	29	61	63
28	30	62	64
29	31	63	65
30	32	64	66
31	33	65	67
32	34	66	68

1721 edition	1758 edition	1721 edition	1758 edition
67	69	111	115
68	70	112	116
69	71	113	117
70	72	114	118
71	73	115	119
72	74	116	120
73	75	117	121
74	76	118	122
	77 [Suppl.3]	119	123
75	78		124 [Suppl.6]
76	129	120	125
77	79	121	126
78	80	122	127
79	81	123	128
80	82	124	130
81	83	125	131
82	84	126	132
83	85	127	133
84	86	128	134
85	87	129	135
86	88	130	136
87	89	131	137
88	90	132	138
	91 [Suppl.4]	133	139
89	92	134	140
90	93	135	141
91	94	136	142
92	95	137	143
93	96		144 [Suppl.7]
94	97		145 [Suppl.8]
95	98	138	146
96	99	139	147
97	100	140	148
98	101	141	149
99	102	142	150
100	103	143	151
101	104	144	152
102	105	145	153
103	106	146	154
104	107	147	155
105	108	148	156
106	109		157 [Suppl.9]
107	110		158 [Suppl.10]
	111 [Suppl.5]	149	159
108	112		160 [Suppl.11]
109	113	150	161
110	114		